Memoirs of an Ordinary Woman

Memoirs of an Ordinary Woman

Margaret Knight

*To Sam & her mum
Best wishes
Margaret*

AMHERST

Copyright © Margaret Knight 2004

Margaret Knight has asserted her right under the
Copyright, Designs and Patents Act, 1988, to be
identified as the author of this work.

All rights reserved.
No part of this publication may be reproduced, stored in a
retrieval system, or transmitted in any form or by any means,
electronic, mechanical, photocopying, recording or otherwise,
without prior written permission of the author.

Some of the names have been changed
to protect their identities.

ISBN 1 903637 25 2

Printed in Great Britain by
The Bath Press

First published in 2004 by

Amherst Publishing Limited
Longmore House, High Street, Otford, Sevenoaks, Kent TN14 5PQ

This book is dedicated to Roger for his love and devotion and for always being there, and to my family and friends for their love and encouragement.

CONTENTS

1	A Childhood	9
2	Ted	19
3	Barbara	21
4	Lili-Anne	25
5	Nellie	29
6	School and Working	31
7	Marriage and Family	43
8	Mum	63
9	Julie	65
10	First of the Gremlins	71
11	Leeds Castle	87
12	Oh, Not More Gremlins	95
13	Holiday	103
14	Another Operation	109
15	The Convalescence Home	113
16	25 Years Married and a Wedding	119
17	Modelling and a Grandchild	123
18	New Home	127
19	Two Weddings	133
20	Holidays and a New Baby	141
21	The Gremlins Are Back	147
22	Venice and More Treatment	159
23	Greece then Radiotherapy	195
24	1994	205
25	1995	215
26	Spain	219
27	An Exciting Year	229
28	Egypt	235
29	A Full Year	247
30	Back to Spain	251
31	A Horrible Year	257
32	Barcelona to Miami - The Cruise	267
33	Our Ruby Wedding Year	275
34	Year 2000, Another Stay in Hospital	289
35	Time to Retire	301
36	Forward to the Future	311

FOREWORD

Margaret Knight has written a moving description of her life and her fight against cancer. She has displayed a fortitude and optimism which has enabled her not only to survive against the odds but also to enjoy life to the full. The support given by her to others is reflected in the love she has received from her friends and family, and in particular from her husband, Roger. As a result, she has been able to make a very successful career for herself at Leeds Castle and, in addition, to train as a Breast Cancer Care Volunteer in order to help fellow sufferers by sharing her experiences. Perhaps this book should have been titled 'Memoirs of an Extraordinary Woman'.

Hugh Vaux, August 2004
(Dr R H C Vaux)

1

A CHILDHOOD

It seemed as if all summers were long and hot when I was a child. I always know when summer has arrived because Mum cuts the toes off last year's sandals, and I am allowed to wear them to play in. It also means a new pair for best although I can not choose the style. It is always a pair of Clarks' brown leather. How I would love a black shiny pair. Out comes last year's cotton dresses, and I can leave off my bodice - a thick white cotton vest with small rubber buttons sewn down the front for decoration.

I was born on the 9th of May 1940, and was eleven years old last birthday. I have four sisters and one brother who are all married. My youngest sister, Nellie, lives at home with us and has a daughter, Valerie-Joan, who is more like a sister as I was five when she was born. At the end of the summer holidays, I am moving from junior school. I do not know how Valerie-Joan will get on as she doesn't like going to school each morning. The bus arrives and she refuses to get on. Her mum pushes while I say she is horrible to make her go but I have to try and pull her on. All the bus drivers know us and are very good-humoured. Once the bus drives off she is okay.

Up until Valerie-Joan started school last year, I had to ride my bike to school, come home for lunch, then go back again. I was very proud of my bike. Before I had it, I had to walk to the village school at Bearsted, come back home for dinner, go back for the afternoon, and walk home again at tea-time. When I asked if I could have a bike, Mum said we could not afford one but if I wanted to have half a bin when she went hop picking, and earn the money to buy one, I could. It seemed a good idea, so at the beginning of September we were picked up in a lorry at 6.30 in the morning, at the crossroads near our house, wearing old clothes and boots with our packed lunch and a flask of tea, with strict instructions from Mum to remember I was going to pick hops and not to play around. Mum was to have a bin next to her friend Mrs Green. We arrived to start picking at 7 o'clock after driving through the country lanes to the hop gardens, picking up other people on the way. Everyone piled out of the lorry and the foreman was there to tell us where our bins were. The hops grew on tall strings between poles in straight rows across the field. The bins were placed at intervals along the rows and we were told to pick clean and without leaves. At least twice a day the bins would be emptied and measured by the bushel. Some of the scratchers (the fast pickers) would have theirs emptied more frequently. I hated first thing in the morning because when you pulled down the binds all the cold dew went all over you, and as the day got warmer it made you itch. The worse days were when it rained because you still had to pick, sheltering under sacks to eat dinner. Amongst the other pickers were the Londoners - men, women, and children came down as a sort of working holiday, staying in the hopper huts on the edge of the fields with the children running wild all day. The earnings of the mothers and fathers were spent in the local pubs, but the nearest village shops would also do a good trade. I had saved my earnings and at the end of the picking I had enough to buy the bike.

My bedroom is at the back of the house. It is small because the ceiling slopes from the middle of the room and down one side. We haven't any electricity, only gas lights but none in my room, so I have a candle or a small oil lamp although I am not allowed to keep it on all night. I have to blow them out as soon as I am in bed, and I hide under the covers because I can hear the mice scampering along the beams in the low ceiling. I still cannot sleep without the covers over my ears and I am sure it is because of this.

There is a white and yellow painted wardrobe, a dressing table, and a chest of drawers, and of course a small bed, with lino on the floor and a rug beside the bed. The rugs all over the house are hand-made. Mum cuts up old clothes and washes any good sacks she can get. The material is cut into strips and then woven into the sacks with a hook. It was Valerie-Joan's and my job in the winter to cut up the strips. These rugs had a tradition that the outside edge was always black or a dark colour – men's old suits were a favourite for this. Red was looked upon as a colour that loose women wore, so red rags were not very attainable, but when you did have some, a red diamond-shape was woven in the centre of the rug. Usually these would lie in front of the fire or range to ward off the evil

A Childhood

eye. If the devil couldn't get into the house through the doors or windows, he could come down the chimney but as soon he saw the red evil eye he went back up again.

The sun is pouring through the yellow curtains in my little room. I love these because we always have floral or shiny brocade, which I hate, but Mum allowed me to have these lovely plain ones. It is never hard to get up. The first thing I always do is to look out of the window. There is a lovely lilac tree which grows over the little building below my room. That is the outside toilet - it has a wooden seat that Mum scrubs every day, and there is lino on the floor and of course a rag rug. We do not use proper toilet paper because we cannot afford it, Mum says, so Valerie-Joan and I have to tear up newspaper into neat squares then thread it onto string which hangs on a hook. If we run out, it is mine or Valerie-Joan's fault.

The view from the bedroom window looks across a meadow, and beyond to the woods. The meadow is a mass of white daisies and bright red poppies. We always have great bunches of daisies in the house as I love picking them for Mum. During the long summer evenings, rabbits play on the edge of the woods, and sometimes Valerie-Joan and I crawl round the side of the meadow with old saucepans trying to catch them. This year there has been a family of foxes.

That summer was the same as previous ones. Valerie-Joan and I roamed the countryside gathering wild flowers and making camps in the woods behind our neighbour Les's chicken shed. After breakfast we decided to go and see Valerie-Joan's mum, my sister Nellie, who helps her friend Mrs Grange with her housework. She has a son, Simon, and a daughter, Jane. I envy Simon his bedroom full of books - he collects the Enid Blyton's *Famous Five* – and how I long to own just one, but Simon is very generous. As soon as he has finished reading a new book, he lets me borrow it. Mrs Grange would tell Nellie all her secrets, and a few years later was to have a torrid love affair with a friend of Simon's. This was only spoken about in whispers between Mum and Nellie, as our Dad would have disapproved. At the Granges, Simon asks if we would like to go to the farm that afternoon as he and the children from the house next door were all going to help with the hay-making. We arranged to meet at the crossroads after dinner - we did not call it lunch as today tea was our evening meal.

Our Mum doesn't go out to work. She is a lovely person - not too fat and not too thin. She has a fresh complexion, and her hair is turning grey. It seems her whole life has been dedicated to our Dad and the family, and the house is always spotless. At 12 o'clock dinner has to be ready. Our Dad has to have everything on time; he has the same routine every day - up at 5 o'clock with cornflakes and tea for breakfast, then he takes a cup of tea up to Mum in the big brass bed with the great feather mattress. He then stokes up the range, Mum's pride and joy which she polishes with black lead, and the hearth has red tiles polished so you can almost see your reflection in them. Brass fire irons and a copper kettle glint in the glow of the fire. Our Dad cycles to work, about fifteen minutes from home, where he works in a small wood yard as a Pallmaker, and sometimes Mum and I go down to help strip the bark off the poles for him.

Monday is washday. This means the big stone copper that is built in the corner of the scullery has to have the fire lit under it; then the copper is filled with water to boil and out comes the big old mangle. This has two rubber rollers which the washing is put through by turning a handle at the side. I do not like washday. The scullery is full of steam and water everywhere, piles of white washing waiting to be boiled and washed, then put through the mangle. We have to help with this, also helping to fold the sheets then hang them on the washing line that stretches across the garden. Mum is not too happy on the occasions the line breaks, with all her white washing lying on the garden. Then it all has to be boiled, rinsed, and mangled again. Everything is washed in order; first the boiling, then the towels, and last the coloured clothes. On Mondays we all hope and pray it will not rain.

On Monday, dinner is always cold meat from the Sunday joint, vegetables all fresh from the garden, and each evening Mum tells Dad which vegetables she needs for the next day. There is no need to buy any as there are rows of potatoes, carrots, onions which are tied with raffia in long columns that hang in the garden shed when harvested, cabbages, and Brussels sprouts. And after the sprouts have finished, the leaves on top of the plant are also used so nothing is wasted. Tall tripods stand down the length of the garden full of runner beans, and, if there is an extra good year, Mum will salt some. This is done by slicing the beans and layering them with salt in jars which are stored in a dark cupboard and used at Christmas. All the salads were grown and there were vegetables for each season, as well as marrows, rhubarb, and gooseberries. Mum looked after the rabbits we had, and these were fattened up because Christmas rabbit meat was very popular. Valerie-Joan and I hated the day a local man came to kill them. We would hide in the house so we didn't hear that awful

A Childhood

squeal they made, and we thought they were cruel to kill them. Mum cured the skins and made fur gloves and muffs which she sold; they were quite a fashion accessory. A lot of bartering went on. Mum would swap rabbits for boxes of apples and pears which were stored under Mum and Dad's big brass bed.

There was a lovely old apple tree in the garden. I felt sad when Dad chopped it down because he could not see what the family who lived in the old cottage opposite was doing. He said it blocked his view from the living-room window. There was great rivalry between Dad and old Mr Gresbey, who lived there, to see who would grow the best vegetables.

Our Dad was rather an unsociable man who did not have much to do with anyone outside the family. He disliked us having visitors, and never took Mum out except for a visit to the local pub. I hated this because Valerie-Joan and I had to sit in the back room all evening and then walk home at closing time. I have never liked going to pubs and I think this is why.

When Mum went shopping she would have to be home so Dad had his meals on time, and he did not like it if she wasn't there when he got in. Dad never seemed to show any emotions. I cannot remember him ever picking me up or hugging me. I always thought this was because Mum became pregnant with me by mistake when she was forty-two and Dad was fifty-one. My eldest sister, Phyllis, was also having her first child at the same time. My brother, Ted, and sisters, Barbara and Lili-Anne, were all of working age, and sister Nellie was fourteen. She helped Mum a lot. Mum told me she was embarrassed at being pregnant at forty-two and all her family grown up, and was much talked about in the village so she hated going there. My Dad also wanted another son, so being a girl did not help. I was to realise many years later why he was so unsociable.

Dad was also very stubborn. One incident happened when the family lived at Scragged Oak near the village of Detling in Kent. He was working for a farmer at the village of Barming, and this was a round journey of approximately 20 miles which Dad would normally cycle, but on this occasion he had walked pushing a home-made wooden barrow with old pram wheels. The reason for this was that Dad had been harvesting potatoes. On the last day, the workers that had been doing the harvesting were given a sack of potatoes, but during the morning the farmer asked Dad to go to the paddock to repair a fence which, as the fencer, was his job, but he would also help on the farm when necessary, hence the potato harvesting. At the end of the day, he returned to the potato field to collect his sack of potatoes. The foreman did not like Dad very much and said that as he had not been there all day he was not entitled to them. Dad was furious. He decided to go to the big house and see the farmer. Normally he would have gone to the back door, cap in hand, but not this day; he went to the front door with his cap on. When the farmer appeared, Dad gave in his notice. The farmer enquired what was wrong, and Dad told him what had happened at the potato field. The farmer said he could see he would not change Dad's mind about leaving so they would go down to the field and get the potatoes. Dad said they could keep their potatoes as he wasn't having any charity and pushed the empty barrow home. When Dad returned from seeking work the next day, Mum told him the farmer had delivered a sack of potatoes. He promptly put them in the barrow and walked all the way back to the farm and left them at the front door.

Simon and the Banks' children are starting off when Valerie-Joan and I arrive at the crossroads. We all jump on to the moving horse and cart, and there is much laughter to see if any of us fall off. We pass the Banks' and Simon's houses, and Bob who lives next door to Simon is standing at his gate. He is large for his age with a lumbering walk - a Downs Syndrome boy who is a bit retarded – and he speaks very little but grunts and smiles as he waves his arms about. He always frightens me and I run when I see him, although today things are different and we accept people with disabilities. He wanders around the woods and lanes and would suddenly jump out as you passed. He was probably very lonely. The boys take great delight in shouting swear words at him, at which he becomes very excited, waving his arms about and trying to repeat what the boys are shouting. Bob's mother appears, to see what all the commotion is about; she knows the boys tease Bob, and as usual will later complain to the boys' fathers. A plain quiet woman in her sixties, she already had another son, an intelligent boy who is at university, when she had Bob - gossip said, during the change of life.

At last we arrive at the field, reaped corn standing in golden sheaves. The driver and the other men in the field stop to chat; and we all scamper off the cart and run wild round the sheaves chasing rabbits. There is an old cottage on the edge of the field where my friend Polly lives with her mother. The local children say Polly's mother is a witch and many stories were told about her. She could make warts disappear, and once put chickweed milk on one I had on my thumb, and yes it did disappear.

A Childhood

I think she was more of a herbalist than a witch. Behind the cottage was a pond. We decide to investigate, and the coots and moorhens scurry for cover in the reeds. This was one of the ponds where we would collect frog spawn.

Twice a week, Mum would walk to the village of Detling, along lanes past the chestnut woods where we would gather chestnuts and blackberries from the hedgerow when in season. All the months of the year would bring their own magic.

In January and February, snowdrops grew in great clumps under the trees, and on the roadside the ploughing and hedging would be going on. The hedges were not almost ripped out with cutting machines as they are today; there was the road man who walked the lanes, cutting the hedges and grass verges. The farmer with the horses ploughing the fields left lovely straight lines of dark brown earth, with the birds swooping behind the plough.

March and April saw the trees and hedgerows with fresh green buds, the woods carpeted in yellow primroses, white violets, purple viola and wild daffodils; and lambs, creamy white against the bright green grass, with skylarks singing overhead.

In May and June, we would gather cowslips and bluebells that covered the woodland floor. This was also the time for finding birds' nests amongst the hedgerows which were abundant with honeysuckle and dog roses. And the sand pit where sand martins swoop in and out of holes in the sand where they nest. It is also time for hearing the cuckoo; we were told if you count the cuckoo's cry until it was out of earshot you add as many years to your life.

July and August was the time for tall foxgloves and bee orchids growing in the woods, and bees and butterflies hovering over fields full of poppies, daisies and hare bells.

In September and October, we would gather baskets of damsons and blackberries for jam and pies, and hazelnuts were a great favourite.

Often we would meet the cows coming from the fields and going back to the farm for milking. They always frightened me - great lumbering animals, huge udders full of milk, on cold days blowing sweet smelling steam from wet nostrils. They could be rather frisky, trying to charge into gardens causing havoc, the farm dogs barking and yelping when the cows kicked out at them. Halfway to the village was a small cottage where the Walklings lived. Mrs Walkling always made sure she was at her garden gate when Mum would pass for her weekly gossip as she did not get out much. Next door to them was a wood yard run by a local family, and all the sons and daughters were involved in the running of the business. Near to the village lived an aunt of ours, and sometimes Mum was invited in for a cup of tea. Next door to her was a family which had six sons, and the parents longed for a daughter. The boys had all inherited their father's, Joe's, bright red hair; his hobby was breeding greyhound dogs. Mum told me Joe had asked her if she would swap me for a greyhound so he could have his daughter, so it was a family joke that I was only worth a skinny greyhound.

The village was centred on the church and school, but there was also the police house, butchers shop and a small garage where we took our accumulator to be recharged. An accumulator supplied the low tension to a radio in conjunction with a high tension battery; the radio being our only form of entertainment. At the top of the village was the Cock Inn, and, in the summer, walkers and cyclists stopped for cool drinks before ascending the downs. Behind the Inn, in tall old trees, was a rookery. In the late afternoon, the sky filled with black clouds of rooks coming home to roost, their loud cries of 'caw caw' filling the air. Whenever I hear rooks now, I think of the village.

The general store was owned by Mr Fancourt, a dapper little man with a huge wart under his left eye which wobbled when he winked, twitched, and sniffed at the same time. The shop had a polished wooden counter with chairs for the customers to sit on while giving their orders which would be delivered later in the day by a boy on a bike with a large basket on the front; if you lived out of the village, Mr Fancourt would deliver the goods in his van. Behind the counter was a selection of drawers in which there were teas, spices, and dried fruit. Hanging above were whole sides of smoked bacon, slices always cut to order. Large round strong-flavoured farmhouse cheeses were under glass domes. Sacks of dried peas, beans, and lentils stood beside the counter with the fresh vegetables, butter cut from a block and weighed out as was sugar which always went into a dark blue paper bag. In the bay window were large glass jars of sweets, lemon sherbet for making lemonade or lovely to have a bag to dip your fingers in.

The bags that the sweets went into were made from a square of paper folded into a cone shape. Sharps' toffee was a favourite, made by a local firm. Ice cream, lovely creamy circles which were put into a cornet, or a small block called a brick was put between two wafers.

A Childhood

When we moved from the house I was born in at Scragged Oak, we lived for a short while in the little house next to the shop before moving to Gidds Hill, Bearsted. I cannot remember much about living there, only that, like most houses at that time, the toilet, or lavatory as it was known, was a small brick building outside the back door. It had white-washed walls with a dirt floor and a rag rug, and the scrubbed wooden seat had a large hole for the adults, and a small one for a child. On the other side of the shop lived the Roots family - father, mother and three girls. Mr Roots had been a prisoner of war and when he came home was like a walking skeleton; he never really recovered from his ordeal. Mrs Roots was a very thin little woman with a short bobbed hair style and round wire glasses. Elizabeth and Edna, the two elder girls, had the same hairstyles and glasses as their mother but were much taller and thin as bean poles. Christine, the younger girl, always looked very healthy compared to her sisters, but was to die very young.

When we moved to Gidds Hill, after my visits to the village with Mum, Edna and I would play games of ball and skipping in the alleyway between Edna's and a large detached house with a lovely walled garden in which we loved to explore and swing on the swing that hung on a big old tree at the bottom of the garden. The house belonged to my Godmother and Mum's best friend, Mrs Green, whom we considered quite well off. The house had a huge kitchen with a large scrubbed table, and in an alcove stood a big cooking range. At one end of the room were cupboards, and a dresser full of fine china. At the other end was a big stone sink. When I was two, Mum had left me, for the first time, with Mrs Green while she had gone into the nearest town, As she had to walk she thought it better to leave me. I was running around the table and ran into a nail sticking out of the draining board. Mum told me she never left me again with anyone until I was older. I still have the scar today.

In their hall stood a lovely grandfather clock, and on the landing, a matching grandmother. The drawing-room had a bureau in which was kept Mrs Green's collection of Christmas and birthday cards made with velvet, silks, and lace. She had two children by her first husband. He was tall and thin, and she small and round. I never knew what his profession was but he always seemed to be sitting in a rocking chair in his study; he never spoke to any of us. Edna and I liked to sneak up to the daughter Florrie's room. There was a child's dresser with a bone china tea-set, a large dolls house complete with carpets and furniture, and china dolls of all sizes sitting around the room in beautiful carved little chairs; how we envied Florrie her collection.

Edna's father was Mrs Green's brother. Times were hard for the family since he came back from the war so she would help out sometimes by buying clothes for the girls, but Edna was often cheeky to her Aunt so I was given the item instead. On her weekly trips to the village, Mum would call into Detling school to see Miss Large the headmistress who ran the penny bank. Your pennies were paid in every week through the year and paid back out at Christmas. My brother, Ted, and sisters, Phyllis, Barbara, Lili-Anne, and Nellie had all attended this school when we lived at Scragged Oak, Detling, near Maidstone, Kent. It was a three-mile walk to the school for them each day. I was born in this house but cannot remember living there as I was only four when we moved into Detling village. My brother and sisters tell me many stories of a time so different from today.

2

EDWARD (TED)

My brother Ted has always been considered a handsome man, tall well-built with bright blue eyes. As a young man he sent many a local girl's heart a flutter. The only boy in a family of five girls, he was of course the apple of Mum's eye, and many a time she got him out of trouble with Dad who in later years seemed to resent Ted becoming successful in life. Ted, as with my sisters, attended the local school at Detling, walking the three miles each day. The walk gave great opportunities for larking about. Before I was born, the family had lived in the house next door to Scragged Oak, a tiny house with only two bedrooms. Next door to us there lived the Scott family, and on one occasion Ted decided that Gladys - one of the girls - only needed one of her very long plaits, so he cut one off. Gladys's father was not too pleased, and threatened to skin him alive if he caught him. As usual, Mum found a way of keeping Ted out of the way when Dad got home.

When, on leaving school at fourteen, Ted went to work in a paper mill at Tovil, near Maidstone, there was no public transport from our house so it was walking or riding a bike. I would think it was about a sixteen miles round trip. At that time, it was a two-bicycle family - one our Dad used, and the other one all the children shared. One particular bad winter, at 4 o'clock in the morning, Dad woke Ted who found it had snowed overnight. He tried to open the back door but the snow was almost to the top of it. Dad said Ted would have to climb out of the bedroom window and clear the snow from the door. No time for breakfast that morning. The lane from our house to the top of Detling hill had hedges on each side except where there were the woods, and the snow was to the top of the hedges. Dad and Ted decided to carry their bikes until they reached the top of the hill, hoping the road would be clearer, but it was too difficult so they left their bikes in the lane to collect on the way home. They knew they would be safe. Very few people went down the lane on a good day; no one would attempt it that day.

Walking as fast as they could, Ted arrived at the mill three minutes late, and was immediately spotted by the foreman: 'You are late, boy, so you can go back home and come in tomorrow, and if you are late again don't bother to come at all. You can set your alarm clock for every hour to check the weather, and then you will not have any excuse to be late.' He smirked, slamming the door of the machine shed in Ted's face. Being only fourteen, Ted began to cry as he walked across the yard. He knew Dad would not be too happy if he lost a day's wages. The manager spotted Ted and asked what the problem was, so he explained where he lived and how he had got up at 4.30 to get in on time, and was only three minutes late. The manager, being a kind-hearted man, took Ted to see the foreman. He said no, he could not start work as he had arrived late so would have to go home and make sure he was not late the next day. Because the manager had intervened, the foreman had thought Ted had complained to him, and, until the foreman retired some years later, held it against Ted. That night, Ted set the alarm for every hour. The winters were very harsh, so many a day he had to walk to work, and then, after long hours, walk back home.

Ted served his apprenticeship at the mill, and then during the war went into the Guards. Very handsome he looked in his uniform, and much admired by Mum and his sisters. After the war, it was back to the mill where he eventually became a foreman and worked there until he took early retirement due to the mill closing down. He married Joyce whom he met when she was in the RAF, and they have two sons and grandchildren. Now in his 80s, he enjoys walking and is very fit, spending much of his time in his large garden and looking after his bees.

3

BARBARA (BARB)

Born on the 26th July 1924, my sister Barb is unlike our brother and sisters because we all have dark hair and she is very fair. At Detling School, Barb won a scholarship but, much to her disappointment, our Dad and Mum said they could not afford for her to go to Grammar school. Everyone at home had jobs to do before and after school. Opposite our house lived the Kitchener family. Their house was surrounded by orchards where chickens run free, and Barb was paid 6 old pence to collect a bucket of eggs. The chickens would sometimes lay their eggs under the hedge, and during the evening one of her other jobs was to collect food for the rabbits that mum kept, so she would hide an egg then pick it up with the rabbit food to take home to Mum. Occasionally Mr Kitchener would give her an egg for her tea. If she worked all day in the garden, again the payment was 6 old pence. Mum and Dad were not at all religious but Ted and the girls had to go to the Methodist Chapel at Yelsted for Sunday school. The chapel superintendent lived near by and would sometimes take them in his horse and trap; if not, they had to walk the three miles.

Barb remembers, while living at Scragged Oak, a local farmer had gone missing while depressed. A search party of local men was organised, of which Dad was one. They were to walk through the woods behind our house in a long line, and if one of the men found anything they were to shout. Dad bent down to go under some low branches, and when he straightened up he saw the farmer hanging above him. He was so shocked he could not shout. The other men found Dad unable to move or speak. It was a long while before he could go into the woods again.

At 14, Barb went into service as a scullery maid at a large house called Godlands. The family, the Barcham-Greens, also owned a local mill. The family was very wealthy; they employed a cook, a house parlour maid, a shoe-boy, and two gardeners. Barb started work at 5 o'clock and did not go to bed until 10 o'clock. In the morning, her first job was to clean out the fireplaces, then take tea to the cook and house parlour maid. It was then time to take hot water to the bedrooms. If there were male guests staying, Barb was not to go into their rooms as this was considered very unseemly, and she was not allowed to wait at table until she was sixteen. She only had one half-day off a week and every other Sunday, also had to supply her own uniform which was a green dress with an overall for the mornings, and a white apron with a mop cap for the afternoons. Her wages were 2/6 a month. The children of the family were very spoilt and would boss Barb around and threaten to tell their mother if she did not do what they wanted. Her next job was at a house called Pollyfield which was only a short walk from Scragged Oak. The owner was a pilot, Squadron Leader Brown, who was Canadian. The war had started when Barb was fifteen, and at seventeen she pretended she was eighteen and joined the RAF as a cook. She made many good friends, especially Nellie who became one of the family, referred to by Barb's children as Nellie Bean. Barb was in London during the bombing, and at the North Weald when Squadron Leader Bader was there.

After leaving the RAF, she had a variety of jobs - one as a waitress for a café called Dockralls. Mr Dockrall was always very smart with dark slicked back hair and a thin moustache. I remember him wearing a check sports jacket and a yellow tie, and he gambled on the horses. Mrs Dockrall, a large lady, made the cakes. Sometimes Mum would take me in for tea when we went shopping, and I thought this a great treat. Although Mum was a good cook, she never made anything fancy. Mrs Dockrall made sponges filled with lemon or chocolate butter-cream and they were delicious. When I moved to the house my family and I live in now, near Willington street, Barb told me it brought back memories of when the family stayed in an oast house at Willington street that has now been converted into a house, but at that time it was just an oast so Mum and the children cleaned it, and the cooking was done outside in what is called a brick oven. The family stayed there during the summer so Dad did not have so far to go to work. On one other occasion, the children were outside playing cowboys and Indians when Ted had been the horse. Barb, the Indian, fell off Ted's back onto her arm, and Ted threatened her not to tell Mum. At tea that evening, Barb could not hold her cutlery properly. Mum always had a hazel twig which was used if anyone misbehaved; the thin twig whipped across the hand usually brought tears. Barb was threatened with this if she did not eat her tea properly. She told Mum she couldn't because her arm hurt. Mum, none too sympathetic, asked what she had done. A sharp kick under the table from Ted, and Barb said she had fallen on it. Eventually, Barb was taken to the local hospital; her arm was broken but she did not reveal how it happened for many years.

In May, most villages would have a May Day celebration. At Detling this was held in the school grounds with dancing, and each year a May queen was chosen. One year, Barb was the queen dressed in a special dress crown and sceptre.

It was 1948 and I was eight. Barb had married Ted who was in the Navy. Everyone liked him - a lovely quiet person, the perfect gentleman - so when they said they wanted to get married, Mum and Dad were pleased. They came to live with us. We were then living at Gidds Hill, near Bearsted. We had moved there from Detling village. It was a bit of a crush; there was Mum and Dad, Nellie and her husband, Tom, Valerie-Joan, and me. In those times, most people started married life with their parents or in-laws. Eventually, they moved into their own home back at Detling. Their first child, Heather, was born, followed by Robin, then Michelle, and by then they were living at Langley. When Michelle was three, Barb developed a problem with her breast. She was admitted to Bart's hospital in the Medway town, and a Mr Towneslay performed a full mastectomy. Losing a breast is naturally distressing, and it would have been very traumatic forty-one years ago. Cancer was not talked about, especially having a mastectomy. After ten years, Barb was discharged and is fit. She has led a very full and active life and has been an inspiration to me. After having Heather, Barb worked for a lady who was the sister-in-law of Hardy Amis, the famous dress designer. When the children had grown up, she worked as a silk-screen printer for thirteen years before retiring.

4

LILI-ANNE

My sister Lili-Anne was always happy and had lots of friends. She was always rushing around and did a lot of work for charity, and had a lovely giggle which made you feel happy. But life had not always been easy for her. When she was six, our brother Ted was in bed ill and Lili-Anne had been shopping with Mum to buy some new shoes. On returning home, Lili-Anne was told not to go up the stairs to see Ted in her new shoes as the stairs were wooden and she could slip, but I guess, like any child, she was eager to show her brother the shoes. My Mum told me the worse part was when she lifted Lili-Anne from the wicker basket that stood at the bottom of the stairs. She would never forget the awful noise made when pulling the broken strand of wicker from her eye. Very few people had a telephone, and the nearest house to have one was about two miles away so Dad cycled there and a doctor and ambulance were called.

The operation Lili-Anne needed had never been performed before. She lay between sandbags, as any movement could have been fatal. She had very little sight left in her eye, and later a tumour developed behind the eye. The surgeon, and the sister on the ward, were to stay friends with her until they died.

Due to where we lived, and no means of transport, Lili-Anne was not fit enough to walk to school - she was still having hospital treatment - so it was a few years before she could have the odd day at school. This was her biggest regret, not being able to go to the village school with her brother and sisters. She taught herself to read and write, when in her late fifties she decided to attend adult education, going on to take her O level English; was about to take A level when she died. She was also helping others, who were unable to read and write, to learn.

With so little education, getting a job would have been difficult. She would have liked to have been a children's nurse but jobs were few in the 1930s so when she was sixteen and offered the job of an in-between maid to a Mrs Standing, whose son was the vicar of All Saints church in Maidstone, she had to accept it. At first she was very homesick and felt like running away but soon settled in.

The vicarage was opposite the church; there had been a house on the site since the middle ages. It was a lovely old house but I found it a bit scary when we went to visit. It was full of long dark passages with stone floors that echoed as you walked along them. I remember the kitchen as a huge room with windows so high you could not see out of them; this was the cook's domain. In winter, Lili-Anne said her bedroom was so cold the water froze in the jug and basin that was there for her to wash in. Her favourite part of the house was the garden, flower beds full of old-fashioned flowers surrounded by lawns, where sometimes they held garden parties. There was also a cobbled courtyard. Although the house had a preservation order on it, many years later it was pulled down for a block of modern offices to be built. All that remains is part of the outer wall and the arched gateway which was the servants' entrance.

When falling down the stairs, Lili-Anne had knocked out her two front teeth so she was fitted with a plate with two false teeth. Unfortunately they were not a very good fit and she had the habit of clacking them up and down. She was a favourite of the local trades people who delivered to the vicarage, particularly the baker boy who called with his basket of fresh bread. On one occasion, seeing him arrive from her bedroom window, she called and waved to him. He stopped for a chat below the window, making her laugh as usual, which made her teeth fall out into the bread basket. He put them on the window sill and she had to run down many stairs and along passages to rush out and retrieve her teeth. She was so embarrassed, that when she saw him coming, she would hide. On another occasion, while laughing and joking, she swallowed the teeth. A quick visit to the doctor and he said all should be well because they would come out as nature intended. He told her to soak them in disinfectant and she could wear them again.

As the years went by, Lili-Anne would help other members of the staff especially the cook and housekeeper, and when they retired she was to take over their responsibilities.

Eventually Lili-Anne was to marry Austin, one of the boys from the family who lived next door at Scragged Oak, a keen gardener who

Lili-Anne

looked after the gardens at the vicarage after he finished work each day.

Reverend Standing was asked to move to Canterbury where he was made a Canon. Lili-Anne and Austin were to go with him, and they were to live in the Precincts of the Cathedral in a large house with a lovely walled garden and a flight of stone steps leading to the front door. During the summer holidays, I would go and stay, and one of my favourite games was dressing up in the collection of 1920s clothes, hats, and jewellery that had belonged to Mrs Standing, who by this time had died. All these things were stored at the top of the house in old chests, and there was even her wedding dress. Many hours I spent parading up and down the front steps. The rest of the holiday I would sit drawing and painting in the Cathedral and Precincts gardens. I wandered the city, watched as the archaeologist worked in the Abbey ruins near the river, and loved looking in the old bookshops.

It was a big responsibility for Lili-Anne, running the house, cooking, cleaning, and looking after her own family as she had had two little boys, Adrian and Andrew. When the Canon entertained, it was extra work cooking and serving the guests. She also helped the Archbishop's wife, who lived next door, when she entertained important guests. The Canon always had his meals in the huge dining room on a large polished table with silver cutlery and crystal glasses. The drawing room had two sets of French doors opening on to verandas. There was a grand piano, and when the Canon was out I was allowed to play on it as at that time I was having piano lessons; it was a great treat to practice my music and try and sing.

As the Canon progressed in his career, it was decided he should have a house built on a plot of ground next door, so work went ahead. Lili-Anne and Austin were to have their own part of the house and garden. The Canon had been working on the Dead Sea scrolls, and had been to London on the day he died. Lili-Anne was in a state of shock and confined to bed. She once told me she loved him more than anyone else. Mum had had a message from Austin asking if she could go down to the house. By this time I was married and had our first son Richard who was three weeks old. I was to drive Mum to Canterbury; this was my first trip out since having the baby and I did not have a carry-cot so he was put in a drawer from a chest. This was of course before seat belts.

When we arrived, Mum suddenly realised I had not been Churched - a ceremony almost unheard of today. In those days you would not enter another house until you had been to Church and been blessed for the safe delivery of the child. It was decided I would go into the little Chapel in the Precincts gardens.

The Canon had left Lili-Anne enough money to buy a house, and an allowance for the rest of her life. She decided to come back to Maidstone to live near the family. They settled in their new home, then one morning Austin said he was not feeling too well and went into the bathroom and died. Lili-Anne seemed to get on with her life. The boys were married and had left home so she found some part-time work and soon had a circle of friends. This is when she went to adult education; she loved going to the theatre and did a lot of work for multiple sclerosis and other charities.

She became unwell and was having various treatments for a stomach ulcer. When she was taken to hospital, cancer was diagnosed, as well as the stomach, and it had spread to other organs. She died soon after being admitted to hospital. I was devastated.

5

ELLEN (NELLIE)

Nellie was fourteen when I was born, and my Mum was forty-two. It was a difficult time for Mum, living in a small village. She was told by one lady she should be ashamed she had been doing that sort of thing at her age. Nellie was a great support to Mum. When I was born, she had to help look after me as well as her other jobs around the house, and my brother and other sisters all had their chores to do each day. One of Nellie's jobs when she was younger was to earn 6 old pennies from a neighbour, Mr Pearson, who owned the orchard next door to our house. She had to go round the orchard singing to scare the birds away. A treat was to have a ride in Mr Pearson's pony and trap.

The postman would give local people a lift in the post van as he delivered the post around the country lanes. On one occasion, Nellie was having a lift into the village when, going round a bend, the door flew open throwing Nellie out. In some way or other, the van ran over her but without any ill effects. This frightened the postman so much he would not give anyone else a lift after that.

Our brother Ted sometimes had to collect milk from the farm. One winter day there had been a heavy fall of snow and, as Ted and Nellie returned from the farm, Mick the road-sweeper was trying to clear the lane. Nellie dared Ted to throw snow balls at Mick. He was very upset by this and threw his shovel at Ted, hitting the milk container and spilling the milk. Nellie had to confess to Mum that she had dared Ted to throw the snowballs. They both had to walk back to the farm to collect more milk. Around this time, the children acquired two bicycles without tyres; great fun was had riding them in the surrounding woods. How different was their enjoyment from today's children with their expensive mountain bikes.

Memoirs of an Ordinary Woman

When leaving school, Nellie went to work at a printing company, Young and Cooper, and at 17 she joined the land army. Hating it and very homesick, she had been given the job of milking the cows living in the countryside. You would have thought this would not have been a problem, but she forgot to clip the cow's tail down and placed the bucket of milk behind the cow who decided to flavour it in a nice smelly way. So after only two weeks, Nellie was back home.

A variety of jobs followed, and then for many years she worked at the West Kent hospital. By this time, Nellie had married Tom, and they had Valerie-Joan. Some years later, Tom was drowned when working on a lightship. On returning to the ship one night in a small boat with a colleague, the boat capsized and the two men were thrown into the sea. The other man's body was found quite soon after, but Tom's was washed ashore some time later several miles along the coast. Nellie and Valerie-Joan had always lived with Mum and Dad when she was first married to Tom as he was in the Air Force and away a lot. Valerie-Joan was more like a sister to me as I was almost five when she was born. After our Mum died, Valerie-Joan was married and left home.

Nellie looked after Dad - not an easy task as he could be quite difficult. He died when he was ninety-two after Nellie had devoted many years looking after him. She had been friends with John for years, meeting him when she had worked at a dairy. After Dad died they decided to get married, this being the only time Nellie and I had words. I was shopping one evening when I bumped into one of my nieces who told me about Aunt Nellie getting married today. I was struck dumb. I was so upset. It was a shock someone else telling me. I respected that she wanted a quiet wedding, and the fact was she had written to tell me but I did not get the letter until the day after my niece told me.

Valerie-Joan's two sons are now married, and Nellie is a great grandmother.

6

SCHOOL AND WORKING

At five years old, I started at infant school at Thurnham. I remember very little about my time there; my memories are from when I started junior school which was opposite the village green at Bearsted.

We had a playground at the back of the school. The boys played football, and skipping ropes were popular with the girls. A game we called film stars was our favourite, and I was good at this as I knew all the stars. My sister Nellie would take me each week to see the latest film because Mum did not like Nellie going on her own.

One girl would stand out front and call out the initials of a film star. The first one to guess the name had the next turn. At the cinema, not only did you see the main film, there was also the B film on first, so I got to know the lesser-known stars. A favourite Christmas present was the latest film annual along with the *Girl* and *School Friend* annuals. The *Girl* and *School Friend* were weekly girls' comics. I could hardly wait for them to come out each week, as we had so few books at home I would read anything I could get my hands on. One Christmas, Lili-Anne asked me if there was anything I would really like. A history book was the answer. I was fascinated by history, and many years later Roger and I joined the local history society and the Kent Archaeology group.

Summertime, and we used the village green as a playground. The green still looks the same today, with the parade of shops, the butchers, a newsagent, and post office. The general store is now part of the butchers and bakers, and the old village inn is still there. On the edge of the green was the pond, surrounded by bull rushes and yellow Iris, and many hours were spent here collecting frog spawn. Nearby was what looked like a lych-gate over a seat where old folk sat in the shade for a chat during the day, and courting couples sat in the evenings. The green was surrounded by lovely old timbered houses, and my best friend Susan lived in a white cottage overlooking the pond. During the summer, the fair was held on the green, and the school supplied the entertainment with the children Maypole dancing; much practice was needed learning how to weave the ribbons in and out.

From the green we could see the lovely old house called Snowfield where we would use the gardens for our summer pageant. One year, I originally I had a smaller part but Pat, whose mother was a drama teacher at another local school, always seemed to get the best parts. Pat had matured more than the other girls in our class and decided, when trying on her costume, to show us she had developed breasts. Unfortunately, at that moment the sports mistress came in so Pat was punished by losing her part, which I was given.

Our classroom had a stove surrounded by a guard, and in winter the teacher would put our little bottles of milk that we had at break time on it to warm.

In one of the old timbered houses, the local doctors held their surgery. The waiting room had an old black leaded stove. In the winter we warmed our hands and feet as it was about half an hour's walk from home to the surgery. Any patient who noticed the fire going down would top it up from the coal bucket. It was so different from today; there was no receptionist, you just waited your turn. If a woman came in with a sick child, someone would always give up their place so the child did not have to wait. The doctor only kept a limited supply of drugs so, if he did not have what you needed, he put them in a tin which was on the wall outside the surgery for you to collect later in the day.

At eleven years of age, we took the eleven plus exam, and we all left Bearsted School. It was hard leaving a school where we knew all the pupils, and going, to what seemed at the time, large unfriendly buildings in the town. I went to East Borough, which was a mixed school, and found it hard to settle in. Eventually the school had a different system and I moved to another part, Vintners Girls. I was very introvert, and missed my friends as we had been split into three different schools - my friend Susan going to a grammar school. I met Beryl at East Borough and we became great friends until leaving school at fifteen, but then we lost touch until recently after many years we were able to meet up again.

For the next two years, I struggled to settle down to school. I had reached puberty, having started to menstruate a month before I was ten. I

School and Working

awoke with violent stomach pains, and went to the outside toilet, but back in the kitchen I fainted. Mum asked what was wrong, and I replied that I thought it was all the beetroot I had been eating as my toilet was like blood. On investigating, Mum realised I had started menstruating. This was not something to be spoken about, and sex education was never discussed, especially when you were only ten years old. These things were supposed to start when you were a teenager. The next thing that happened horrified me. Mum said I would have this once a month, and was not to go up the woods with the boys. I could not understand this. I certainly did not want any boys knowing I had this awful thing. I was not even going to tell my best girl friends. Mum said I would have to wear a sanitary towel. I had never heard of one, but she showed me a square of cotton made from an old sheet. This was folded and made into a sausage shape with the two ends turned over and pinned down with a safety pin to form loops. Mum then gave me a length of elastic to make a belt which was threaded through the loops. Next I was given a bucket, and Mum said I would wash the soiled ones myself. We had a small washing line at the back of the house where I was to hang them to dry. When years later I was telling some young girls at work about this, they were appalled at how different things were then. I told the girls we could not afford proper sanitary towels, and I did not see one until I started work.

Although I was very shy, I had lots of friends, played netball for the school, and belonged to the local Brownies. When I was thirteen, I thought I would like to earn some pocket money. Mum suggested putting a card in the village shop to say I would like a job baby-sitting and would charge 1/3d an hour. A week later a smart well-spoken lady knocked on our front door and said she was Mrs Wallis and lived at Thurnham, and was checking that my mother approved of me baby-sitting. It may be quite late when they got home as they often went to London to the theatre, and would I be allowed to stay the night sometimes? She would pay me five shillings, the equivalent of fifty pence today. Would I go to the house the following Saturday to meet their little boy who was six months old and called Timothy?

I arrived after lunch, and a loud barking greeted me. Mrs Wallis had not told me they had a dog. Although we always had a dog at home, I have always been rather nervous of dogs, and this one was a very large Bull Mastiff. Mrs Wallis suggested I take Timothy and the dog for a walk to get to know them. The dog Oscar I found to be a great softie, and as the house was in quite a lonely lane I was pleased to have him with me. The Wallis family owned a local building firm. They had a very full social life, so most weekends I was there. They had a radiogram with a large selection of records. Fats Waller was their favourite, not my sort of music; I was a great fan of Mario Lanza. During the school summer holidays, I would often go down for the day while Mrs Wallis had one of her days in London, shopping and having her hair styled, which I thought very grand. While the baby had his nap, I would often have a look in her wardrobe. I could not believe one person could have so many clothes. The wardrobe was the length of the large bedroom. On one occasion she had bought a new swimsuit so I thought I would try it on. The bedroom faced the front of the house, and between the two large windows was a full length mirror which I was admiring myself in. I saw Mrs Wallis returning early so I pulled off the swimsuit, grabbed my clothes, ran into the bathroom, dressed, and pretended I was using the toilet. I had learnt my lesson about trying on her clothes. If the Wallises were going out for the evening, I would go to the house early to give Timothy his tea, and bath him while Mrs Wallis was getting ready. He was a good baby and very rarely awoke during the evening so I would often do the ironing. She had good value for the 1/3d [7 pence] an hour that I would earn.

During the school holidays, Mrs Wallis asked me if I would take Timothy to stay with her mother who owned a guest house at Worthing in Sussex so they could go away for a few days - quite a responsibility for a thirteen-year-old. Mrs Wallis drove us down to Worthing, a quiet seaside town which was a popular place for people to retire to. Timothy and I were to share a room at the top of the house with a lovely view over the roof tops. I was left completely in charge of the baby. We would have breakfast with the other guests in the dining room, all of whom were old ladies who were delighted to have the baby staying with his nanny, as they called me. After breakfast, Timothy would have a nap while I washed his nappies and clothes. We would then have a walk along the sea front, return for lunch, and go out walking again. He loved sitting in his pram watching the sea-gulls. When I had my own children, I used to think no way would I allow a girl of thirteen to look after my children. Having been brought up in a big family, I was quite mature, more so than most girls of my age.

I had a very well-developed body with a thirty-four B bust and, at school, the boys would tease me. I hated being called names referring to

School and Working

my breasts. It was at this time that I really got to know Roger, who became my husband. He was unlike the other boys, much more of a gentleman. One of his friends had wanted to take me out, but Roger said that, as he was attracted to me himself, he did not pass on the message. Instead, he asked me out.

The first time Roger and I went out on our own, I did not tell my Mum. She thought I was going to see my friend Beryl. The only place to go would have been the cinema but we could not do that because I had to catch the last bus home which left the town at nine o'clock. Very few dances were held during the week, and I would have been too shy to have gone to one anyway. In fact, no-one would have gone to a dance unless in the appropriate clothes. This is before discos and clubs where now jeans are quite acceptable. Women did not wear jeans, and men only wore them for work.

Roger suggested we went for a walk along the river. To be quite truthful, I was nervous about being on my own with a boy. We walked until we came to what was called the high level bridge, and he said he wanted to kiss me. Before I could reply, I had had my first kiss. I thought, oh my goodness, now I will have a baby. The old saying of, 'ignorance is bliss', is not always true. I just kept thinking: what have I done? Although I had older sisters, neither they nor my Mum had ever discussed the facts of life; even when I had started menstruation, Mum did not explain why I was having it. We walked back to the bus station, and before I could get on I had had my second kiss. I could not get on the bus fast enough and hoped there wasn't anyone I or, worse still, my Mum, knew.

Miss Browne was the sports mistress. She also taught an extra activity, square dancing, which a group of us joined. Miss Browne was very enthusiastic and asked if we would like to do some demonstration dancing at local village fetes. My partner was a tall boy with auburn hair, but unfortunately I cannot remember his name. The last year Roger and I were at school, Miss Browne married and went to live in rooms in a large house near our house. It was owned by our French teacher, Miss Dibble, a precise, thin, very 1920 looking lady with short, straight, bobbed hair and round gold-rimmed glasses who was always immaculately dressed. Twenty-five years after I had left school, and was working at Leeds Castle, she attended a function and looked exactly the same. When I introduced myself, she said, 'Oh, you used to come to tea with Miss Browne, now let me think, your surname was Tapp.' This was true; Roger and I sometimes went to tea with Miss Browne and her husband.

If I wanted some extra pocket money, one way of earning it was to take Dad's empty beer bottles back to the local pub where I would get two old pence back for each bottle. It was about half an hour's walk to the pub, and I had been lots of times, so on a warm summer evening I took our dog Sukie. It was quite a lonely road past a little hamlet of houses, then the rest of the way woods were on one side of the road and open fields the other. I was in sight of the pub when I could hear the music and sounds of the fair which was being held beyond the woods in the park. The dog stopped and pricked up her ears at the sound of whistling. When I turned to look towards the woods where the dog was looking, I saw a man standing with his trousers down, exposing himself. I was too frightened to run and, because he was whistling, the dog kept pulling towards him. I then saw, coming towards us, a man on a bike who, as he got nearer, I recognised was John. He lived in the next road to us; he was disabled as he had been born with a hump on his back. I called out to him, 'Please help me, there is a man in the woods with his trousers down.' He told me to carry on to the pub as he had seen a police car parked there, then he left his bike on the side of the road and went chasing into the woods after the man. I thought this was very brave of him. I ran to the policeman and he said, 'Go back home,' then he joined the chase into the woods. Not long after I arrived home, a policeman and woman came to see me, asked lots of questions, and said if I saw him again to ring them as he had escaped through the woods.

A few weeks later, riding my bike to school, just as I got to the top of the hill by the pub, a motorbike slowed down. The rider did not have a helmet on - it was not compulsory then - and I recognised him as the man in the woods. Just past the pub was a telephone box so I rang the police and told them the number of the bike. That evening the police came to our house and said they had caught the man; he lived in an old cottage not far from us beyond the woods, hence the reason he escaped them. Sometime later I went to the local magistrate's court where he was charged with indecent exposure, and fined.

Around this time, Roger told his Mum he had a girlfriend. She asked if I would like to join them on a visit to the seaside one weekend. He said he thought I would, except I was attending court that week, but he didn't explain why. Sometime later, she said she had been really worried and thought I was in trouble with the police. She was very relieved when I explained.

School and Working

When I started to write my memoirs, we retrieved our boxes of love letters, mainly written when Roger went to sea. Amongst them was the very first letter he wrote to me in pencil saying he would meet me after school at the crossroads, but try and see him beforehand, also that his Mum had invited me to go to the seaside the following weekend. I had also kept a postcard he had sent the week before when he had been on holiday staying at Hastings with his Mum, her partner Harry, and Roger's grandma.

The following Sunday, I met Roger's Mum and Harry. We went on the bus to Folkestone; Harry did not drive. I wanted to go but, being so shy, found it quite an ordeal, especially as I knew I would have to eat out. We never went to restaurants. The only place I had been to was Lyons Corner House tea shop. When Mum went shopping on a Saturday morning she would meet her friend Mrs Green, and I was allowed to have tomato soup and a bread roll. When I think about those times, I can almost taste that soup and warm fresh bread. If I did not have that it would be a toasted bun and tea - having this was a great treat.

Roger wanted to kiss and cuddle me when we sat on the beach. I found this very embarrassing in front of his Mum and Harry. While they sat and dozed in their deck chairs, we went into the old town. Roger wanted to buy me a present. I always wore earrings so he bought me a sparkling pair. I didn't like to say I didn't like them, so I wore them on and off for many years and still have them.

Roger's Mum is quite an outspoken, forceful person. She had Roger when she was eighteen and, having had a private education, her parents thought she was too young to have a child but she lived at home with them and they adored Roger. Her Mum's family had been wealthy and had owned lots of property. The family house was near the village of Aylesford, next to the sandpits they owned. The house was called Kit's Coty House, named after the famous Kit's Coty, the remains of a prehistoric burial chamber. It consists of three enormous upright stones with another high stone resting on top. It is impossible to imagine just how they got the stones up there. This would have once been buried under a mound of earth and was probably a communal site for religious leaders. The lovely old family house, built high on the hillside, overlooked the burial chamber and the Medway valley. The family sold it many years ago; it is now a restaurant.

When Roger's Gran married his Granddad, she realised he liked to drink. Gradually over the years, Gran's family furniture and treasures, such as oil paintings, glass, and china, were sold. They sold the large house they lived in and moved to a smaller one on the outskirts of Maidstone. The front of the house was a shop selling practically everything, and Roger's Mum ran the shop with his Granddad while Gran looked after the house and Roger. About two years after I met Roger, his Granddad died. His mum hated running the shop so she closed it down and converted it into another room.

When I started going out with Roger, it was at the time I began baby-sitting for the Wallises. I asked Mrs Wallis if Roger could come along with me, and she said she would have to check with Mum who said it was all right with her. After he stayed a few times with me, if I was staying the night, he would go back to my house at about ten o'clock and stay there. Then Mrs Wallis said she was sorry but he would not be able to stay any more. Her neighbour, a severe tall thin woman whose husband owned the village butchers, had said it was not right we were there on our own. Her evil thoughts which she must have had were unfounded as we only ever sat on the sofa holding hands.

Art was my favourite subject, and Mr Herbert, my form teacher who was also my art teacher, suggested I went to the local Art College on Saturday mornings. I wanted to do fashion design. Mum said I could go but would have to take Valerie-Joan so she would make soft toys while I designed and learnt how to make the pattern, then the garment. During my last term at school, I was thrilled when I was told there was a place to go to the college full-time when I left school. I could not wait to tell Mum and Dad at tea that evening. 'Are you going to earn any money?' asked Dad. I tried to explain it was a privilege to obtain a place, but Dad's answer was that I was to get a job to give Mum some money. He said I was getting above myself thinking I wouldn't have to work.

Mrs Wallis knew I was due to leave school. The next time I baby sat, I told her how upset I was. I had hoped I could go to the art college, but Dad said I was to get a full-time job. Before I went home, she said we should have a chat, and asked if I would like to work full-time looking after Timothy, but only of course if Dad approved. Back home it was decided I could, and it would also mean I would not have any bus fares as I could ride my bike. The day after leaving school, I started. Mrs Wallis had been to London and bought me a uniform, blue and white check dresses for the mornings, and pink for the afternoons. If there were visitors, I had to wear

School and Working

a white frilly apron. Sometimes I would also look after the children of some friends when it was their nannies' day off.

I stayed at the Wallis home for almost a year. I liked looking after Timothy but it was very solitary not meeting anyone of my own age, so I thought I would look for another job. When in the town shopping, I saw a card in a dress shop window advertising for a junior sales assistant. The shop was owned by two Jewish brothers. I found it difficult telling Mrs Wallis I was going to leave, also leaving Timothy who I knew would miss me as he was with me all the time. Roger had stayed on at school an extra year, so he left the same time as me. He had obtained a place at a sea training school, the T.S. 'Warfleet' in the village of Botley, near Southampton. Looking back at that time, I did not realise Roger would spend more time at sea than at home over the next five years until we were married and had our first son.

During the time he was at Warfleet, he did have some leave. My brother Ted offered to drive Roger's Mum, my Mum, and me down to see him. When we arrived, Roger was feeling ill; he had a whitlow on his finger and was in a lot of pain. Ted took the two mums to the cinema, whilst all Roger and I could do was sit in the car. We could not even have a cuddle because he was in so much pain when he moved his hand. The next day he had the whitlow lanced. I think Roger found it hard as this was the first time he had been away from home. The discipline was very strict, but he now says it was a good start for him. I would send him parcels with cigarettes, toiletries, and writing paper as he was not earning any money.

Then the letter came to say he had passed his exams and had a position on a liner, the Winchester Castle, going to Capetown in South Africa, stopping at Durban, Las Palmas, and Madeira. This must have been an exciting time for him. At around this time, we had my Dad's mum living with us. She had very long white hair. I don't think she had ever had it cut, and only washed it twice a year. It was in beautiful condition, and she always wore a long black dress with detachable white lace collars, and black boots that laced up the front. She liked Roger, and when she became ill she said she was waiting for him to come home, but she died shortly before he arrived home from sea. She was ninety-nine; we were hoping she would live to be one hundred.

I had started work at the dress shop as the junior. I was not allowed to approach the customers. The first sales lady would enquire if she could help; my job was to make sure all the dresses, suits, and coats were in sizes and hanging correctly. Then after the customer tried a garment on, I would hang it back up again. As time went on, I became second sales which enabled me to earn commission.

The first sales was a lovely lady, Sybil, who was to become one of my dearest friends. She had a hard life; her husband Cyril worked for his relations who owned a fish and chip shop so he worked all hours. They found it hard to manage on his wages so Sybil had decided to go back to work. They had two sons; the eldest went to Grammar school and eventually to university. This was all extra expense but Sybil was so proud of her boys. The younger one did well and became a headmaster of a school. Sybil always said I was the daughter she had not had. I had been working at the shop about a year when we were told the shop was closing down. I had been in a bright new shop selling modern clothes so I asked the manageress - a well-built lady with short auburn hair; she wore heavy make-up, but well applied, and was wearing a smart black suit - if there were any vacancies. She said she would take me on but it was a different sort of selling and I would be on the sweater counter. I felt sad leaving Sybil, and had been at Jax, the new shop, two weeks when Sybil came in to see me and said she did not know what she would do; she only had a week before the dress shop closed. I told her how I enjoyed working in the new shop, and they were looking for another assistant. The next week Sybil joined me, and the other girls took to her straight away. She became the shop mum.

Before I left school, I had a flair for hairdressing. It wasn't possible to train because you had to serve an apprenticeship with a very small wage, and sometimes you had to pay to be trained. My Dad would not have agreed to that. Home perms had become easy to use so I would cut, perm, and set my Mum's, sister Nellie's, Barb's, and Valerie-Joan's hair. One day as Mum waited at the bus stop, a lady who lived near by said Mum's hair always looked nice and asked who her hairdresser was. Mum said I did hers and the rest of the family. She asked if I would go and see her as she would like me to do hers. I had half a day off on a Wednesday so I went to see her and started going every week; then her neighbour asked if I could do her. Next door to her lived a family whose daughter Jo I had been to school with. They lived in a bungalow with a large conservatory at the back and a lovely garden. Valerie-Joan and I envied Jo who seemed to have everything, nice clothes and lovely birthday parties, a handsome Dad and attractive young Mum, but their lives were to be turned upside

School and Working

down when Jo's Mum in her thirties had a stroke. She had always been very smart, very house proud, and loved cooking, and then suddenly she could not do any of these things. She was hardly able to get herself dressed, so Mum went round each week cleaning and preparing the food. She became another customer on a Wednesday afternoon.

Valerie-Joan had blonde hair. I cringe now when I think how I used peroxide to streak the front of her hair. How it did not all fall out, I will never know, but she was the envy of the girls on the school bus. I had a large vanity box with my make-up in. When I was out, Valerie-Joan and my niece, Heather, would have a great time trying all the make-up but of course I did not know until many years later. Heather, my sister Barb's daughter, used to stay with us frequently, also Jean my eldest sister, Phyllis's daughter, who was only a few months older than me. Mum and Phyllis had been pregnant at the same time, and Jean would stay with us during the school holidays. We would all get on well riding our bikes around the lanes - it was a carefree childhood.

7

MARRIAGE AND FAMILY

I settled in working at the shop and we all got on really well. I was still quite reserved, but working with girls who were older than me brought me out of my shell a bit. As with most young girls, the talk was mainly about boyfriends. When I first started at the shop, Roger went to sea for six weeks to South Africa and back, and then had two weeks off. Mrs Filmer, the manageress, allowed me to save up my overtime for when he came home. Patsy, who was the window dresser, came from a very nice family which lived in a select part of town. Patsy was a bit of a rebel and had a boyfriend her parents did not approve of. My ears nearly fell off when we were in the staff room one lunch time. Patsy, and one of the other girls, Gill, would tell what they got up to with their boyfriends. Patsy told how the night before, her boyfriend had gone to sleep on the sofa so Patsy had got out his penis and drawn a face on it with lipstick; to my innocent ears this was scandalous. I did not dare tell my Mum or Roger.

Eventually, Patsy left so I became the window dresser. It was a responsible job, and if the shop's takings were not very good one week, we would get a visit from Miss Yates, the supervisor from head office. Everything would come out of the windows and I would have to think of a new theme and colour scheme. The clothes chosen would then have to be pressed. Blouses and jumpers would go on wire bodies after fine tissue paper was laid over the frame, the garment was pinned and fitted on, and the frame would hang from fine threads along with a display of skirts, dresses, and lingerie. I loved the job, especially at Easter and Christmas when we would use props such as a large sleigh with a Father Christmas.

Roger had changed ships, and the letters were fewer. After a long time not hearing, a letter came to say they were in Cuba in dock and not allowed to leave due to the war and a leader called Fidel Castro. Soon we were all to find out who he was. Troops had boarded the ship, confiscated the cargo, and then next day returned and gave them Havana cigars and white rum. The day the letter arrived I was going up to Roger's Mum after work. I usually went up once a week to do her hair. By this time, Roger's granddad had died and they had closed the shop; his Mum was working in a dry cleaning shop. Sometimes my Mum would meet us both and we would go up to their house for tea, which I usually cooked. Roger's Mum was not very domesticated and did not like cooking so Gran did that, and they had a cleaning lady. As soon as we got to the house, Mum gave me my letter. After reading it, I told them the bad news that when they could leave Cuba, the ship would go to America, Japan, Hong Kong, Cape Town, Lisbon, India, and Hamburg. He would be gone in all just over nine months. I was so upset.

After tea, walking to the bus stop to go home, we saw Sybil. I ran across the road to her crying, 'Roger is stuck in some port in the middle of a war and will be away at least nine months.' Sybil put her arms around me, saying not to worry, the time would soon go.

To keep busy I would work any extra Friday night. We stayed open later as the local factory girls were paid then; most of them worked at the Sharp's toffee factory. In they would come to buy the latest fashion to wear that night to the local dance held in the Star hotel. I was going for ballroom dancing lessons with one of the girls we called Cash (because she was the shop cashier), a tall well-built girl with lovely natural blond hair. She later had an operation to pull her jaw back which jutted out. Her jaw was all wired up and she had food and drink through a straw. Once a week after work we would go to the Peter Pready dance school. The only trouble was we would have to dance together, and I would be the man, so Roger now complains I always take the lead when we dance.

The girls at the shop found out I did my hairdressing so I started to do some of theirs. I would go home after work with them, and perm, colour or set their hair. Sometimes I would do three of the girls. By now I had a portable hair dryer, just like the salon dryers. We would often go to my lovely friend René's home, and we did face packs and manicures while their hair was drying; we had such great fun on these occasions.

My best friend at work was Ella, very attractive with very blue eyes and black hair, and I got to know all her family. She lived at home with her Mum and had older sisters. Sometimes I went home with her to do her, and her Mum's and sisters', hair. I knew Ella had a boyfriend although I had never seen him, but she said her Mum and sisters did not approve of him. Ella asked me to keep a secret; she said she was thinking of running away with her boyfriend. I did not really believe her until, a few days later, a policewoman came into the shop and asked if anyone knew where she had gone. None of us could help but they soon found them. Ella did not come back to the shop and I never saw her again, although sometimes her Mum or sisters would come in the shop. I missed her. Many years later, David, our youngest son, came home from school talking about a girl in his class. I recognised the name and asked him to ask if her Mum was called Ella and, if so, did she remember Margaret from Jax, and sure enough it was her.

With Roger away, the girls were always trying to encourage me to go out with other boys but I was not interested. On one occasion I was in the shop window, working on a display, when there was a tap on the window. This was always happening - boys acting stupid - but this time I turned to see two very handsome American servicemen. They were asking me to go outside. I tried to ignore them but they were quite persistent and went into the shop and asked to speak to me. I went outside, and the tall dark one asked if he could take me to dinner and dancing at the Star hotel. I said I was sorry but I could not, and returned to the window. He went back into the shop and asked the girls if they would persuade me. As they were leaving, he tapped the window and said he would wait in the foyer of the hotel at eight o'clock. The girls said I was crazy to refuse, but I was not going to be a one-night stand for a handsome American.

Before Roger had gone on his long voyage, he had bought me a dog, a black standard poodle called Whizz. She was very nervous and hated traffic, but eventually she calmed down. I would usually wear a black suit to work. I would not have considered going casually dressed, and all my accessories had to match whatever the weather. I always had a long umbrella - they were the fashion accessory. I would cover it with material to match the blouse I was wearing. On one occasion I had a black and white striped blouse, a matching umbrella, and I had painted stripes on my earrings. When I had Whizz, she always wore a bow to match my outfit. On the evenings I went up to Roger's Mum, either my Mum or Valerie-Joan would bring Whizz to the shop for me to take up with me. Valerie-Joan said I was a pain always saying she had to brush and comb her and put the right colour ribbon on her. When Roger and I had our engagement party, Whizz had a collar and bow to match my dress.

Eventually, Roger came home from his long trip. Some of the crew hired an old Dakota aircraft from Hamburg, otherwise they would have gone deep sea again and it could have been months before they came home. Roger would sleep in my bedroom, and I had a spare bed in Nellie's room. Mum allowed me to go in to say goodnight to him that first night home. I lay on top of the bed, and Roger held me and said, 'I just want to hold you and drink you in.' It must have been very hard for him to control himself but he did not take advantage.

Roger decided he wanted to learn to drive so we bought a car, a Ford Special, made from fibre glass - a snazzy little sports car. We borrowed the money from my brother, Ted. Roger had money sent home to pay Ted back. It would be difficult for Roger to have driving lessons as he was at sea most of the time, so Ted said he would take him out when he was on leave. As Ted worked shift work, he was often home during the day. Well, he did not get many lessons. During his first leave home after buying the car, his test came through. He took the test and passed. This was great. It gave us such freedom when he was home; we would drive out into the countryside. We rented a garage which was about fifteen minutes from our house. Once a week, I would walk there and wash and polish the car. I thought it a bit silly that it sat in the garage for six weeks while Roger was away at sea so I decided to learn to drive.

There were not many women drivers, and only one driving school in the town, so I enrolled, had one set of ten lessons and, much to my amazement, passed my test first time. I wanted to surprise Roger when he came home. He always came to the shop first to see me when he arrived home, so as usual he called round to the shop and said he would go home and get the car to pick me up when I finished work. I said, 'There is no need, the car is in the car park behind the shop.' 'Oh, did your brother bring it down for you?' he asked. He was quite taken aback when I replied, 'No, I did.' Once I could drive, I would sometimes help out in other branches of the shop, so would often work in Oxford Street or Tunbridge Wells. I was able to drive Roger back to the docks and, if I was not working, go to meet him when he arrived home.

When Roger was on his nine-month trips, he wrote and told his Mum he would like to get engaged to me, but to keep it a surprise until he arrived home. His Mum replied to him saying she was all for us getting engaged and he had known me long enough to know his own mind. 'I know she has some funny ways at times but I will say she has stayed true to you while you have been away. She has never stopped coming up to see me and she will do anything for me.' We never did find out what the funny ways were! His Mum told me she wanted to have a party for Roger when he came home as he had been away for so long. She found out what sort of rings I liked, and my size. As soon as he arrived home he went out and bought the ring. That night, we went up to his Mum and, beside their house in an alleyway which was very dark, Roger said he wanted to ask me something. He kissed me and asked if I would I marry him; then he put a ring on my finger. It was so dark I could not see a thing, so we went back into the street under a lamp, and the diamond sparkled in the lamp light. I then started to panic. 'What do you think your Mum will say?' 'Well, go in and see,' he replied.

We went in and I immediately asked his Mum to come to the outside toilet with me. It may seem strange now, but, even at home, if anyone wanted to use the toilet at night, we always took someone with us to wait outside. In the garden, I said I did not want to use the toilet but had something to tell her. Roger has bought a ring and asked me to marry him. 'That's all right,' she said, 'I know all about it.' When we went back inside, she told me how it had all been a secret, and that the coming home party was really to be an engagement party. All the family were pleased, and the party, held in rooms over a local pub, was a great success. We had sixty guests and, for the entertainment, a pianist who cost one guinea.

I was seventeen, and Roger eighteen, when we got engaged. We planned on getting married the following year. I had always wanted a winter wedding, and a friend had said that if I designed my dress she would make it; she had been a court dressmaker. I wanted white velvet with red velvet bridesmaids. I prepared the designs, and then asked my friend if she was still willing to make them. She said she was sorry but she now worked full-time so she was unable to. I was very disappointed so Valerie-Joan and I went to London. I saw a white ballerina-length lace dress, completely different to the plain long dress I had designed. I tried it on and it was a perfect fit.

On my way to work the next day, I saw a silvery blue dress I thought would suit Valerie-Joan who was going to be my chief bridesmaid. I wanted to have my niece Heather as well, and when I told Roger's Mum this, she said her sister's girls would have to be bridesmaids too, and she had four girls. My Mum said it would be too expensive, so it was decided

I could only have Valerie-Joan. I don't think Heather ever forgave me.

As we went ahead with the arrangements, it proved difficult as we had to make sure Roger's ship would dock in time. The only date available was January tenth, 1959. My parish church was in the village of Boxley, a lovely country church with a lych-gate, but Roger wanted to be married in his church where he had been a choir boy. Saint Paul's was on the outskirts of Maidstone, a large church with beautiful stained glass windows. I was so pleased we decided to be married there, as three years later we had our first son Richard christened. Then not long after that some small boys set fire to the hymn books, and the church was almost burnt to the ground. Eventually demolished, a block of flats was built surrounded by the grave stones.

A month before Roger came home for the wedding, he sent me a poem he had written.

> Soon the bells will be ringing, just for you and me
> For we will soon be married, my darling wife to be.
> We'll be there at the altar, and side by side we'll stand,
> And take the oaths of marriage to make us man and wife.
> For when I put the ring on your finger, dear,
> We'll bind our love forever until eternity.

Roger was due to arrive home the night before we were to be married, so we hoped and prayed the ship would sail on time. I had to make all the arrangements, choosing and buying the wedding rings. The tenth of January was a cold frosty morning, and the garden had a sprinkling of sparkling snow. The day before, Mum had made a large pot of stew as we were not getting married until the afternoon. As always, Mum stuck to the rules that we would all eat midday. When I make a stew today, it always reminds me of that day. I am sure there are not many brides who go off to their wedding after a meal of stew and dumplings.

Dad and I were the last to leave the house, with strict instructions from Mum to make sure everywhere was locked up. I had worried about my Dad giving me away, as he had not spoken to me for nearly two years. Roger had asked him if we could get married, and he said yes. He was always pleasant to Roger. I said previously that Dad could be difficult to get on with and hated mixing with people. When I went to work for the Wallis family, he said, 'That's it; get in with the posh knobs.'

Marriage and Family

He was always funny about Roger's family as they had their own business and owned their house. Many years later I found out why he acted like he did. I think he felt a failure because he had wanted his own business. He did not like Mum having visitors, and this was part of the reason he was not talking to me. Roger's Mum and Harry had the habit of turning up sometimes. Mum enjoyed this, but Dad would sit and read his paper most of the time as if they were not there. Dad also had the habit of drinking his tea out of his saucer. On one occasion he was doing it and I clicked my tongue as I did not approve. He was very annoyed and shouted that I was getting too much of an upstart, mixing with the knobs. 'I don't suppose they drink their tea out of the saucer up his house,' meaning Roger's home. He did not speak to me for the next two years until we were leaving the house to go to the church, and he asked me if I was all right.

Waiting at our front gate was a group of ladies who had come to see the wedding party leave. The church was full of relatives and friends, and we had the traditional wedding service. There had been a sprinkling of snow while we were in church, and while we waited to have our photographs taken, the photographers put their overcoats round Valerie-Joan and my shoulders to keep us warm. The wedding reception was held where we had our engagement party. My sister Nellie had some friends who had a hotel so she paid for us to spend our wedding night there. I was very embarrassed that the owners knew it was our wedding night, and made Roger pick up all the confetti that fell out of our clothes. I doubt that many couples today are that shy and naive.

Roger had only a week at home, and then he was back at sea. We hoped to get a house and start a family straight away. I was not too knowledgeable on the subject of sex, and thought I would become pregnant immediately, but with Roger away at sea for six weeks, and only home for two weeks, I did not become pregnant for a year. We had very little time on our own when Roger was home, with Mum, Dad, Nellie, and Valerie-Joan all sharing the house.

At the end of our first year of marriage, Roger came home and everyone was out. We did not have a bathroom, so to have a bath we had to light the copper in the scullery and bring out the tin bath. I had mine first, as I would still undress in the dark. Roger had his, then in front of the fire we made love and our first son Richard was conceived.

Back at sea Roger wrote me another poem.

I believe that God above
Created you for me to love,
He picked you out from all the rest
Because he knew I'd love you best.
I had a heart once good and true,
But now it's gone from me to you,
So look after it, as I have done,
For you now have two, and I have none,
This is my prayer I send to you,
My darling, I love you.

Mrs Filmer, the manageress at the shop, always said she looked forward to me taking our first child into the shop to see her. That was not to happen; she was taken ill before I became pregnant and, after a short while, died. She had a daughter, Christine, sad to say, who also died young leaving small children.

Mrs Gresbey, who lived in the cottage opposite, called Mum to the fence one morning, a few weeks after we were married, and much to Mum's annoyance said,

'I see that young daughter of yours got married. Which one was it? She seemed to have a variety.'

'What do you mean?' Mum demanded.

'Well, I have seen her bring home a sailor, a solder, and one in a suit,' replied Mrs Gresbey.

Mum was so annoyed. 'If you must know, that is the same young man. He was in the army cadets; now he is in the navy, and he wears the suit when he is home on leave.' Mum stormed into the kitchen, saying to my sister Nellie, 'nosy old so-and-so.'

Six weeks after we had made love in front of the fire, Roger was back at sea and I realised I had not had a period. I wanted to go to the doctor, but knew I would have to wait until I had missed two more. In the fifties, you could not get a pregnancy test from the chemist as you can today. The surgery was still in the old house in the village, with its coal fire in the waiting room, and the tin box on the wall outside where the medicines were left for patients to collect - not something safe to do today. I saw our family doctor who confirmed I was pregnant and arranged for me to see the local midwife, Sister Paul, who was so pleased when I told her who I was. She had been the midwife who had delivered me, and had known our family for years. When we lived at Scragged Oak, Mum would assist Sister Paul when women in the village went into labour. Now she was due to retire at the end of the year and was very excited that I had been one of her babies, and would now deliver my child.

Jax, the shop where I was working, was going to close down. All the staff was really sad, and I decided I would have to find another job before I became too pregnant. Paiges, a dress shop in the town, was advertising for a window dresser saleswoman. I went to see the manageress who said I was what they were looking for and I could start the following week. Sybil was worried she would not have a job when Jax closed so when I had been at the shop for two weeks and they said they needed a first sales, I recommended Sybil. She came to the shop for an interview and was taken on; she was so pleased. We enjoyed working at the shop, but not as much as Jax. It was a more formal atmosphere. At Jax we were one big family sharing everyone's joys and sorrows.

Roger was overjoyed I was having our baby. He was on the 'SS Silvo' in Stockholm when he received my letter telling him I was pregnant. He replied:

> My own darling wife,
> I was so glad to get a letter from you today, darling, but what pleased me most of all was hearing that you were really having a baby. I cannot believe it is true, and cannot wait for you to have the baby.

During the next few weeks, I write and tell Roger I can feel the baby moving. It is a funny sensation. If I lay a newspaper on my tummy, you can see it moving. The next time Roger was home, we were discussing having the baby when I said to Roger I was not sure how the baby was going to get out of my belly button. He laughed and said he would have to have a talk with me. When he told me how the baby would be born, I was horrified.

I went into work one day when I was seven month's pregnant. I had been serving a lady and her husband when the manageress called me into her office. I had put on quite a lot of weight, as I had only been wearing a size eight before I became pregnant. 'I saw the customer's husband looking at you. Now you are showing you are pregnant, you will have to give up work.'

The following week I left, and the girls had bought me lovely presents for the baby.

It had been quite difficult driving as I had to sit near to the steering wheel. I am only five foot one and a half, and by the time I was nine months I weighed fourteen stone so I had been pleased to give up work. It had also been a hot summer. A few weeks before the baby was due, Roger came home from his last trip to sea. He thought he would find it difficult to get employment having been at sea for so long but was offered the position of operator at a tarmac plant.

At two o'clock on the twenty-eighth of September 1960, I awoke with the most dreadful pains. Roger was sound asleep but the pains were so bad I thought something must be wrong so I awoke him and asked him to wake my Mum. 'You have started to have the baby,' said Mum. 'We will have to get everything ready for the doctor and the midwife, Sister Paul.' The bed was remade with old sheets, and the copper in the scullery lit. Roger and I had moved out of my little bedroom, down into the front room, so when the baby was born, Mum wouldn't have to keep running up and down stairs. At that time you had what we called a 'lying in' after the baby was born. You had to stay in bed for a week to ten days, and the midwife would call every day.

I had never had such awful pains. I felt I could not sit down, and the best position was leaning over the armchair. Ten hours later, I was feeling exhausted. The doctor arrived with a new doctor who had recently joined the practice. My waters had broken before they arrived, and after they examined me they said the baby should be born soon, but it was another two hours, after another agonizing pain, before Sister Paul became very excited. We have the head coming, but it wasn't only the head, one of the baby's arms was over the head, and all I could see was a head, with lots of black hair and a little hand waving about, yelling its head off. Dr Newberry, the new young doctor, had become concerned that the labour had been going on too long and had thought I should go to hospital. Sister Paul had not been happy about that. 'There is no need for that - we are doing fine, are we not dear?' she had said to me, but dear just wanted to get it over and did not think we were doing fine. I had never had pains like it. During the time I had been in labour, my Dad had gone to work, come home for dinner, and gone back to work again. As no-one had been to tell him I had had the baby, he came back home to find Roger still pacing the kitchen. He had not been allowed in to see the birth. Sister Paul would not allow that. She said the fathers had done their bit so there was no need for him to come in. It is so different today when fathers are welcome at the birth.

One last push and out came a baby boy still yelling his head off. Mum wrapped him in a blanket while Sister Paul attended to me. Seeing that all appeared well, after the afterbirth arrived, the doctors left 'You need stitching,' she said, 'this will hurt a bit.' Could anything hurt as much as the baby being born? I had had no gas and air or pain control. Sister Paul did not believe in it, and she just stitched me up. Mum went and told Roger, Dad, and Nellie that we had a son, and now I was going to have stitches. Nellie said, 'I cannot stand anymore. I am going round to see my friend, Mrs Grange.' I saw her run past the window. During the time I was giving birth, Sister Paul had given Mum a camera and said she wanted her to take photographs to record this special event, as she had delivered me and was now delivering my child.

The baby was bathed and put in a long white night-gown; boys and girls were all dressed the same. Sister Paul, when weighing him, had said, 'oh my goodness, he weighs ten pounds two ounces. We cannot put that, so we will put ten pounds - that is big enough. She was a law unto herself and you did not argue with her. Roger was at last allowed in to see his son. We had already decided that if the baby was a boy he would be named Richard. Roger was over the moon with his son.

That evening, mother-in-law, Harry, and Gran came to see the baby. Mother-in-law was pleased because she had a grandson; she did not like girls. The next day, other members of the family came to see the baby. There is always great excitement when anyone in the family has a baby. Sybil and René came to see the baby. Sybil was holding Richard. 'I hope this is not catching,' she laughed, and three months later Sybil was pregnant with her daughter Jane. Poor Sybil found it hard to manage on her husband Cyril's wages. It would mean she would have to give up work, plus she was forty-six, but her family and friends all rallied round and helped out with things for the baby. When Jane was four years old, Cyril was taken ill. He had for some while been having problems with his stomach, unable to eat properly and passing blood, so he was admitted to hospital and in a very short time, died. Sybil coped really well.

I found having my own baby quite different from looking after Timothy or baby-sitting for nieces and nephews. This little person was my responsibility. He was not a very good baby, mainly because Sister Paul insisted I breast fed him. Although I had lots of milk, Richard was a big baby and it was not enough for him, plus he was quite a sick baby as well. When I took him to the clinic, the health visitor suggested I put him on solid food and also try him on tinned baby milk; this did the trick. At first Mum did not approve as this was a modern way, but Richard settled down and slept better and was not so sick. I was finding it difficult with us all living in the same house and I felt as if I could not do as I wanted with the baby. He was constantly being picked up as so many people were coming and going all the time. My sister Barb and family were living in a flat in the village of Detling where we used to live and were hoping to move into a house as they now had three children. Roger and I thought that if they got a house, perhaps we would get the flat. Barb came in to tell us they had got a new house at Langley, a small village about fifteen minutes' drive from Gidds Hill. That night in bed, Roger said, 'I wonder if we will get the flat.' The next day we had even better news. We heard we had a house next door to Barb.

Because I had had stitches after having Richard, Roger and I had not made love until Richard was three months old, and I became pregnant that first time, once again out of ignorance. Because I had not become pregnant as soon as we were married, we thought the same thing would happen again, plus I had been told that all the time you breast-feed you would not become pregnant. I did not tell Mum I had been sick a few times, but you cannot hide things from mums and one morning Mum said, 'Are you pregnant again?' I replied I thought I was as I had not had a period and had been sick. The doctor confirmed I was pregnant.

As soon as we got engaged we had started saving and buying furniture, so when we got a house we had all the basic things we needed. We went to view the house. We were next door to Barb and Ted, and were very excited - a new three-bedroomed house with a good size garden. Richard was six months old when we moved in.

Mum wanted us to go back and stay with her when I had the new baby. It would be better for Mum because Dad did not like her going away. On the seventeenth of October 1961, I awoke with what I knew were labour pains. Roger helped me pack the last of the things we needed to take. With one young baby already, I had quite a lot to take. We and Mum did not have a phone so we had no way of letting her know we were on our way. Having sorted ourselves out, the pains were quite frequent so we made our way to Mum. As soon as we arrived, Roger was dispatched to the local phone box to ring the midwife and, half an hour later, two young

Marriage and Family

midwives arrived. They examined me and said it would not be too long. Sue, one of the midwives, gave me an injection to help with the pain, and just before two o'clock that afternoon our daughter was born. Roger was allowed in straightaway. It had been a much better experience than with Sister Paul and her old-fashioned regime. Everyone was so pleased that we now had a little girl, although she was not so little - she weighed nine and three quarter pounds. We decided to name her Julie. Richard was brought in to see his sister, and although he was only thirteen months old he seemed such a big boy to the baby.

After a week, we decided to go home. I needed to get into a routine, plus I felt Mum had run around enough. It had been nice to be waited on but it was also good to be in our own home. Sybil and René came to see the new baby and our house. Sybil had had her baby, a little girl, Jane. We had a lovely day with lots to chat about. Julie was six months old when another of the girls from work, Sylvia, wrote to say she had a few days off and could she come for the day.

When we had Richard, Mother-in-law said she wanted to buy the pram. She chose a large black and white coach-built pram, which was lovely but cost a fortune. It was a bright sunny day, and Julie was sitting up in the pram in a white dress and frilly bonnet. We walked to the bus stop to meet Sylvia, and Richard had a seat at the end of the pram. Many years later when I met up with Sylvia again, she said she always remembers Julie in her bonnet and Richard sitting on the pram. At that time she was desperate to have a baby. She was married but we did not know it was a very unhappy marriage. She did eventually have a daughter.

We were very happy in our house. Most Sundays, Mum and Dad, or Mother-in-law and Harry and little Gran, would come for lunch or tea. I enjoyed looking after the children, cooking and cleaning. I had had good training from Mum. Around this time, Mum had started to have trouble with her stomach; sometimes the pains were so bad she would lie on the floor. When at last she saw the doctor, he said she had an ulcer. I think it took her so long to go to the doctor because she was frightened; her mum had died very young with stomach problems.

When Richard was three and Julie two, I started to get broody again. After I had Richard, I told Mum it was the most awful experience, with dreadful pains. She had not told me it would be like that, and I said I was not going to have any more children. 'You will change your mind; it is something you soon forget,' she said. So, becoming pregnant with Julie had been a good thing; the young midwives made it a much better experience. After I had had Julie, the doctor said we should wait before having more children because I was only small and, because they had been large babies, my body needed time to recover. In October 1963, I became pregnant again and found I was feeling more tired with this baby. When I was nine months, the doctor said if I did not rest I would have to go into hospital as my legs were swelling and my blood pressure was up. Two weeks later, on the fourth of June 1964, I woke at three o'clock in the morning with pains. I paced the bedroom trying not to wake Roger. Behind our house were some bungalows, and in one lived Mary and her husband. They had one little girl, and Mary was pregnant again. While I paced up and down, I heard a car, looked out of the window, and saw it was the midwife. Mary must be having her baby. Sure enough, when the midwife came to me later, she said Mary had had a little girl, Jill.

When she was in her teens, she developed cancer and died in hospital the same time as my sister Lili-Anne. I was so shocked when we went to visit Lili-Anne and saw Jill; it seemed so unfair as she was only a teenager. While she was in remission, Jill helped raise funds for a local charity, the Kent Leukaemia and Cancer Equipment Fund which had been started by Peggy Wood who is my brother Ted's wife's sister. When her grandson was diagnosed with cancer, she found that some of the equipment the hospital needed, they did not have, so Peggy set about raising funds for them. Some of the children had to travel by train to London. This was not good because they had to avoid getting any infection as this could be fatal, so sometimes they went into the goods van so not to sit with anyone with germs. Peggy set about raising funds to buy a specially equipped ambulance for the children to travel in. The fund has raised over two million, not only for the children but equipment for many other departments at the local hospital including the breast and oncology units. Peggy started by running the charity from a shed at the bottom of her garden.

My waters had broken, and the pains were more frequent so I woke Roger and said he would have to go and get Mum. We dressed Richard and Julie. They both had red jumpers; Richard had little tartan trousers, and Julie a tartan skirt. I thought how small they both were, and with a new baby I was going to be very busy. Roger took them with him to get my Mum, and he said he would ring the midwife on the way. When he had gone, I got the rest of the things ready. I suddenly had a strong pain and felt as if I needed to go to the toilet. As I sat on the toilet, the pains were very frequent. The midwife arrived and she said she would examine me, 'Oh my goodness, the baby is nearly here,' she said. Mum arrived with Roger, Richard, and Julie, and the midwife asked Mum to get some water ready. Once again, Roger was sent out of the room. It is something we both regret that he did not see any of the children born - today fathers are welcomed into the delivery room. 'One more push and the baby will be here. Good job you did not push when you were on the toilet or you would have had it down the loo,' said the nurse. 'You have a boy.' She laid the yelling baby on my tummy. She cut the cord and called Roger and Mum in. 'You have a lovely big boy,' she said as she weighed him - Eight and three quarter pounds. After I had had Richard, Mum told me any more children I had would probably get bigger. Thank goodness they did not.

We have a crib in the family, and whoever was having a baby would make new drapes for it which I had done. Julie had always loved dolls, so having a real baby in the crib was wonderful for her. She would tuck in the covers on the crib, and the baby only had to make a whimper for her to be there. We had decided to name the baby, David. Mum stayed until the weekend. By this time, family and friends had been to see the new baby, and I soon was into a routine. I did not have a washing machine so first job in the morning was to rinse out the nappies that had been soaking in a bucket over night. These were then boiled in a small gas boiler, followed by lots of rinsing. It was a messy business; I put a small bath under the mangle and hoped that the water, which was squeezed out, ended up in the bath and not on the floor. I had a washing line the length of the garden, and I still think it is a lovely sight - white washing blowing high on a line and, with three small children, my line was full each day.

There were no big supermarkets. We had the milkman, baker, butcher, and the greengrocer who would all call at the house. I would go shopping for the rest of my goods once a week; I did have a fridge, but not a freezer. Our leisure time was taking the children to the local park, and our holidays were staying in caravans. David was six months old when we thought it would be a nice idea to foster a child on a short-term basis - better for a child to stay with a family than going into a home. We had to have references from the health visitor, doctor, and a neighbour, so I asked a lady who lived opposite to us. She had had a large family and had known us long enough to know what sort of a family we were. Some weeks later, after visits from the local social worker, we had a letter to say we had been accepted. I had told them I would prefer to have a baby so as to fit in with our family. Two months went by, and then the social worker called to say there was a baby girl they would like us to foster. The baby was still in hospital where she had been born six weeks ago. Previously her mother had been on the contraceptive pill but had still fallen pregnant, and then had had a stroke which had paralysed her all down one side. She had not wanted any more children as she already had a little girl of two. They lived on a farm and she loved horse riding. When the baby was born, she had rejected her; she seemed to blame the baby for her stroke.

There was great excitement the day Sarah arrived. Julie was very pleased to have another baby in the house. Coming straight from the hospital, she did not have many clothes but I had a good supply. It was hard work, four children under four. I was quite organised, and my days were typical of a mother in the 1960s. I would get up with Roger, and the days were spent washing, cleaning, and cooking. We always had meat, fish, and fresh vegetables, and I would often make my own bread, and all our pies and cakes were home-made. In the afternoons, I would take the children for a walk - the baby one end of the pram and David the other, while Richard and Julie walked. There was little traffic so it was quite safe to walk around the country lanes. We would pick the blackberries, wild damsons, cob-nuts, and chestnuts, when in season, the same as Mum did, and I'd make my own jams and marmalade. After the children had had their tea, Sarah and David would have their bath in the sink in the kitchen, then they would have their bottles and go to bed. Richard and Julie would have a bath together in the bathroom, and sometimes Roger would be home early before they went to bed. He says some of the best memories of when they were young is coming home when they were all ready for bed, Julie in her pretty night-dresses and the little quilted dressing gown I had made, Richard in his pyjamas and blue dressing gown with red ladybird buttons, and the babies tucked up in their cots and all smelling of the clean fresh smell of baby powder.

As the children grew older we would all have our main meal together, always sitting at the dining room table, everyone trying to talk at once to tell what they had done with their day. We did not have a television so there was no watching while we ate as a lot of families do today. In the evenings we were still busy, me knitting or sewing, and Roger always doing something around the house. Sarah settled in well; her mother did not come to see her, but her grandmother did and, on the odd occasion, her father. The childcare lady would come every so often to see things were all right. Sarah was a lovely little girl who had the same blue eyes as David, and her hair the same as Julie's, so when I first took her to the clinic they thought she was mine. After we had had Sarah for about eight months, her grandmother arrived one day with her father and said they thought we should adopt her. As much as we loved her, it would have been easy to say yes, but she had a mother, father, and sister, plus the family was financially able to have a nanny if physically her mother could not cope. In fact, her mother had improved a great deal and had some feeling back in her limbs, so was able to ride which was her great love, and had also started to drive again. I told Sarah's grandmother I thought it would be a good idea if everyone encouraged her to come and see Sarah. After a while she started to visit. Some weeks later, she came and said she had decided to take Sarah home the next week. Late morning, I saw the car stop outside. Sarah was put in the car seat, the clothes and toys she had acquired were put in the boot and she had gone. I was fine until it was time to get the children's tea ready. I was about to put Sarah's dish on the highchair when I realised we did not have her anymore, and I stood and cried. About a month later, Sarah's mother arrived and asked if I would look after her for the weekend. I was over the moon. I thought, great we will still get to see her occasionally. We had a lovely weekend. When Sarah's mother arrived to take her home, she had brought me a present; it was a teapot. Nearly forty years later, we still use it when the family comes, and whenever I see it I always think of Sarah.

We did not see or hear from Sarah's family again until, about ten years later, Roger and I were helping at an archaeological dig. We had to walk along a lane leading to a riding school, and as we walked past a parked car I felt the urge to look in the car and recognised Sarah's mother. She looked at me, then looked away, and sitting in the back was Sarah and her sister, two pretty little girls with blond hair. I would have loved to have spoken to them, but knew their mother had recognised me and did not want to. Sarah was too young when we had her to remember us, and I certainly would not have said anything to upset her.

A week after Sarah had gone home, we had our next little girl, Mandy. She arrived looking a poor little thing. Her vest was all in holes, and Julie would get the vest out when we had visitors and say, 'look what the baby came in.' The first thing I always did when any of the children arrived was bath them and put them in clean clothes. This particular little girl I took into the childcare office, after she had been with us for two weeks, to see her mother. While we were waiting, a tall smart lady with her face make-up and hair all done, arrived and went into the office. I was amazed to discover this was the child's mother, seeing how poorly dressed Mandy was when she arrived at our home. The next to arrive were a sweet little brother and sister. I had the two so they did not have to be split up. They did everything together and they would follow me into the garden when I was hanging out the washing, always holding hands. When we were looking after Mandy I started to have migraine headaches. We were on holiday in a caravan, and had taken Mandy with us. The headaches always started with flashing stars before my eyes, and as the day wore on I was feeling awful. I had washed the children and was getting them ready for bed. While dressing Mandy, it became so bad I could hardly see and Roger had to put her nappy on. This really frightened me so when we arrived home I went to see my doctor. He said I must come off the contraceptive pill - I had started to take it after I had had David - and would Roger consider having a vasectomy. We had already discussed this as Roger did not like me taking the pill.

A few weeks later he went to the Marie Stopes clinic. I felt a little sad because I would have liked four children but we felt we were lucky to have three healthy children, and even if something awful had happened to any of them you cannot replace them. As soon as I stopped taking the pill, the headaches disappeared.

We continued to foster until David was four, then Roger said he thought I should have a rest as I had been washing nappies for the last eight years, and David would soon start school. We had also during this time had children from London who had never had a holiday or been to the countryside or seaside. Around this time, Roger had bought me a white Spitfire sports car. It was not very practical with three children, and we now had Seamus, a large Irish Setter, a scatty dog. Roger was the manager of a sewing machine shop and had gone to see a customer in her home. She had just moved into a small flat and had been told she was not allowed to keep the dog so Roger came away with Seamus. The lady did not tell him he chased cats when given the chance.

We had a lovely silver and grey stripy cat named Catty. The shop Roger managed was in Sevenoaks, and at the back of the shop there were feral cats. When one of them had kittens in a shed behind the shop, Roger started feeding them and eventually took one into the shop. A few weeks later we had Catty. Her favourite place to sit was on the sill of one of the kitchen windows. The first morning we had Seamus, he spotted Catty in her usual place and made a flying leap at the window. Next moment, with a great bang, the dog had gone through the window. We had glass everywhere, and a dog with a cut nose. It took months for us to stop him chasing her, but in the end they would sleep together. When I took the children to school, Seamus came too. I had our three children, the dog, and my niece Michelle, in this small sports car - no seat belts in those days. My sister Barb and her husband Ted were still living next door, and Michelle was three months younger than Richard. We would all pile in the car each morning and, after I dropped them off at school, I would take Seamus for a run around the playing fields. She had a habit of catching rabbits and bringing them back to me. She never killed them, just dropped them at my feet. We had both Seamus and Catty until they were seventeen, and when Seamus died, Catty was soon after. I'm sure she missed him.

Richard, Julie, and David attended the primary school in the village of Sutton Valance. The headmaster was Mr Cash, a lovely man well-built with a snowy white beard who, like all the teachers, had a great sense of duty and good old-fashioned values. It was sad that he retired early and, not long after, died. Mrs Morgan was the headmistress; Mrs Coot, the infant teacher, was the local vicar's wife, and Mrs Malby, who I still exchange Christmas cards with. David was five when he joined Richard and Julie at the school but he was not keen on starting. The first morning we arrived in Mrs Coot's class, he decided he wanted to go home with Mummy darling (he always called me this). After a great deal of persuading, and Julie coming in from her class, I was able to leave him. I had no trouble with Richard on his first day, but my niece Michelle, who lived next door, started with him. Julie, on her first day, decided she wanted her Dad to come and kiss her before I left. Roger was at work so Richard was brought in from his class.

When Richard was eleven, he went to Cornwallis secondary school. Mr Cash had told us he was grammar school material and should do well. I think he found it quite hard at first, going to a large Secondary Modern after a village school where you know everyone, the same as I had done. He settled in, with good results, and went on to Maidstone Grammar school.

8

MUM

I would go to visit Mum and Dad once a week, and do her weekly shop when I did mine. During the school holidays, Richard, Julie, and David would stay with Mum while I was shopping. They loved being at Mum's. She would sit on her swinging seat while they played in the garden, or they would walk along the hedgerows picking the wild flowers.

Mum had always had problems with her stomach, and had a stomach ulcer for sometime. Eventually, the ulcer burst. She was taken to hospital and then she developed angina. It was the twenty-eighth of April 1972, and my brother Ted arrived at our house with the most devastating news; Mum had died. We all knew Ted was Mum's favourite, and I don't think he ever came to terms with losing her. I remember being quite calm when Ted told me, but I just wanted to be on my own. It did not seem true. Mum had not been feeling well with the angina, and the doctor had said she must stay in bed and rest, so Barb, Lili-Anne, and I had been taking it in turns to go for the day to do housework and cook lunch for Mum and Dad. My sister Nellie, who still lived with them, was working. I had been the day before Mum died and she had seemed her usual self, frustrated because she had to rest in bed. The next day Lili-Anne was going later in the day, so in the morning Dad had pottered about tidying up. Mum seemed her self but said she felt tired so would have a little sleep while Dad did what he called his outside jobs, getting the coal in and chopping his morning wood. She asked him to wake her, when he had finished, with a cup of coffee. He made the coffee and took it into Mum but she had died as she slept. Dad could not be consoled; he cried all the time.

After Ted had gone, I had to collect the children from school. How was I going to tell the children and Roger? He was very close to Mum. I parked in the school grounds, and the children came running out and got in the car. I said I had something sad to tell them, and Julie immediately asked if something was wrong with her Dad. 'No,' I said, but gently told them Nan had died and gone to heaven; no-one spoke. I told them I had to phone Dad from the telephone box on the way home, as we did not have a telephone. I could not tell Roger without crying. I tried hard to be brave, but once I started to tell him I could not stop. He said he would come straight home.

We went to Mum's. All the family was there. Mum had been taken to the chapel of rest. Ted, Barb, Lili-Anne, and Nellie all said they wanted to go and see her. I think Lili-Anne went everyday until the funeral. I did not want to go; I wanted to remember Mum as I last saw her. Losing your Mum is one of the worse things that can happen to you. Mums are always there for you. Our Mum was what I call an old-fashioned mum whose whole life had revolved around the family. She had wanted to be buried at Detling village, Saint Martins, a lovely old church. The graveyard is across the road from the church through a lych-gate.

It was a bright, cold April day, and many of the people from the village were at the service. Mum had been well-thought of, having been part of the village for many years.

We all went back to the house that would never be the same without Mum. I always think it strange that people, who hardly ever visit, turn up for funerals and end up laughing and telling stories about old times. It was good to see my eldest sister, Phyllis. I hardly knew her. I can remember visiting her home very occasionally and being rather frightened of her husband, Horace. He was very strict and, although he had a full-time job, he waited on Phyllis, doing the housework and cooking. We would visit on a Sunday and he had always made cakes. As I have said, my Dad was rather unsociable so he hardly ever visited Phyllis, but I realised why many years later.

Dad found coping with Mum's death very hard to come to terms with, and for days he just sat and cried. In the end I asked the doctor what we should do, and he said,

'Nothing. When you have been with someone for many years, it is very hard so we must give him time.'

Richard, Julie, and David have great memories of their days spent with their Nan. I wish Mum had known that Richard obtained a place at Grammar school and went on to university. She would have been very proud.

9

JULIE

We had now moved into the village of Leeds, in Kent. It is very picturesque, the church with its Norman tower and history of bell-ringing, the remains of an Augustinian Priory, and the magical Leeds Castle. A year after Richard started at Cornwallis school, Julie joined him. She had been there about a year and a half and, like any girl of her age, thirteen, loved the latest fashion and pop music. I would take her and friends to their favourite stars' concerts; she also had ballet lessons and was a member of the school netball team. Doing well at school, the teachers said she would go on to Grammar school but we were to have some devastating news.

I enjoyed dress-making and made most of Julie's clothes. One evening I was making her a skirt but was having trouble making it hang properly; it kept pulling to one side. With us was a friend of Julie's, Carol, and it was her who said one hip was higher than the other. I saw she was right and that her spine was not straight; it seemed to curve. We were not too worried but decided to see our GP. Thank goodness we did. He sent us to our local hospital to be X-rayed that morning and also made an appointment for her to see a specialist. A few weeks later, we saw a consultant at the hospital who said he would like her to see a specialist at a London hospital, a Mr Manning, and all this time it had been worrying us as we were kept in the dark; nothing had been explained to us.

It was October 1974 when Julie and I travelled to London. This was to be the first of many visits to the Great Portland Street Orthopaedic hospital. Julie was X-rayed, measured, pricked with pins, and we were thoroughly questioned. Then the problem was revealed; she had Scoliosis. Her spine was rotating and curving, causing her body to twist, and was affecting her ribcage which was losing its symmetry and pressing on her lungs. It meant she would have to spend three months in hospital so that her spine could be straightened.

On the way home, Julie and I did not talk much; it had all been too much of a shock. Arriving home, Roger wanted to know what had happened. He was taken aback at the news and the length of time she would be in hospital, but little did we know that this was only the beginning, and there was to be a lot more involved than three months in hospital.

We arrived at the Royal National Orthopaedic hospital at Stanmore, Middlesex, on the twenty-third of March and went straight to the ward where we were introduced to the staff. Another girl arrived with the same problem, except that like most of the other girls on the ward she had one leg longer than the other. By the time we left, Julie had made friends with the other girls. The next day, she was X-rayed again, and the following day, a huge plaster from her shoulders to her hips was put on; around the bust it measured forty-two inches. Bolts were fixed, in the front, which were progressively tightened so that she gradually straightened. After one week, the curve of seventy-two degrees had been reduced to forty, and on the twenty-second of April, it was down to twenty-seven degrees. During all this time she had to lie flat on her back, and rolled on her side for her meals. During the whole time she never complained but, although it must have been very uncomfortable, she appeared happy and cheerful every time we visited. When some of the girls became tearful and depressed, she always managed to cheer them up by drawing or telling jokes Richard and David had told her.

We were not very well-off, and the journey involved catching two buses and two trains, so it was quite expensive. I would go every weekend and take Richard or David, and Roger every other week, and of course members of the family visited.

When the curve was down to twenty-seven degrees, Julie had major surgery. On the day of the operation, I went up to stay for a week and had a room in the nurses' home. I had been told to arrive after the operation. I was taken to the intensive care unit where Julie lay with pipes and tubes coming from everywhere, it seemed. She looked so ill; it frightened me so much I rang my sister Nellie. We were both crying. The problem was that no-one had told me what to expect, and I had never seen anyone in intensive care. I did not ring Roger until the evening; he was worried enough so I rang when I was not so upset.

I would go in and sit with her every day, but for the first few days she

Julie

was heavily drugged because of the pain. The doctor told me the operation had been a success which was great news. The operation had involved a twelve-inch steel rod being fused to the spine. When opened, the spine produces a jelly, and then strips of bone taken from the hip are placed across the rod. The jelly fuses it together so the operation is called a fusion of the spine. This had brought the curve down to eighteen degrees which was excellent seeing how big the curve was originally. When we were shown the X-rays taken before the operation, we could see the ribs had closed. Now they were opened and not pressing on her lungs.

At the end of the week, Julie was back on the ward recovering rapidly. Even though she was still in a lot of pain when she moved, she never complained. While she was in the theatre for her operation, another plaster had been put on. May the third, and the strips came off the incisions where the bone had been taken. Nine days later she was fitted with a slimmer plaster which went down to her hips and just above the knee on one leg. It was lighter, but unfortunately went up to her neck to give support to her head and neck. There was a hole in the middle to enable action for any emergency stomach problems.

In May, on my birthday, we went up to see Julie. I had made a cake for her and the other girls on the ward, but when we arrived one of the nurses accidentally revealed that Julie had a surprise for me. Somehow, lying on her back, she had managed to knit me a tea cosy. We were all very emotional. It had taken a great deal of effort, and the nurses were very impressed. I still have that tea cosy. Since the day she had her first large plaster fitted, she had not been allowed to stand so she had been lying down the whole time. The nurses would roll the girls on to trolleys where they would manoeuvre themselves around the ward, and on nice days go outside on to a patio. They also had tutors for their school work, and Julie won an award while she was there. It was reported in the local newspaper, with a photo of her receiving the award from the Chief Supt. of Harrow police, also the beat officer at Edgware who had visited the hospital encouraging the children to take part. They had to do three written tests, think up a road safety slogan, and paint a picture of the police at work.

At last the day came for her to come home. Two days before, she had been allowed up for the first time since being admitted, in order to learn to walk again whilst balancing the plaster as it was quite heavy. After two weeks at home, she wanted to go back to school. The doctor agreed she could, but because we were now living quite a long drive to her school it was suggested that Julie change schools and go to Swadelands at Lenham. A bus would pick her up at the end of our road because it was difficult for her to walk very far with the plaster on. The staff and pupils all helped, realising her difficulty. She had to wear the plaster for six months and, as it was one of our hottest summers for years, it must have been unbearable. Some days we would tip talcum powder down her neck to try and cool her down.

When the day came for her to have the plaster removed, we were excited, but also apprehensive. We went to the ward to see the nurses who thought she had coped really well. She was put in a harness hanging from the ceiling. When the plaster had been cut off, she was lowered into a bath. Julie says that was the best bath ever. The talcum powder we sprinkled into the plaster had formed a sort of coating of mud, and it must have been a wonderful feeling to have it all washed off. Julie was then fitted with a Milwaukee brace; this had a neck brace with a bar down the front and two bars at the back to which was fitted a wide leather band over her hips. It looked like a piece of torture equipment. She was not allowed out of the brace standing up, but after a month she would lie on the bed and I could roll her out of it for half an hour. She had to sleep in it which must have been so uncomfortable.

After three months we were back at the hospital, and - great news - she could take the brace off at night. It must have been wonderful the first night sleeping without it. Another three months later and the hospital said she could leave the brace off for good, the fusion was excellent and the treatment was over apart from check-ups every six months. The only things she could not do were trampolining, and diving when swimming. At last she could wear what she liked, instead of trousers and smocks, so we had to go clothes shopping. One thing that did worry us was whether she would be able to have children, but the doctors assured us she would. The only problem she may have is backache due to the rod down her spine. When you look at her now, there is nothing to indicate that she has had the operation except for a hair-line scar along her spine and on her hip where the bone was taken.

Julie had settled into school, but it had been a very stressful time for all of us. It was a very serious operation, and there had been days when I had gone into her bedroom, sat on her bed, and cried, wondering if the operation would be successful.

Now this was behind us, I started helping at Sutton Valance School

Julie

three afternoons a week. David was still attending there, but the following year he started at Swadelands with Julie.

Richard had obtained a place at Maidstone Grammar School and was doing well. He was a member of the school orchestra, playing the trumpet, and was also a member of the Maidstone youth orchestra.

Around this time, I started having pains in my stomach, and after some weeks I went to see our local GP, Dr. Vaux, who had been our GP for a number of years. He had just joined the surgery when he came to visit David. Richard and Julie had had chickenpox, and now David who was three months old was covered in watery spots. It was the usual procedure for the doctor to visit for any contagious disease. This was my first meeting with the new doctor. He looked at David and said, 'Poor little fellow.' He had on a cotton night-dress (no baby-grows then) to keep him cool, and mitts so he would not scratch himself. We had been on holiday in a caravan when Richard said he did not feel well, and soon he had the watery spots. I did not know what they were until we were back home and Mum told me. Julie was next, then David. Two weeks later, I found one watery spot on my breast, and very soon I was covered, even my head. My sister Barb who lived next door would talk to me through the kitchen window. I looked such a sight she sent my brother-in-law Ted to look at me.

When I thought it was over, I had pains around my middle. The doctor diagnosed shingles, and I was quite ill. I had to stay in for a month which was hard work with the baby and two small children.

Mum had died two years before Julie had her operation. I missed her, but I was to miss her even more.

10

FIRST OF THE GREMLINS

It was the end of 1974 when I made my first visit to the doctor for my stomach pains. He gave me medicine to take when the pain was bad, and told me to go back if the pain continued. The medicine did not help much and sometimes the pain was so bad it frightened me. I went back to my GP, Dr. Vaux. He thought I should see a colleague of his, Dr. Stevens, at the West Kent Hospital because they had an endoscope (long flexible tubes that transmit visual images). The tubes would go into the stomach, and the doctor can take a biopsy and watch what he is doing on a screen. It sounded awful, but when I arrived I was put at ease by the nurses. I was given Valium, a tranquillizer, so I was relaxed and sort of knew what was going on and could swallow the tube. After that I remembered nothing until the nurse awoke me with a cup of tea; once I could swallow, it was safe to go home. I was not allowed to drive so Roger came to collect me and have a chat with Dr. Stevens. I was still very sleepy. He told Roger there was an ulcer, but they would keep an eye on it and hopefully treatment would get rid of it. In charge of the ward was Kate Wrelton who looked after me for the next seventeen years until she retired. On one occasion she said I should have a gold star as I had been one of the first patients to be gastroscoped in the hospital, and must hold the record for having it done more times than anyone else.

From 1974, Dr. Stevens had gastroscoped me on several occasions, and on each occasion had seen a linear white slough running down the high lesser curve with excoriated areas. This area was gastroscoped and biopsied three times, in December 1975, in January 1976, and again in July 1977. The pathologist report showed some malignant infiltration. A barium-meal showed a slightly abnormal appearance on the lesser curve of the stomach. Dr. Stevens gastroscoped me again and then went on holiday, asking a colleague of his, Dr. Hardwick, to see me.

After the last gastroscope, I expected to see Dr. Vaux as usual, but this time I had a letter from Dr. Stevens to say he was sorry he could not see me as he was going on holiday, but would like me to see a colleague of his. I thought this strange and, as it had never happened before, I was a bit worried. The children were on holiday from school so Roger was having his annual holiday. My appointment with the consultant, Dr. Hardwick, was at the West Kent Hospital, Marsham Street, Maidstone, our nearest town. I suggested that Roger and the children went into town while I had my appointment.

I was shown into a small room, and the consultant Dr. Hardwick had with him someone who I guessed was his secretary. He must have introduced me, but the only thing I can remember was that she looked at me with compassion, and it frightened me. Dr. Hardwick told me that Dr. Stevens did not want me to wait until he came back from holiday, so had asked him to see me. He told me the biopsy had shown abnormal cells and that I should have an operation to remove them. At this stage I said a silly thing and told him that Dr. Stevens always said he would try and cure the ulcer without an operation as I was quite young. He looked serious and said I had no option, and he had made an appointment for me to go to the Westminster Hospital in London to see a Professor Ellis.

I sat in the garden behind the hospital to wait for Roger and the children. Our insurance lady came past and asked what I was doing sitting in the garden on my own. I did not feel like telling her too much so I said, 'I had an appointment and am waiting for the family.' I just wanted her to go as I wanted to cry on my own. She left, and Roger and the children appeared. It is funny the things we remember on such occasions, but I had asked them to buy a loaf and they had a large bloomer. Whenever I buy one now, I think of that day.

Roger was eager to know what Dr. Hardwick had said. I told him and said I wanted to go and see Dr. Vaux, my GP. We drove the ten minutes in silence; even the children sensed things were not right, and they were quiet. The surgery was empty so I asked the receptionist if I could see Dr. Vaux. I did not realise he was standing behind the screen but he said he would see me. I said I had been to see Dr. Hardwick, and told him what he had told me, and I wanted to know if I had cancer. He paused for a moment and said he could not say for sure until I had seen the professor, who would probably keep me in to operate to see what was going on but, yes, I did have abnormal cells. He suggested I take my things and be prepared for a stay.

I must confess, at that stage I thought he would cut out whatever the problem was, and that would be it. How wrong I was to be.

We thought that we should tell the family - my Dad, brother, sisters, and Roger's Mum - so if they did keep me in the hospital it would not be such a shock. When we arrived at Dad's, Nellie and Dad were sitting in the garden. I wanted to tell Nellie on her own so Roger suggested Dad went indoors for a chat. Nellie and I went round the back of the house. I can see us so vividly standing by the outside toilet. I told her the doctors said I had abnormal cells, and that it could be cancer of the stomach. I had been referred to a London hospital and most probably would have to stay in when I went to see the professor. Nellie started crying and this made me cry. I told her I would be all right. I said I was not frightened and I would have it cut out and I'd be fine. She said she would not tell Dad everything, only that I probably had to have an operation, and she would also tell the rest of the family.

The professor's clinic was held on a Saturday morning so we were up early. My bag packed, we drove to the hospital, parked the car and, as we were early, took the children over Westminster Bridge to see the Houses of Parliament and Westminster Abbey as we walked along the river. I wanted to get back to the hospital and get it over with. Perhaps he wouldn't keep me in. Perhaps there would not be a problem; it would be fine and I could go back home with the family.

Back at the clinic, after a short wait, I was called into the examining room. The nurse said to leave my pants and slip on, and the professor would be in shortly. After undressing, I sat on the edge of the bed. I had to keep wiping my hands on a tissue as I felt I was getting hotter all the time.

The Professor peeped round the door and asked if he could come in and bring some of his students with him. He introduced himself and shook my hand, and from that moment I felt safe and confident with this dapper nice looking man. After examining me and asking a lot of questions, he said he would like me to stay in so he could have a look inside me and take some biopsies, and then he could tell me what was going on. Now they had to find me a bed. A nurse told me they would try and sort out a bed as soon as possible. I dressed and went into the waiting room to tell Roger. After a while, we were taken down to the wards. As we walked along the corridor, the sister was waiting with a man, and a woman whose name I was to find out later was Pam. Apparently, when the sister saw us coming, she said, 'this is the lady that is an emergency.' Pam told me later they had found a bed for her, and then said, 'sorry, but there has been an emergency admitted and we need the bed.' So the poor woman had been asked to wait in the corridor. When she saw me, she had said to her husband, 'well, she doesn't look like an emergency to me.' To a stranger, I would have looked a healthy young woman.

Pam and I ended up on the same ward, and she told me this after I had had my operation, and said how guilty she felt thinking there wasn't much wrong with me when she first saw me.

The sister on St Mark ward said Roger and the children could stay a while until I was undressed and the doctor came to talk to me. It was hard when they had to go, all standing waving at the door and looking sad. I wanted to cry but had to be brave. A young student came to see me and made notes about my stomach problems leading up to coming to the hospital. The usual pre-op things were done such as blood taken, urine sample, and blood pressure. Everyone thought I looked pretty healthy. I may have been on the outside, but the gremlins were lurking on the inside.

Two days later, at nine thirty am, I had my pre-med. One of the nurses came down to theatre with me, holding my hand. I was wheeled into a bright room where the Professor came and patted my hand, and said I would be all right. Next, the anaesthetist came; one little prick in my hand and he told me to count to ten. I think I only got to two, when the next thing I remember is the nurse calling my name.

My medical notes say at twelve o'clock noon I had not returned to the ward, but by two o'clock a partial gastrectomy had been performed; in fact, two thirds of my stomach had been removed. My operation was on the twelfth of August 1977. I cannot remember much about the next two days. I had a temperature and was not sleeping very well. I was having two-hourly observations, and had been given a blanket bath. I was in quite a lot of pain when moving. I was allowed sips of water. On the third day I was helped into a chair, and sat for a while, having sips of milk. When I was able to drink a whole glass, I could start on solids. The fourth night after the operation, I was still not sleeping very well. I was worried about the biopsy reports.

One morning after the Professor's rounds, one of the nurses asked me to tell Roger when he came to visit that the Professor would like to see him. I was still in some pain. Moving was difficult and I could not straighten up properly. On his next two visits, Roger asked to speak to the Professor but he was always unavailable.

At last he saw the registrar in the corridor near the ward, and asked, 'Do you have the histology report?' The answer, Roger describes, almost knocked him off his feet. The young doctor told him, 'the outlook is very grim. Your wife has a carcinoma of the stomach, a malignant tumour. The Professor has removed two thirds of the stomach but she will be lucky to live three months, and has not got one in a million chance of surviving. There is a possibility of chemotherapy, but if they decided to give it to her it would not be a cure although it could increase her life expectancy.' Roger thought he was going to pass out. A nurse sat him down and gave him a cup of tea. The doctor told him it was not a good idea to tell some patients. They gave up if they knew, so it was best to keep it to himself. If he told one person in the family, they would have to tell another; that is human nature and in the end I would find out.

As Roger walked to the ward, he saw my niece, Valerie-Joan, and her husband, Sid. As I was only allowed two visitors at a time, Valerie-Joan said she would go in first to see me. After she had gone, Sid asked Roger if he was all right as he looked awful, and, although the doctor had told him not to tell anyone, he felt he could trust Sid. He had to tell someone, and he knew Sid would not tell Valerie-Joan because she would have been too upset and would have told her Mum, my sister Nellie.

Valerie-Joan and Sid left for a while so that Roger and I could have some time on our own. I remember Roger holding my hand and saying he missed me so much and felt like lying on the bed and giving me a cuddle. Valerie-Joan and Sid came back to say they would take Roger home as he had travelled up by train. Sid was worried about him - none of them had eaten - so he said they would go for a meal. It has always been a family joke that Roger never says no to food, but this time he was still in shock and could eat very little.

At the weekend, Roger brought the children and his Mum, and her partner Harry, to visit. After the children had been in, Mother-in-law and Harry came in on their own. She proceeded to tell me that, when anything happened to me, she had decided Roger would not be able to look after the children so she would sell her house, buy a bigger one, and the children would live with her. When they had all gone, I was beside myself. It was my worst nightmare - someone else looking after our children. For a start, Mother-in-law had not looked after Roger, his Gran had. I don't think she had a clue about what was involved in looking after three children, washing, ironing, cooking, running them around for all their hobbies. Harry did not drive, she did not cook, or even do the ironing, and they had a cleaner, plus she went to work. She was not used to being a housewife at all. Roger was more than capable of looking after the children and the home. He had had good training in the navy. In fact, no-one had told her what the doctors had said, she was only surmising.

I decided I would leave a letter in my diary for Roger. I wrote:

My darling Roger,
If anything happens to me, I want you please to keep the children at our house and look after them yourself. I do not want anyone else to have them.
I love you all.
Margie (I was christened Margaret Katharine but the family called me Margie).

I lay there wondering whether the doctors had told Roger I had only so long to live. The only thing Roger had told me was that I may have to have some treatment. So why had Mother-in-law said that to me? I did not want to tell Roger what she had said, as I thought it would upset him. I decided not to think about it too much. She was just assuming I would not get better.

The Professor was due on his rounds, and I was sitting up in bed feeling much better, although moving about was still difficult. At last the Professor and his entourage arrived. He sat on the bed and held my hand. He said I was a young woman with a lovely family, and he thought it a good idea for me to have some treatment. After the Professor moved to the next bed, I hid under the sheets and cried. I thought I really have got cancer. Suddenly, all the things Roger and I had planned to do, would not be possible. I so wanted to see the children grow up and get married and have children. The next thing I knew, the Professor pulled back the sheets and asked me what I thought I was doing getting upset. I would have the treatment and be fine.

Roger has told me he was beside himself with worry, and would have tried anything to make me well. He was talking to a colleague at work, Peter, who said, 'You should talk to my Aunt Millie.' A few days later he took Roger to meet his aunt. They had a chat and she felt she could help.

First of the Gremlins

She was a healer. Roger had never believed in this sort of thing, but he said he felt desperate. He was to go home, and she gave him a time when he was to fill a glass with water, empty and refill it three times, and then sit and think of me, and she would do the same.

Roger had not been able to sleep very well since I had been in hospital, but on the evening he had arranged to do as Peter's Aunt Millie had told him, he arrived home from work exhausted, but followed her instructions and thought of me at the same time. When he went to bed, for the first time since I had been in hospital, he went straight to sleep. He told me he had woken to find the whole room bathed in a bright white light. I have asked him if he was dreaming but he says no, he got out of bed and looked out of the window, but it was in darkness outside. The light in the room faded, and he tells me he thought I had died, although he felt a great peace. As soon as he could, he rang the hospital and, to his surprise, the nurse told him there had been a great improvement and I was sitting up in bed looking much better.

I continued to improve, but was still quite poorly. The doctors had told Roger they would like me to go into a hospice for a week, and then if I was still holding my own, I would start treatment. I did not realise what a hospice was at the time, but just wanted to go home. I told Roger and he said he wanted me home too, but I had to be able to drink first. At last I could drink a whole glass of milk, so it was time to try and eat. I had had tests to see if there were any leakages but all seemed well. I was looking forward to something different from milk. When the food trolley came round, the male nurse who I had not seen before put a tray in front of me, and on the plate was a sort of beef burger, chips, and beans. 'I don't think I can eat that,' I said. He replied that, as I had not ordered yesterday, that is all there is left so I had to eat that or nothing. The procedure for ordering food was that each day you had a list of food given to you and you ticked off what you wanted the next day. If, in the meantime, you went home, the next patient in your bed had what you had ordered. As I had not ordered, I was given what was left.

When he had left the ward, I called Nurse Sue over and told her what had happened. I said I thought the doctor told me not to eat solid food; I was to start with soup or jelly. She nearly had a fit, and said the nurse should have checked my diet, and eating any solid food (especially what he had left me) would have caused all sorts of problems.

I did not have much of an appetite, and just having soup and jelly was a bit boring, but although I did have some discomfort when eating, I was keeping it down, so that was good.

I was improving every day. I was walking out to the bathroom to wash; one of the nurses had washed my hair and I had been able to dry it. I felt a new woman as it had not been washed since I had been in there. Sometimes when Roger and the children came, he would take me down in the lift and we would sit in the garden.

I had been very spoilt with lots of cards and flowers, but one morning Nurse Sue brought me the post, and I opened a large envelope to find that Mrs Malby's infant class at Sutton Valance school, where I was helping in the afternoons, had all written a letter hoping I would get well soon and saying they missed me. They had also each included a drawing. I felt very emotional and had a few tears; even the nurses were touched.

One day when Roger came to visit, he said he had had a beef sandwich in a pub just down from the hospital. It made me really fancy one, but Roger was worried about me digesting it. We asked the nurse, and she said as long as the meat and bread were very thinly sliced, I could try. Off Roger went, explained to the barman, and they very kindly made me a tiny beef sandwich. It tasted wonderful.

At last the Professor came on his rounds one morning and said I was doing so well that, after I had had my sutures (stitches) removed, I could go home for a week before returning to start the chemotherapy treatment. The next morning, alternate stitches were removed, and the rest the following day. I was so excited I was going home, but I had strict instructions that I was not to start cleaning, washing, and ironing. They said I could make a cup of tea but I wasn't sure I would be able to do that. We would see. I was going home, and I was going to get better.

I was ready when Roger came to collect me. I still had trouble moving, and it was painful when I tried to straighten up, but it was a wonderful feeling going out into the warm fresh August day. The children had gone back to school after their summer holidays so we arrived home on our own. There was something I had to ask Roger before the children arrived home. We stood in the hall and I asked him if I only had so long to live. He answered no; I had had the operation and would have the treatment and be fine. He says we sometimes tell a lie so as not to hurt the people we love, but this was the hardest lie he was ever to tell.

Seamus, our dog, came to greet us. Normally he was rather boisterous but he seemed to know he should not jump up me. I sat on the sofa, and

Roger said he had a present for me. When I had gone into hospital a new record by Rita Coolidge called 'We're All Alone' had just been released so he had bought it for me. He put it on the record player and the words filled the room. For the first time since I had been diagnosed with the cancer, I cried in front of Roger and he hugged me. I cannot hear that record without becoming emotional.

The children all arrived home from school. It was so good to be home with them that I did not want to think about going back to the hospital the next week. That night, Roger held me as close as he could. It was difficult as I could only lie comfortably on my back, and he said how good it was to hold me and have me home.

During that week I read a magazine in which there was an article about a young girl with cancer. It said she was having chemotherapy and showed a photo of her; she did not have any hair! The word chemotherapy jumped off the page at me. That was what I was going to have. I read the article. It said the girl had lost all her hair due to the treatment, and it also made her very sick. I read it again and again, and I could not believe I was going to lose my hair. No-one at the hospital had told me that. In fact I had not been told anything. I had never heard of anyone losing their hair. My thick dark reddish hair was almost to my shoulders. Would it grow again if I lost mine?

As soon as Roger came in from work that evening, I showed him the article. Had they told him I would lose my hair and be really sick, I asked him? He looked shocked. No-one had told him that but, not to worry, wait until I was back at the hospital and ask them.

One week later and I was back at the Westminster Hospital. Arriving on the ward, pretty Nurse Sue said jokingly, 'oh no, not you again.' After Roger had left, Nurse Sue came for a chat. I asked her if I would lose my hair, and she said to ask Sister when she did her rounds. That evening, Sister came for her nightly rounds. I asked her and she said that, when I went down to radiotherapy (they did not call it oncology then) in the morning, the doctor would explain everything I wanted to know.

In fact I did not start the next day, but had to wait until the following morning. Richard the porter came into the ward pushing a wheelchair. 'Margaret Knight,' he called. I waved across the room and said, 'That's me, but I don't need a wheelchair,' I laughed. 'You will when you come back,' he replied. The radiotherapy department was on the ground floor. In the lift on the way down, I asked Richard, 'Why will I need a wheelchair?' His answer was that the treatment usually makes patients a bit wobbly on their feet, and sick.

The Westminster was an old hospital which has closed down now. We went down to the radiotherapy department along dull corridors in need of a coat of paint. When I go to the new oncology unit at Maidstone Hospital now, I think how lucky we are. It is full of light, has a garden in the middle, and it even has a pond with ducks. It also has the most up-to-date equipment, but the care I had at the Westminster was second to none.

Richard wheeled me into a small room and left me with the lady doctor. My first question was, 'will I lose my hair?' 'Yes, you will, and you will probably have diarrhoea and sickness, but we can give you anti-sickness drugs to help.' She dismissed the fact I would lose my hair. The chemotherapy was given by intravenous drip. I do not have very good veins but at last she found one and the treatment started. It took about three quarters of an hour. I thought it would never finish but at last it did. I got up to find my legs were very wobbly. It knocked me for six. Richard was right, and I did need a wheelchair to get me back to the ward. I had been back about half an hour and was sitting on my bed chatting to Rita, a patient who was waiting to have hysterectomy. She asked how I was feeling. 'Well, I haven't felt sick yet; perhaps I won't,' I said, a bit too confidently. Fifteen minutes later, I started feeling sick, retching as if my whole insides were coming out, but all I could bring up was bright gold liquid. My notes say I had the chemo for five days and was nauseated, but slept quite a lot due to the anti-sickness drugs which made me feel sleepy. When I had the sickness spells, I would ask the nurses to pull the curtains around the bed. As I was the only patient on the ward having chemo, I felt it was distressing for the other patients to hear and see me retching.

For the next six months, Roger would take me up to the Westminster on a Sunday evening. I'd start the chemo on Monday for five days, and go home for the weekend. The first week Roger came to collect me, the nurses gave me a sick bowl to take with me as I would probably be sick on the way home. The other side effect was diarrhoea, but that time we made it home before I needed the toilet. Due to not having all my stomach, any food I managed to eat had me needing the toilet soon after. Having the chemo was making it worse so I learned not to eat near to going home. It was lovely to be going home. Roger held me close that night and said he would give anything for me not to have to go back at the end of the weekend.

First of the Gremlins

I awoke Saturday morning to find long strands of hair all over the pillow, and when I washed it, even more came out. It was very distressing; if only I had been told more about the hair loss. With long hair, it is a good idea to have it cut before starting treatment. No-one had given me any advice about hats and scarves, only that I would get a wig.

When I went back for my next treatment, one morning a man arrived with a case of wigs. He opened the case to reveal short, medium, and long synthetic ones, not a bit like my hair-style or colour. He thought the long one was more me. After he had gone, I felt rather down. I could not imagine myself wearing it, so what would I do? Later, speaking to one of the nurses, she said I could go to the shop and then I would have a chance to try some on. On the way home at the end of the week, we went to the wig maker and they changed it for another one that I felt a bit happier about.

The next six months seemed to revolve around going to the hospital. When I was home at the weekends, I seemed to spend most of my time sitting on the toilet, with my head over the sink retching. It would feel as if the rest of my insides were coming up, and it would also make it very sore.

After the first time Roger made love to me during the chemo, I turned over and silently cried. I looked so thin, had no hair, and I was overwhelmed that he still wanted me. When I told Roger this some time later, he said it made him want me even more. He thought he was going to lose me, so what I looked like did not matter; it was still me. He said we take so much for granted, but my having the cancer brought to mind a quotation we saw on a grave once when we were on holiday:

'From how slender a thread hands all that's sweetest in life'

The doctors had not mentioned that I might have to carry on with the treatment, so I could hardly wait for the last week. I really thought that would be the end of it. My big disappointment had been, after three months, when Roger came to the hospital to collect me as usual, and the sister said we had to go to the radiotherapy department to see Dr. Hanham who, with Dr. Phillips, had planned my chemo. The news was not what I expected. It was such a blow. Was I hearing this right? He was saying that, as I had tolerated the chemo better than they thought, I should continue with it. I was devastated. Would this sickness, diarrhoea, and not being able to eat properly, ever stop?

At the end of the next three months, I was so excited this would be the end of it all, and that my hair would grow again. The doctors had assured me it would. Once again we were back seeing Dr. Hanham. During the last few days, I had had tests such as liver scans, barium-meal and X-rays. Dr. Hanham was saying there did not seem to be any recurrence, but there was uncertainty. He felt I should continue the chemo for at least two years. I felt as if I had been smacked in the face. Two years. Would I survive that long? I looked as if I had been in a prisoner-of-war camp. I was so thin, my skin was grey, and I had no hair, eyebrows, or eyelashes. Not only did I have the awful diarrhoea and sickness, I would feel so cold yet the perspiration would run off me.

We did not talk much on the way home. Roger was as devastated as me. It must have been awful for him trying to keep up the pretence - not only to me but the family as well - that I was going to be fine while the doctors were telling him I would not survive. Family and friends have since told me I looked so ill they feared the worse.

Roger told me some years later how, when we were in bed asleep, he would wake up to make sure I was still breathing, as there were times when I was so ill that he thought I would die in bed. He got into the habit of waking up and checking on me.

I made an appointment to see my GP, Dr. Vaux. He had received a letter from Dr. Hanham to say I was to continue the chemo once a week. Dr. Vaux said he was willing to administer the chemo for me so that I did not have to travel up to London every week, and said to ask at the clinic the next week. Dr. Hanham agreed he could for three weeks, and then on the fourth week I was to go back to the Westminster because I would need a blood count and check-up. They would then also supply me with the drugs and butterflies, to use for the injections because I was running out of veins, to take to Dr. Vaux.

I can never thank Dr. Vaux enough for how he looked after me. He thought it would be a good idea to have the chemo on a Monday so that the worst days of sickness would be Tuesday, Wednesday, and Thursday; then by the weekend it would not be so bad. He also suggested the best time was at the end of surgery as the injections were intravenous and my veins not too good. I would take my sick bowl because, five minutes after leaving the surgery, Roger would have to stop the car as I was retching so much. Now when I drive past that way, I still think, oh, there is my sick stop. After a few weeks, I was having quite good weekends, so I hated

First of the Gremlins

Mondays. Roger would come home early from work to take me. I would be ready but say, 'I don't want to go.' He was always patient with me and say, 'don't be silly, you know you must go.' The days seemed to drag. I was still having a bit of trouble moving about, and the doctors had told me I must not do anything, only rest. I had other ideas. After Roger had gone to work, and the children to school, I would get myself going slowly. I found a way of getting the cleaner without lifting it. Being a man, Roger thought that when he cleaned at the weekend, it lasted the week so he did not realise what I was doing. With three teenagers, there was a lot of washing and ironing so I would sit at the table and iron. Then I did not have to lift the ironing board. I would do jobs in the morning, so then, if I had visitors in the afternoon, no-one saw what I was doing.

One morning, after David had arrived at school, a boy went up to him and said, 'I hear your mum's got cancer. Chris Payne's mum had that and died; they usually do.' I suppose the school was an hour's walk from our house, but David picked up his school bag, left, and walked home. He came into the house and said, 'You didn't tell me you had cancer; a boy at school had to tell me,' and with that he refused to leave me and go to school. When I had been diagnosed, Roger and I decided to tell Richard, who was seventeen, and Julie, sixteen, because we felt they were old enough to understand what cancer was. However, Roger never told them he had been told I had no hope of surviving, because I still did not know. As David was only thirteen, we thought it best to let him think it was my stomach ulcer. Looking back, we realise we should have explained it to him; children accept and understand far more than we sometimes give them credit for. We should have told the schools, but we didn't, and I think this was due to the fact that having cancer was something people did not talk about. It was almost as if it was wrong to have it, and some thought you could catch it. Everyone avoided the word cancer, the hospital, family and friends. Thank goodness this has now improved, especially with doctors, hospitals, and support groups and counselling.

David was still at home, and it was beginning to get us down. He would lie in bed, and had become very irritable, so we went to the school and asked for help. They said we should have told them what was happening when I first went into hospital. It was decided David should see the school psychiatrist.

I did not look in the mirror when I had a bath, then one day I thought I must look at myself. I took off my clothes and stood in front of the mirror.

I was horrified, faced with this almost skeletal figure, a scar nearly the length of my body, and almost bald with just a few long strands of hair. My skin was grey and, for the first time, reality struck me; was I going to die? The first thing to do was cut the wispy strands of hair off. I think I thought that all the time they were there, I had some hair; it was silly. Another couple of days and it would have all gone, so out came the scissors and I cut them off, had a bath, dressed, put some lipstick on, put a bright scarf on my bald head, and I was ready to beat the gremlins.

Valerie-Joan and her friend Barbara came frequently. On one occasion, she told me, I had looked so ill when they came; usually I would have a scarf on, but I had opened the door without one so, for the first time, they saw me bald. When they left, they drove around the corner and both sat and cried.

Roger had been doing the weekly shopping, and I had only been out to visit my Dad and Nellie, but I thought I would go shopping with him one evening. Roger would usually go on a Friday after work. He had been so good, he would come home with little delicacies that we could not really afford, to try and tempt me to eat which I was still finding difficult. I took extra anti-sick pills, got myself ready, wig on, and took my sick bowl. The supermarket was in town, and we parked on the roof car park. It was really windy and, as I got out of the car, the wind took hold of the wig. I pulled it on and held onto it until we were safely inside. We started the shopping, and everything was going fine until we arrived at the meat counter. The moment I saw the raw liver, the only thing I could think of was my operation and blood and transfusions. I had to get to the toilet as fast as I could. I don't know what the women in the other cubicles thought, hearing all the retching coming from my cubicle. At last I stopped, waited until I thought everyone had gone, and crept out. I was not going to be put off so we tried the next week, but as soon as I saw the meat I was off again. We decided that in future I would avoid the meat counter.

When we knew I was having chemo, Roger had been to see Mr Cash, the headmaster at Sutton Valance School, and said I would not be able to go back. I was not allowed to drive while on chemo, because the anti-sickness drugs made me sleepy and I obviously wasn't fit enough anyway. After the doctors had said I would be on the chemo for at least two years, we had to think what to do about my little Spitfire car. We only had one garage so it had to stand out all that time. We decided to sell it. Roger soon found a colleague at work who was interested for his daughter, and they arranged to come one evening. I watched from the window as they went for a drive, and the girl looked really pleased when they came back. I knew they would buy it and I had so hoped they wouldn't. I felt quite down the next few days; it was like part of me had gone. I had been so excited when Roger had bought it for me, and I had so enjoyed going out with the children and the dog. Then I thought how it would be for Roger if I did die, and him having to sell it, so I put it out of my mind.

The appointment for David to see the psychiatrist was on Friday afternoon. We had arranged it for then, hoping I would have a good day and not be too sick. David had gone off on his bike after lunch and had not returned when Roger arrived home; he had had to leave work early, so was not too pleased to find David not home. He arrived fifteen minutes before our appointment and said he had forgotten. I made him wash and change, but he obviously did not want to go. There were two psychiatrists, a lady, and a man who looked like a mad scientist, short with long bushy hair. They decided to talk to us together first, but David was not very communicative. We had to tell about my illness, how Roger and I had coped, also Richard and Julie. I felt as if we were being interrogated. Then Roger and I went into another room while David stayed. Then it was our turn again. They felt we were coping well with the situation, and we were a nice happy family, but thought we should have explained that I had cancer to David from the start. After the boy at school had told him everyone who has it dies, he felt if he left me I would die, so that was why he wouldn't go to school. It was decided a home tutor would be a good idea, and David had agreed to this.

The following week, Mrs Grey arrived. She was a nice lady who David took to straight away, and the one-to-one teaching was a great benefit as he had always found it difficult to concentrate. He had speech therapy at infant school and was later diagnosed as dyslexic, but with Mrs Grey his English and Maths came on a treat. We were having trouble getting him to go to his sessions with the psychiatrist, and after some time I suggested that Mrs Grey should take David to school for his lessons, to try and get him into the routine of going back to school. We discussed it with the psychiatrist, Mrs Grey, and the school, and they all thought it was a good idea. The school said they would make a room available.

We at last seemed to be getting into a routine, although not exactly normal as I was still very sick half the week. Roger did not get paid when he had time off work, and he had to leave work early on a Monday to take me to the surgery for the chemo. Sometimes my veins gave up; the six months of chemo had caused havoc with them. I looked like a drug addict as my arms were black and blue with bruises from the injections. Dr. Vaux was very patient, trying in my arms, hands, anywhere we could, to get a vein. I would wear gloves to try and keep my hands warm on the way to the surgery, putting my hands in hot water when I arrived, but sometimes we just couldn't get a vein. Sometimes, Dr. Vaux would say he felt I had had enough and I should go back in the morning to try again. This would mean Roger would lose another half a day's work, and every three weeks when we went up to London to the Westminster, that was another day lost. I don't think people realise sometimes how being ill can cause financial hardship. Fortunately we had never lived above our means, so we cut down on what we thought were luxuries rather than necessities.

During the time I was having the six months chemo, and staying in hospital during the week, I did not have visitors. It was a long way for people to travel, and I was so grotty and sleepy due to the drugs. I did not like anyone seeing me being sick and retching, so family and friends would pop in when I was home at the weekends. When I started the weekly chemo, everyone was very thoughtful and did not visit at the beginning of the week because they knew they were my bad days. Some days I don't know how I sat and made conversation, I felt such a grot, but people had made the effort to visit so I did not want to be rude. My nieces Heather and Valerie-Joan, and her friend Barbara, my sisters Nellie, Barb, Lili-Anne, and my brother Ted were all frequent visitors; also my best friend, Trisha. We had been friends since the children went to infant school. She is married to Jim, and they have two children, Tony and Lisa.

After about half a year of being on the weekly chemo, my hair started to grow. It was just like a baby's, a soft down, but it was a great boost, and there was a bonus. It was growing curly, not the reddish-brown it had been, but dark brown. I was getting stronger and did not feel so much pain when eating. I was being checked all the time, having liver scans, barium-meal and X-rays. On the weeks we went up to the Westminster, while I was having my chemo, Roger would have a chat with the doctors. He would tell them I was doing well, but they told him not to get his hopes up as things still looked grim.

David started back to school at last, and I was still having the chemo at the surgery for three weeks, then back to the Westminster for the fourth, but was gradually tolerating it better.

11

LEEDS CASTLE

It was about a year later, and I was still having the chemo once a week but, as time had gone on, I was still having problems Monday, Tuesday, and Wednesday, not so much being sick but retching up the foul-tasting gold liquid. Also I still had the diarrhoea but by the weekends, my body was learning to cope better. Something was to happen which was to change my life completely. We had very good neighbours at Leeds, Ernie and Pat and their two children. They were the sort of people who kept to themselves, but if you needed anything they were there. One day, Ernie asked Roger how I was getting on. Roger said I was coping well, but he felt I was on my own too much. I needed something to do so as not to have too much time to think about things. Ernie and Pat both worked at Leeds Castle; the Castle was about twenty minutes walk from our house, set in beautiful park land with a duckery, woodland gardens, and aviaries with a wonderful collection of birds, plus its own vineyard and greenhouses.

A fairytale castle surrounded by a moat, described by Lord Conway as, 'The loveliest Castle In The World.' The first holder of what was the manor of Kent, in the year 865, had been Ethelbert IV. Through the ages, the holders had included William the Conqueror, Odo, Bishop of Bayeau, and some of the Crevecoeur family, and in 1278, Eleanor of Castile, and various holders including, in 1509, Henry VIII. The first private owner, in 1552, had been Sir Anthony St Leger, plus six more owners, then in 1632, Sir Thomas Culpeper in whose name the lovely Culpeper garden was created in 1980, which for hundreds of years had been a vegetable plot. It also has a herb garden planted along the old wall which would have pleased a later namesake, the seventeenth century herbalist, Nicholas Culpeper. In 1710, Catherine Lady Fairfax became the first of the Fairfax family to own the Castle. The Fairfax Hall, a lovely Kentish tithe barn dating from

1680, and which is now the setting for banquets and other functions, is named in their honour. There were a few more owners, then in 1821 the first of the Wykeham-Martins and, in 1926, the last owner, the Hon Olive Lady Baillie. She immediately set about restoring the Castle which had been described as quite unique in antiquity, but needs a large sum of expenditure to make it habitable - not a bath in place, and only oil lamps for the servants' quarters in the dungeons. Under her care, the Castle became, in the 1930s, one of the great houses of England, and a centre of lavish hospitality. Visitors included members of foreign royal families and the British royal family, including the Prince of Wales, afterwards Edward VIII, the Duke of Windsor, the Duke of Kent, and his wife Princess Marina. There were also ambassadors, ministers, members of Parliament, and stars of the screen, Errol Flynn, James Stewart, and Douglas Fairbanks. But Lady Baillie was very shy, so Leeds Castle was seldom in the news.

Before I became ill, Roger, myself, and the children all became members of the Maidstone and the Kent Archaeology society. We loved going on digs so when we were told the society was going to do a dig in our village, we could not wait to get involved. The excavations were the site of Leeds Priory, an Augustinian Priory founded by Robert de Crevecoeur in 1119, which continued in existence until the dissolution in 1539. It was part of the Leeds Castle estate. Mr Peter Tester was in charge of the excavations, a lovely, quiet but very knowledgeable man who sadly is no longer with us - a great loss to archaeology. One very hot day, Lady Baillie, with the curator of the Castle, came to inspect the dig. I can remember this slim lady in 1920-style dress, a large straw hat, and carrying a sun shade. At the time I had no idea that, sometime in the future, I would work at the Castle.

Ernie suggested to Roger that perhaps one afternoon a week I would like to work at the Castle with Pat. She worked housekeeping in the Castle some mornings, and then in the afternoons served teas in the Fairfax Hall. He said he would ask Christine the manageress if I could possibly work one afternoon. She said to go down with Pat at the end of the week; Ernie had explained to her about my treatment. I was excited but apprehensive about going to the Castle, having not worked for so long and also not being very fit. The one good thing was that although very short, I did have hair. Pat said we would leave home after lunch. We had to walk down to the Castle through the village, past the old pub and up a leafy lane into the park. The view was wonderful; as we were looking down on the Castle surrounded by a shimmering moat, we could see the wood gardens, the tennis courts and old summer house, and we could also see the aviaries and greenhouses. I never failed to wonder at the beauty of that view every time I went through the park.

Christine said I could stay for the afternoon to see how I got on. She introduced me to the other staff. Tina was the supervisor, a lovely, tall, slim young girl, and we were to become great friends. I always say I am her other mum. Then there was Diane. Her husband had died very suddenly and she had moved into a cottage near the Castle. She was to become a dear friend. Heather had decided to come to work at the Castle because she was coping with losing her youngest son who was fourteen and had cancer. She was a lovely, slightly eccentric, lady, and I became very fond of all of these ladies who have given me such great support over the years.

We were having a Women's Institute group for a cream tea so we had to lay the tables, serve tea, and clear away when they had gone, then we sat and had a cup of tea ourselves. Christine asked if I would like to come next week; I was so pleased and enjoyed it so much. The journey back home wasn't so easy; it was all up hill, and the last part through the village was very steep. Back home I thanked Pat and said how much I had enjoyed the afternoon. Indoors, pleased I had prepared dinner before going, I felt so tired. I sat on the sofa and it was as if my whole body had collapsed; I had not had so much exercise since my operation. I could not move. Roger, arriving home from work, came straight into the lounge and asked how I had got on. He said he had worried about me all day. I told him it had been a lovely afternoon, and then had to tell him I could not get up. It was as if my whole body had seized up. He was upset and said he should not have suggested that I went, and that I was not to go again. That was the best thing he could have said because immediately I decided I would be going again. The next few days, I felt completely worn out but was determined I would be going the next week.

Soon I was into a routine, going to the Castle one or two afternoons a week. It had started to get busy at the weekends, so Christine asked us if we had any family who could help; Richard and Julie came in to help.

I was really excited one afternoon when Christine told us we were to have a tour of the Castle. We had got to know the staff at the Castle; there was John and Lucia, the chef and his wife, the butler, the housekeeper, and Lord Geoffrey-Lloyd. He had been a friend of Lady Baillie's for over forty years and, in 1974, was the first chairman of the Leeds Castle Foundation.

Lady Baillie had become ill at her house in the Bahamas, and was in the South of France for the last few weeks of her life. She died in London on ninth of September 1974 without returning to Leeds Castle again. She had wanted the Castle to be available to the public, and to be a centre for medical conferences and the arts, and so the Leeds Castle Foundation was set up. Lord Geoffrey-Lloyd had been a member of Churchill's wartime ministry and was secretary of state for education 1957-59. He devoted the last nine years of his life to establishing the foundation on lines laid down by Lady Baillie. He was a lovely man who spent a lot of time at the Castle, and he would come for his afternoon cup of tea and scone in the Fairfax Hall tea-rooms, always making a point of speaking to all of us ladies and bringing the Castle's two Great Danes, Boots and Danny (this of course would not be allowed in the tea rooms today). The dogs were part of the inheritance left to the foundation. Mrs Walsh the housekeeper looked after them when Lord Geoffrey-Lloyd was not at the Castle, and we would often see her walking around the grounds with them. There have always been dogs at the Castle, and now there is the famous Dog Collar museum.

We started our tour in the cellar, and then went into the kitchens, the Queen's room and bathroom, the Queen's Gallery, the wonderful Henry VIII Banqueting Hall with its ebony wood floor and carved oak ceiling, both introduced by Lady Baillie, then on to the Seminar room, the Chapel and the bedrooms. These were the private rooms at that time, not shown to the public, but they are now used when there are conferences. We continued downstairs into the Yellow drawing room, the lovely Thorpe Hall, the library and dining room, and out through the front Hall. We all enjoyed our tour.

A few weeks later Christine asked if we could work extra time as we were having an important conference. They would arrive on the Monday, so I said I would have to go and have my chemo, take extra anti-sickness pills, and hope I did not feel too drowsy. By this time we had a few more staff, and one of these was Vera; we became friends and usually worked together. We were going to look after the security but little did we know how many guests there would be.

The next morning, Pat and I were picked up by the Castle mini-bus and we were to be ready for 8.30. It would be a long day. Pat had to work in the Castle as the main guests would stay in the Castle. The staff did not know who was coming, and Christine had said we would have a chat before we started work. There was lots of activity with police dog handlers, helicopters, and underwater equipment so I thought something important must be happening. Christine told us it was a very important meeting. The foreign ministers of Egypt, Israel, and America were to have the vital preliminary talks which led to the signing of the Peace Treaty at Camp David later that year. The ministers were Mr Cyrus Vance, Mr Mohammed Ibrahim Kamel, and General Moshe Dayan. Our job was to feed all the security people, and as we had to have staff on duty twenty-four hours, Tina, Heather, Diane, and Julie worked the night shift. Vera, Richard, and Christine's relations and I did the days. It was very hectic, and we were to be picked up by taxi on entering the Castle grounds. There were soldiers and police, and after being checked and the taxi searched, we drove through the grounds where there were security helicopters circling above, and police dogs patrolling; it was a bit frightening.

Christine and Richard went to get the food. With so many different nationalities, and some not eating meat, others not eating ham, we had to have a wide variety for them to choose from. At around five thirty, I went off to the doctors to have my chemo. I did not tell Dr. Vaux what I was going to do, as I did not think he would approve. When I had told him I had started work at the Castle, he had not been too impressed. I was only going back for about two hours, and everyone was rushing around trying to get everything ready for the next day. After about half an hour, I had to quickly make my way to the toilet hoping no-one realised I was starting to feel sick. I knelt on the floor retching over the toilet, and as usual it was a foul-tasting gold liquid.

As always when I was sick, I would feel like lying down. The drugs made me sleepy anyway, but because I had taken extra they were taking effect. I sat on the toilet, leaning against the wall, wishing I did not have this cancer, then pulled myself together and went back to help the others. That night, I went home feeling so ill I thought I would just go to bed and hope I would be all right for the morning.

The taxi would drop Julie off from the night shift, and pick me up, so I had to be ready for eight o'clock. I really had to force myself to get up and get ready. At the Fairfax Hall, we were preparing for lunch. Vera and I were to serve the lunches, and the other staff prepare the food. How we managed I will never know. As soon as we started serving, some of the men said they cannot eat that for religious reasons, so back to the kitchen we would go. At that time, we did not have the large kitchens they have now. Although hectic, we had some fun. Two Arabs said they would buy Vera and me in exchange for two camels. Apparently this was a compliment. After lunch, things quietened down but by this time I was feeling ill, and taking more anti-sickness made me feel even more drowsy. I started retching and had to rush to the toilet. Christine sent one the girls down to me and said I was to go and lie on the bed in the room that one of the secretaries sometimes stayed in. It seemed sheer bliss; all I wanted to do was go to sleep. I awoke to the sound of voices. I peeped out of the window; it was time to feed them again. I had a quick wash and went down. For the next two hours, Vera and I took plates of food, made tea and coffee, and cleared tables. It was such an experience, and at the end of the talks, the police and security made a collection for us; they said we had all worked so hard. Leeds Castle had provided a secure and private venue for a special occasion.

After the publicity the Castle received for the conference, it seemed everyone wanted to see the fairytale Castle, and the following weekend we were so busy. This was the beginning for dinners, lunches, conferences, weddings, and filming. I never thought then that Roger and I would make a documentary and that part of it would be filmed at the Castle.

The Henry VIII series for BBC2 caused us ladies great excitement as the cast would be in the Fairfax Hall for all their meals. It was a great cast list, with John Stride as Henry, Timothy West as Cardinal Wolsey, Claire Bloom as Queen Catherine, and Barbara Kellerman as Anne Boleyn. One of the older actresses was Sylvia Coleridge; she was a lovely person. There were quite a few actors who are still on our screens now, John Nettleton was one, and also there were Peter Vaughn and Jeremy Kemp.

I am sure that working at the Castle was the best thing I did while on the chemo. I will always be grateful to Christine for taking me on, and for everyone who worked with me. Some days when I was being sick in the toilets, someone would come down discreetly to see that I was all right. Some days I felt so ill when I got up, I would get my jobs done, get ready, and go into Julie and lie beside her on her bed until it was time for me to go to work. I really had to make myself get up and go. After my chemo on Mondays, I was still very sick. I would feel so cold, but at the same time felt hot. Sometimes I thought it would never end, but I never thought I was going through all this, only to die. I just wanted to get back to normal.

Every third week when we went up to the Westminster, I was constantly having tests. Near the end of the two years, the registrar thought it a good idea to have an endoscope and liver scan to check if there were any problems. As usual, Dr. Stevens at Maidstone Hospital did the endoscope, and the results were good. Back at the Westminster, the liver scan went well too. At the end of the next month, Dr. Hanham said I had done so well in the last two years it was perhaps appropriate for me to stop. The feeling was unbelievable. I was to have one more month's chemo, and that seemed the longest month of all the chemo treatment. I was so frightened when I went back that they would change their minds and not stop.

Dr. Vaux was on holiday on the last week of my chemo, so I saw a colleague of his, Dr. Manners. I was so pleased when I went into his room, but his words knocked me back. He said I was not to become over confident. His words stung. Did he mean I would have to have more treatment? I decided not to think about it.

After the last chemo session, on my first day back at work, Roger said we would celebrate with the girls so when he came to collect me he brought champagne. I also had a lovely surprise; the girls had bought me a silver charm bracelet so that every year or special occasion I could add to it, and now it is so full it is hard to find room for any more.

One morning, we arrived at work to find the scones had not been delivered. Christine asked if any of us could make scones. I volunteered and they were all impressed, and Christine asked if I would like to make them all the time. I loved my time spent cooking in the kitchen. I would make cakes and pies, and bread pudding which was a great hit with the golfers.

I was getting fitter, but still had to go up to the Westminster for check-ups.

We were becoming busy all the time at the Castle. Christine moved on and we had a new manager, Richard, and his wife Kathy. Richard had worked with Dave who was now our head chef. It was decided we would start to have what is now a very successful event, the Kentish evenings. At first they were held every Saturday. The guests would arrive to a sherry reception, have a tour of the Castle, then dinner in the Fairfax Hall with entertainment such as local Morris dancers and a folk band. The meal was five courses of local fare. My job was to cook a meal for the staff, and help Kathy, the general manager. Mr Buck always came in and made the gravy. I liked Kathy; she was rather quiet but we worked well together. She had two little boys while at the Castle. I think they live abroad now.

Richard, our son, had been working hard at school to obtain his grades to go to university, and we were over the moon when, in the summer of 1979, he had his results. He had taken mathematics, chemistry, and biology, and had passes in all three. This was a great boost to everyone; the previous three years had been pretty grotty. Richard obtained a place at Hull University, and was going to live on campus the first year so we set about getting things together for this big step in his life. Roger and I took him up north to get him settled in. We had a look around the campus; it was in a nice area, and he had his own room. He was a bit home-sick as most people are at first, but soon settled in making lots of friends. It was a great experience for him.

12

OH, NOT MORE GREMLINS

About five months after I stopped chemo, I was having the same sort of pains as before my operation. I told Dr. Vaux who thought it a good idea to see Dr. Stevens for an endoscope. The result was that there was a possibility of a recurrence, Dr. Stevens told me, and the results from the biopsy showed the appearances are suggestive of recurrence of carcinoma. What a blow. The words of Dr. Manners rang in my ears, 'don't become over confident.'

Professor Ellis said he would see me straight away, so once again, on the twenty second of February 1980, I am back in St Marks ward at the Westminster Hospital. I had been feeling sick, poor appetite, and had a weight loss of eight pounds over the last two months. The nurses say, 'oh no, you are not back again.' They all work so hard, and such long hours, but are always cheerful. Professor Ellis came in to see me for a chat. The next day I had a barium-meal. From my notes, it seems I was quite calm. My operation was due three days after I was admitted. The day before the operation, Simon, one of the young doctors, came and asked me to sign the consent form. I thought I had better read it before signing. It states that I am to have a total gastrectomy. And what exactly will that mean, I ask nervously.

'It means we are going to remove all the rest of your stomach.'

'Bloody hell,' I said, 'I didn't realise that.'

'You should have known what it would mean. As you have already had two thirds removed, there is no other option now but to take it all! Thanks a lot,' he says, taking the form as if I had just signed a cheque, and then he had gone.

I don't usually swear, and felt embarrassed that I had. So many questions ran through my mind. How will I be able to eat without a stomach? It had been difficult enough since having two thirds removed. I sat and imagined all sorts of horrors. Would I need tubes or a colostomy? No-one had actually explained what would happen. Also, would it mean more chemo? I would know tomorrow.

Up until the night before my operation, I had slept well, but that night I was very restless. I had my pre-med at seven o'clock am, went to theatre at eight o'clock. My notes say twelve o'clock and patient still in theatre. Next note was, returned from theatre at twelve thirty following total gastrectomy, observations to continue half-hourly. I had a fair evening and was stable. It was strictly nil by mouth, but frequent mouth-washes. Six days after the operation, I went for a barium-meal to see if there was any leakage. It was very difficult and painful trying to move about on the machine. There did not appear to be any problems, so, for the first time since the operation, I was able to have a sip of water, although, of course, I was on saline drip. Roger came again that evening; he was eager to know how the barium-meal went. My notes say I was always cheerful and had lots of flowers delivered. The only problem was a temperature, and I did not like having the physiotherapy with the steam inhalations. I found it quite painful; in fact any movement was painful. At last I was able to have small amounts of milk, and once I could drink a whole glass, real food was next I hoped.

During this time, I had lots of visitors and did appreciate their visits as it was a long journey for everyone. Roger and I always liked the cartoon character in our newspaper, a man and woman with the caption always starting, 'Love Is...' So he would draw me cards and send them to me, one of me in hospital with the caption, 'Love Is missing you when we're not together.' Then inside the card, him washing up with, 'the house work bit is nothing darling, not having you to cuddle is.' These made me have a few tears. I missed Roger and the children so much.

At last I could drink a whole glass of milk; not in one go, it took a whole day, but at last I could try to eat. Soup and jelly and ice-cream.

I had been dreading the Professor coming to tell me I would need more chemo, but what a relief when he explained how he had done the operation. Removing all the remaining stomach and part of my oesophagus, he had made a pipe joining the oesophagus to the intestines and also checked my liver and lymph glands. The good news was I need not have anymore chemo. I was so pleased I wanted to hug him. I could hardly contain myself, and as soon as Roger came in that evening, I told him the good news. He was so relieved; it had been such a worry for him, and he said he wanted to hug the Professor as well.

My hair felt and looked awful. It had not been washed since arriving at the hospital, and I was so pleased when Valerie-Joan and Heather arrived with her hair dressing gear. Valerie-Joan had told her when she visited me a few days before that I had said I wish I could have my hair done. I felt a new woman afterwards, and even the doctors said how much better I was looking.

I was moving about more, so I would help the other ladies on the ward. One older lady said she wished she could wash and set her hair. I knew how she felt because, when Heather had done mine, it really perked me up. I told her that, if one of the nurses would wash it, I would set it. The nurses thought it a great idea and were only to pleased to wash it for her. I set it in rollers and dried it, and brushed out it looked really nice. She was so pleased, and could hardly wait for her husband's visit. He came across to my bed and thanked me, saying it had made her feel so much better, so I became the ward hairdresser. One of the patients was a young girl Paula, in her twenties, who had a twin sister. They were a nice family, and seemed very close. Both girls had very long hair, and one day Paula asked if I could help with her hair. I often wonder what happened to her.

When I was admitted back to hospital, Roger phoned the university and explained the situation. They were very good, and asked Richard if he would like to go home, so it was a lovely surprise one afternoon to see him coming into the ward. After Richard had gone, I felt sad, wondering if I would see him get his degree. Was I going to survive long enough?

I could only eat a small amount. The doctors suggested I try baby food when I went home, to have some variety. At last I could go home; what a wonderful feeling. I was going home sooner than we thought, but there had been some press coverage about getting more patients through the system. In fact, they had the television cameras in to film. I think it was for the news, and I was one of the patients chosen to be filmed but I never knew if it was shown.

I had to go back in one month. The first week back home, I had lots of visitors; really it was a bit too much and I was still very weak. I thought I would go home and be back to normal, but it was major surgery and it was going to take time. The hospital had sent me home with dressings for my wound, which was still a bit messy. I think really I should have had the nurse in to dress it, but being independent I did it myself.

In my notes is a lovely letter Professor Ellis wrote to Dr. Vaux: 'I was delighted to see this lady in the follow-up clinic today.' I feel very touched as to how caring they all were to me. He continues: 'She is progressing well following her total gastrectomy. I think it would be advisable to commence a monthly injection of vitamin B12 because IF she is a long survivor she will inevitably develop a B12 deficiency after a total gastrectomy. Twenty-five years later, and I still have my B12 so I think we could say I have been a long survivor.

Eight weeks after my operation, I was finding eating very difficult. It was very painful, and the doctors had told Roger I would only be able to eat tiny amounts of soft food and half a cup of tea. I write in my diary that the first time I tried to eat some bread it was so painful it made me cry and I wished I had not had to have the operation. It did not last long. I resigned myself to eating baby food, soup, jelly, and ice-cream.

There was another blow to us that year. Roger had been offered a job starting up a branch of an American company importing clay to make cat litter. They over-produced and it did not sell as well as expected, so the company closed down and Roger was made redundant. I was upset that he had left a good job for them, and it could not have come at a worse time with all his other worries. I was feeling very low, with my weight getting worse instead of better; David was worrying because he kept missing going to the psychiatrist.

On the first of May, I heard the cuckoo and saw it sitting on the tree opposite the bedroom window. This perked me up; I thought summer is coming. It was a good omen, as a few days later Roger got another job.

When Julie was seventeen, she had met Kevin and, at nineteen, he was still her boyfriend. He was not the sort of person we thought she would choose, but we did not interfere and he was welcome at home. Richard was settling in well at university and had made lots of friends. May the ninth 1980 came, and it was my birthday. I had lots of cards and presents. Roger gave me a lovely Art Nouveau silver butterfly on a chain. Roger asked if I would like to go for a drive as it was a bright sunny day. We went past Scragged Oak, the house I had been born in, and up into the hills where we could see the oak trees, lovely with golden bronze foliage, the hedgerows, some starting to blossom, and primroses all over the banks. We sat watching the rabbits hopping about, and there were bluebells and violets everywhere; it was good to be fit enough to enjoy it. We called into mother-in-law who gave us some plants. Driving home through the lanes, we stopped in a gateway. The bluebells below the coppice wood were like a blue carpet. I opened the car window to see a little field mouse scampering up the gate post. I remember all the details of this day because Roger's next words were to stun me. He said he had something to tell me, that when I was ill the first time he had not told me the truth. He went on to say how the doctors had told him I would be lucky to live three months, and had not got a one in a million chance of surviving. He said he could not believe what they were telling him, and he had asked if I could have treatment. They said I was too ill, and they thought it a good idea if I went into a hospice; that was when he decided he wanted me home.

But, of course, I did make enough improvement to have treatment. I could not put into words what my feelings were when Roger told me this; how awful that he had had to live with this all through my chemo treatment. When I had been so ill, he must have wondered why I had to go through with all this if it wasn't going to do any good. I wanted to know everything the doctors had told him. Roger said he had told me now because I had a right to know, and I am sure he felt he had to share it with me so we could fight it together, because it could still come back. Those little gremlins may still be lurking somewhere in my body.

As we sat in the car, I suddenly felt like getting out and running into the fields shouting how glad I was to be alive. What a birthday present it had been; I was even more determined to beat the gremlins now.

Richard was getting on well at university, and David did not have to see the psychiatrist so much. Julie was working in a bank, and she was finding my illness hard to cope with. If we talked about me being ill, and especially if we watched a programme on television about cancer, she would flounce out of the room saying, 'Do we have to watch this?' I know whenever my Mum was ill, I would worry I would lose her, so I know what she was going through. It had not been easy for any of the family seeing me look a totally different person the last three years, so thin, with no hair, and being sick most of the time. But now I was looking so much better; my hair had grown dark and curly, and my skin looked a good colour, not grey. I had looked dreadful.

A week after my birthday, Roger started his new job so I was on my own at home and thought I would get back to normal and do the washing, and clean through the house. I had made arrangements to go and see Trisha after lunch. I finished my jobs, and thought I would sit down for a rest when I had finished, exhausted. My arms and my whole body ached, and the next thing I knew, I awoke to find it was four o'clock. I rang Trisha and apologised. The next few days I decided not to try and do everything in one day, and to sit down for an hour each afternoon. The weather was dry and sunny so I would sit outside in my rocking chair. We had a blackbird that had nested in our hedge. She would come to the kitchen door to get crumbs, and now she brought her baby. We also had a hedgehog that would come in the evening and rattle the dish we left out for it; another one joined it, and eventually they brought their babies.

The tiredness lasted for some while, and also the eating problems, but I found that as long as I ate very small amounts, I did not have as much pain. I was still on baby foods, soup, and milk, and everything had to be very fresh or I would be in the bathroom in a flash.

Another person who was very kind to me was my dentist, Dr. Baldwin, a lovely man who had been our dentist for years. He was great with the children, and genuinely concerned when I told him I had stomach cancer. As a doctor, he probably thought the future looked grim for me. I worked with his wife, Anne, who was the castle florist then.

After my next visit to the clinic at the Westminster, my notes say: 'I saw this lady in clinic today and I am pleased to say she is doing remarkably well following her total gastrectomy. There was no sign of recurrence of the tumour and on abdominal examination the wound had healed. There was no hernia. A nylon stitch in the scar I managed to remove.' I did not see the Professor on this occasion, but saw his registrar instead. I saw the Professor on my following two check-ups, and he wrote that he was delighted to see me and I was making excellent progress but had lost some weight, so suggested I have Complan which I would be able to digest. If I had any problems he would see me before my next check-up.

At the end of the summer, I went back to work at the Castle. I was seeing Dr. Vaux once a month for my B12 injection, and when I said I was going back to work he thought it was a bit early, but I had missed the girls and the lovely surroundings. I could not carry anything heavy, or lift, so it was suggested I sat at the till in the Fairfax Hall restaurant. I really enjoyed being back; everyone had given me such encouragement. It was great fun sitting at the till. Diane liked to serve teas, but she sometimes got a bit cross with visitors. She would pour out the teas before they had time to tell her how they liked it. She always put the milk in first, and a lot of foreign visitors liked it without milk. They would say, 'may I have one without milk?' and she would reply, 'you didn't ask.' The fact was she hadn't given them time. After they had paid me, she would say, 'I don't know how you can sit there all day and be so polite to everyone.' I am very fond of Diane and we often laugh about her pouring the teas; she is a great character. A new lady, Jan, had joined the staff, and was to become a great friend.

The year, 1981, was special for the Castle; we were to have the Queen visit. It was the year of the disabled; the Castle had always welcomed disabled visitors, and improvements had been made to make the Castle more enjoyable for them. The Queen was to meet invited disabled guests in the Fairfax Hall, and the staff was to stand around the hall. We had been briefed on how to curtsy and address the Queen if she spoke to any of us. The children from Leeds village school were invited. At last the moment arrived and the Queen was in the hall. She smiled at us as she walked around the room and chatted with various people before leaving. I feel very privileged working at the Castle, and meeting so many interesting people. Princess Margaret came on a few occasions; one of her visits was in the summer, and she had dinner in a fabulous marquee in the grounds. Once you were inside it was like a beautiful room; it had drapes on the walls, chandeliers, sparkling crystal glasses, silver candelabras, and beautiful flower arrangements. It was a wonderful sight. After we had finished work, Heather and I sat on the grass to see the Princess arrive for dinner. I had seen her many years before when staying with my sister Lili-Anne in Canterbury. She is not very tall but, like all the royal ladies I have seen, very slim with a lovely complexion, and she wore shoes with very high heels.

When we had seen all the guests arrive in their finery, Heather and I walked home. We always had something to talk about; Heather had travelled and had a wealth of knowledge. As we walked up through the park, we stopped and looked back - the Castle had a backdrop of pink streaked sky, and we both said, 'pink sky at night, a shepherd's delight'. I think it was our delight to work in such lovely surroundings. My sisters were very excited when I was meeting a royal visitor at the Castle, and always wanted to know the details of the visit. Sometimes I was allowed tickets for them to come in as well, which they loved.

13

HOLIDAY

Roger thought we should have a holiday, and felt it would do us both good. He needed a rest, having had so much worry; he hated me having to have the chemo because of how ill it made me. We decided to go to Scotland. Roger had told his Mum we were going to have a holiday, and the next time we went up to see them she said Harry and her were going to treat us to the holiday. They had some brochures, and we were thrilled when we discovered they were for Italy. It had always been my dream to go to Pompeii because of our interest in archaeology.

Two weeks later and we were on the plane to Venice; I could hardly contain myself I was so excited. This was my first experience of flying and going abroad.

Arriving in Venice, I fell in love with the city - a painting come to life. We were staying in a wonderful old hotel with a balcony, and that night there was the most dreadful thunder storm. Venice had not had rain for months so all the local people were standing outside. As the ground was so dry, the rain seemed to bounce off the dry earth. We stood on our balcony watching them dancing and getting soaked. The next morning it was as if it had not rained at all. The ground was dry again and it was very hot. We took a water bus across the Lagoon to the city. The facade of St Mark's glittered with gold and mosaics, and beside it rose the tall pink Campanile from which there is a panoramic view of the whole Lagoon and its islands. The pale pink and white Doge's Palace with its Gothic arcades is breathtaking, and the Rialto Bridge with the little shops full of glass, lace, and jewellery. I did not want to leave, but we were moving on to travel through Tuscany and then Padua, an ancient university city. We visited the shrine of St Anthony, and the frescoes by Giotto in the Scrovegni Chapel. In Verona, we visited Juliet's balcony and, like all the tourists, I went up and blew a kiss to Roger from the balcony. We also saw the Roman arena where they hold the operas. That evening, we had our first view of the beautiful Renaissance city of Florence across the river Arno where, towering over the roofs, was the Santa Maria del Fiore Cathedral, the third largest in the world. It was designed in 1296 by Arnolfio di Cambio, and after his death the work was continued by Giotto who also started on the Campanile. I could hardly wait to start the next morning; there was so much to see. The Baptistery was the ancient Cathedral of Florence before Santa Maria del Fiore was built; it dates from the 11th century. It has three gilt bronze doors, each one depicting different stories. The interior takes your breath away; the roof is 14th century Byzantine mosaics. The Palazzo Vecchio, with its wonderful sculptures, has a copy of Michelangelo's David. I loved the Uffizi Gallery with Botticelli's The Birth of Venus, and other works by Titian, Leonardo da Vinci, and Raphael. In the gallery of the Academy is the original David by Michelangelo; it is truly a masterpiece. Every building was wonderful, but it was times like this when I became sad thinking, would I survive the gremlins and be able to go back sometime?

Our next stop was Pisa. We only had half a day so had to cram in as much as possible. The Leaning Tower of Pisa must be the best known tower in the world, originally built in the late twelfth century as the bell tower of the Cathedral, although the building of this was started in 1063. It is a masterpiece of Italian architecture. We bought an icon and sent more cards home. From here we drove to Naples, and then, for the rest of the holiday, we were to be based in Sorrento. When we arrived, there had been a mix-up with the hotels and we ended up in a new hotel, the Grand Hotel Vesuvio, which was a marble palace and the most expensive in Sorrento, so we were very lucky. We had a suite of huge rooms with a balcony and a stunning view.

Positano is the first town along the coast; it is a cluster of pastel painted houses and little coves. We stopped at Praiano, a fishing village, and a little further on is the Emerald Grotto, discovered in 1932 by a local sailor who, seeking refuge from the rain, chanced upon the Grotto. It is a wonderful sight; the sunlight filtering through an underwater opening, colours the water with beautiful emerald reflections, and the half-submerged stalagmites and stalactites are also a spectacular sight. The next town was Amalfi; I loved it here - the old white houses, many built with their backs against the cliffs, joined together by little alleyways and

Holiday

steps. The town hall was once a Benedictine Monastery, and the spectacular Cathedral, the Duomo of Amalfi, situated at the top of an impressive flight of steps, contains a wealth of art treasures. We walked through the lovely Amalfi villa gardens, and after we left, all along the coastal road, our guide pointed out villas of the rich and famous.

It is hard to say I had a favourite place, but it has to be Ravllo. At the end of the Piazza Vescovado stands the villa Rufolo, surrounded by a lush garden rich with exotic plants and fragrant flowers and ancient trees. The chemo had made me lose my sense of smell, but Roger said the perfume from the flowers was overwhelming, and the view from the terraces is never to be forgotten. Richard Wagner came here in 1880 when he was working on the second act of the 'Parsifal' which tells of Klingsor the Magician's enchanted garden. In this wonderful setting, as if moved by a vision for which he had been searching for a long time, the maestro is quoted as exclaiming, 'Klingsor's Zaubergarten ist gefunden!' (Klingsor's enchanted garden has been found). Every summer, a festival of symphonic music takes place here with orchestras from all over the world, and I would love to bring Roger here to one of the concerts. A walk through the streets takes us to the villa Cimbrone where D.H. Lawrence stayed.

The drive back to the hotel was an endless succession of bends, at certain points scaling dizzy heights and then plummeting almost to sea level, sometimes meeting little old lorries and having to back to the mountain edge - nerve racking. Everywhere there were lemon trees, lush vegetation, and flowers all against the backdrop of the blue sea. Back at the hotel we had a leisurely bath, changed, and went down to the dining room which overlooked the bay.

Our next place to visit was Capri and Anacapri, a small island which was reached by an early morning boat trip. Of all the places we visited, Capri did not excite me. There were vaulted houses, labyrinthine streets, and expensive boutiques. We looked over the cliff down to a house in a bay, built overlooking the sea, where the singer Gracie Fields lived. At Anacapri, we went to the villa San Michele, built by the Swedish doctor, Axel Munthe, on the site of the villa of Tiberiu.

At last our day to visit Pompeii, Herculaneum, and Vesuvius had arrived. First we went to Vesuvius. It was quite a difficult walk up a winding path; it was like walking on cinders and, arriving at the top, there was steam and smoke. We had the usual tourist photos taken of us on the smoking edge of the volcano. I could not wait to get to Pompeii, and although the journey seemed to take forever, it was only a short drive. It was wonderful; we were walking along a Roman street bordered by kerbed foot-pavements and, at regular intervals, stepping-stones for the pedestrians. There were inns, shops, stables, and the houses with their frescoes, colours so bright it was as if they had been painted yesterday, and beautiful mosaic floors. The forum adjoined the Basilica and the temple of Apollo. There is a lovely garden around the villa of Julia Felixit; it seems to have been a luxury hotel with residential area, an inn, shop, a bath for public use, and a series of rooms. Under the tiled roof are marble columns, and in the garden, marble fish ponds. Behind the villa is the amphitheatre. Lots of the treasures found here are in the Naples museum. I had such a great day, and although it was very hot with lots of walking, there had been so much to see.

The next day we were going to Herculaneum, another town that had been destroyed with Pompeii. I did not think anything could surpass Pompeii, but how wrong I was. We drove into the town, and there were so many houses with their roofs intact, you imagined the town was still alive. Shops with shelves holding pots with carbonized cereals and other foods, while a hearth placed on the same counter was used to pour out hot drinks and prepare foods. The houses were wonderful; one still had a wooden balcony; another, beautiful decorations, a covered loggia, and an open terrace to the sea. The baths of the forum consist of two sections, one for men, another for women, the latter being smaller and less decorated. A long narrow passage leads to the gymnasium, and the dressing room with seats and brackets for dresses; and there was a beautiful mosaic floor. I could go on and on as I fell totally in love with Herculaneum, and I promised myself I would beat the gremlins just to come back here. It was farewell to Sorrento, and on to the splendour of Rome, the city of the seven hills; again, so much to see in such a short time. The Roman forum must have been truly magnificent, as is the coliseum. In the Piazza di Spagna, where the great stairway called the Spanish Steps, leads up to the church of Trinita'Del Monti, there are flowers all up the steps; a sight not to forget. Everywhere there are beautiful statues and works of art.

I could have spent a whole holiday at the Vatican City. 'Pieta' by Michelangelo is so beautiful, and the Sistine Chapel is the most outstanding of Italian art. After a long day we went back to our hotel for dinner. We were to visit beautiful Trevi with its myriad Fountains, but we were warned to be careful as there were pick-pockets everywhere. I felt quite frightened.

Holiday

You could hear whistling all the time. This apparently was their way of communicating with each other. The next day we arrived at Assisi, the city of St Francis, where Giotto went to paint the life of the saint in twenty eight scenes. Arriving at the church, we were told we could go in but there was a wedding ceremony being held. As we entered we had a lump in our throats as the soloist sang Ave Maria; it was so beautiful, everyone stood still. We also called at Monte Casino on the way to San Marino which I loved. It is famous for being the smallest and oldest republic in the world. It seems to be perched on top of a mountain, and has its own form of government. The male inhabitants run the shops and businesses, but when necessary are the army in uniforms like tin soldiers. There was great excitement when we arrived because the Pope was visiting the next day. During the evening, we wandered around the town which is famous for its local wines and sweet Moscato. Every shop invited you in to sample, and if you refused they were most upset, so we went back to the hotel rather happy. Unfortunately, our hotel room overlooked the main street, because all night they were cleaning the narrow streets and fronts of the houses for the Pope's visit. Up early the next day, we had been given permission to go to the area where the Pope would arrive; there was great excitement, and at last we could see the helicopter. We were so near we could have touched him, and he blessed us as he passed which for me in my circumstances was a wonderful moment.

We had our last night in Venice, so we had one more chance to explore the sights and waterways of this magical city before our flight home. It had been a truly wonderful experience, and had given me a taste for foreign travel.

14

ANOTHER OPERATION

I was going to Dr. Vaux for my B12 injections once a month, and to the Westminster Hospital clinic every three months. The Professor was still pleased with me. I was eating powdered baby foods which were mixed with water, but only liked the sweet ones and could now manage half a marmite sandwich and biscuits. Not a very good diet but, with the milk drinks, I was not losing any more weight. It could be difficult. On one occasion at work, a new girl started and at our lunch break said, 'no wonder you are so thin if that's all you eat.' Tina was really annoyed and said, 'if you had her problem, you would have trouble eating. It is not easy when you have had your stomach removed because of cancer.' The poor girl was so embarrassed and said she was sorry.

A year after my operation, I was starting to have quite a lot of pain so Dr. Vaux asked Dr. Stevens to gastroscope me. He found all was well but I also had a liver scan. There was slight enlargement of the liver which was a bit worrying in a lady of my age, so he suggested another scan in three months for comparison.

I had been having problems with my periods for some while, and it was decided that the pains I was having was to do with this. Some of the treatments I had tried had made me sick. I told the Professor this during one of my check-ups, and he suggested I should see a gynaecologist, a colleague of his, a Mr Roberts. Once again I am back at the Westminster in Mr Roberts' clinic, and immediately I like him. He suggested I try hormone treatment which unfortunately made me sick, and I could not afford to lose any more weight.

It was 1982 and we had some good news. Richard had passed his degree with honours. Roger and I drove up to Hull the day before the ceremony for the Conferment of Degrees. We booked to stay at bed and breakfast in a town called Beverly. I was a bit apprehensive about going away because of my eating. When we arrived where we were staying, they did not serve evening meals but suggested a restaurant not too far away. When we ordered our main meal, I said I'd like a small portion and asked what the vegetables were. I said I'd have just one vegetable, the green beans, but when the plate arrived it had the biggest portion of beans. The waitress told us that the chef had said, if that was the only vegetable I was having, I should have a large portion. For dessert I asked for a very small slice of the chocolate cake; back the waitress came with a big smile and a huge slice of cake, saying that was the last piece so I might as well have it all. Breakfast next morning, I asked for just bacon, and once again a smiling waiter brought me a large plate full of rashers of bacon. Roger was doing well because I hated to leave it, so had to pass it on to him.

I was now beginning to try to eat more things as I felt I could not just live on the baby food extra. But I did spend a lot of time in the bathroom after I had eaten, so I had to be very careful about what I ate.

The ceremony was held in the city hall. It was a super day which started with an organ recital, then various pieces of music and the procession started; it was all very moving. The graduating students went up to receive their degrees, resplendent in caps and gowns, and it was a great moment when Richard received his. Outside the city hall, everyone was taking photos. Then we went for tea at the university; it was a warm sunny day, and we were served drinks on the lawns so we had a chance to meet Richard's friends and their parents; a great day.

During this time, my Dad became ill. He was still living with my sister Nellie, but was in bed all the time. Nellie was still working at the hospital so it was hard for her. Then dad became very poorly so he was taken into hospital, and when we visited overnight he had become a frail little old man. Dad died on the twenty-seventh of October 1982 and was buried with our Mum at Detling. He was ninety-two.

After trying various treatments, Mr Roberts' advice was to have a total hysterectomy. He felt it radical to remove the ovaries as I was comparatively young, but with my previous history there might be strong indications following the cancer of the stomach. He left it for me to talk to Roger and Dr. Vaux, but in order not to waste time had put me on his list. If I had the operation on a Friday, Professor Ellis would be in the operating theatre, and Mr Roberts said he would value his assessment of the upper abdomen.

Another Operation

My menstrual cycle was out of control and I was constantly having heavy periods all the time, so we all decided the operation was the right thing to do. I was admitted on the twenty-fourth of March 1983, and had the operation the next day. All went well; Mr Roberts opened the wound from my previous operations so although I had had three, I only had one scar. The Professor was present, and was pleased how things looked from his previous operations. When the day came for the stitches to be removed, the staff nurse asked if I would mind a nurse who had not done it before. I agreed as the Westminster is a teaching hospital. I was a bit nervous though because the poor girl was shaking. She wore thick glasses and seemed to get really close to see what she was doing; I held each side of the wound so the stitches were taut and she did a good job.

There were quite a few ladies on the ward having hysterectomies, and Mr Roberts wanted some of us to go to convalescence homes. I was not at all keen, but everyone felt it was for the best. If I went home, I would start doing things and I was supposed to rest, so I reluctantly agreed. Some of the ladies were going to a new home near Brighton, but I was to go to the seaside town of St Leonards. Another lady, Sheila, would follow a few days after me, so I thought, well, there would be someone I knew.

15

THE CONVALESCENCE HOME

Roger came to collect me from the hospital. We said goodbye to the nurses and the other ladies, and Shelia said she hoped to see me soon. It was a lovely spring day as we drove out of London into Kent. The gardens were full of daffodils and the trees were bursting with green leaves, but I wanted to go home. Roger said I had to go because the doctors said I needed the rest. I had not only had the hysterectomy, but had to consider it had not been long since my other operations.

Roger suggested we stop for lunch at Bodiam, a village which has a castle surrounded by a moat. We went to the pub near the castle. We enjoyed our lunch; eating out was of course still difficult, so I had soup. It was so nice to be on our own. Reluctant to move, I was very apprehensive of going to the convalescence home. Roger went to pay for the meal, and I moved out into the cold fresh air, lovely after being in hospital.

We arrived late afternoon at St Teresa's, a Victorian house near the sea front. The Matron greeted us and invited us into the drawing room for tea. It was as if time had stood still; the room was large and quite dark with long, heavy velvet curtains. There were paintings, Art Nouveau ornaments, and a large cabinet full of delicate china. Matron said she would leave us to have our tea, and then she would show us around. A little plump woman arrived with the tea, also scones, butter and jam. I felt she should have been wearing a black dress, white apron, and a frilly cap to go with the atmosphere of the room. I whispered to Roger that I did not want to stay, but he said not to be silly. 'Anyway,' he said, 'Shelia will arrive soon to keep you company.' Matron arrived to take me to my room on the second floor with a view across the roof tops. The first thing I noticed was the screeching gulls, and whenever I hear gulls now it reminds me of the convalescence home. Matron informed us that Roger could stay while I unpacked, and then he was to leave. I was then to have a rest before dinner and would be called when I could go down to meet the other ladies. After she had gone, I once again told Roger I did not want to stay. I wanted to cry but it would have made it worse for him. He cuddled me and said that it was only for two weeks and he would see me at the weekend. When he had gone I lay on the bed and realised the day had exhausted me.

The whole house seemed to be in a time warp. The dining room had high ornate ceilings, and French doors led to a large garden surrounded by a high wall. The round tables had embroidered table cloths and napkins, silver cutlery, and sparkling glasses. Each table had fresh flowers. Matron introduced me to the other ladies; Maud was a tall thin woman of about fifty who looked as if she had been crying. I later found out she cried most of the time as her only son had died five years ago and she had not got over it. Betty was obviously the sort of person who complained about everything. 'It will be vegetable soup. We always have it on a Monday. I am sure it is the left-overs from the weekend,' she whined. Phyllis was small with soft brown curls which framed her child-like face. She constantly fiddled with her little lace handkerchief, and she told me she was staying there for her nerves.

I thought: much more of this and I will need to be here for my nerves. The rest of the tables were occupied by a variety of ladies. It appeared that everyone took it in turn to say grace. After dinner we all assembled in the sun lounge that had been built at the back of the house. The room was furnished with modern armchairs, a sofa, and wooden upright chairs arranged around a television; at the far end of the room was a pink velvet chaise longue. Elizabeth, a rather bossy lady who seemed to think she was in charge, said we could watch television if it was a programme Matron approved of, and as it was the singer Cliff Richard, a born again Christian, we could watch. What followed next made me want to go home even more. Cynthia was small and had bright pink rouged cheeks and lips and, what I can only describe as pink hair in a riot of curls. I was wearing a jumper with embroidered flowers across the front, and the next thing I knew, Cynthia was sitting close up to me running her hand across my breast. 'Oh I do like your jumper,' she was saying. I cringed. 'Do stop, and leave her alone,' Elizabeth almost shouted. 'I want to sit next to Margaret,' said Cynthia. Elizabeth's patience was running out. 'Well you can sit on your own chair.' Cynthia unwillingly sat on her chair sulking.

The Convalescence Home

The woman sitting next to her moved her chair closer and held her hand. Jean was a fussy woman who liked lace - it was all over her blouse - and she had a bow in her hair. She looked at me rather smugly. I was beginning to think I was having nightmare. I glanced at the small old lady dressed in black with a beret pulled over her hair who was lying on the chaise longue. Elizabeth saw me looking, and whispered that she was a retired doctor who lived in a small castle in Ireland. She stayed at St Teresa's three times a year, but I never saw her speak to anyone while I was there.

At nine o'clock, the Cliff Richard programme finished. 'We do not watch the news because it upsets some of the ladies,' I was told. 'Matron likes us in bed by nine thirty.' We also had to make sure all the plugs were pulled out and the lights turned off. I could at last escape to my room, but was not happy to discover there were no locks on the bedroom door or the bathroom. I hoped Cynthia did not walk in her sleep! I had not been in bed long when Matron tapped on the door. She went into all the ladies to say goodnight. She told me I would have breakfast in bed, and was not allowed downstairs until ten thirty when I would have to see the visiting doctor. Well, thank goodness, I was tired so I soon fell asleep.

The next morning when I went downstairs, the ladies were sitting in the large hall waiting to see the doctor. It seemed to be the highlight of the week for them. I was called into a small room with a double bed on which was a Gladstone bag, which when I was young was known as a doctor's bag. I had not seen one for years. Scattered all over the bed was what looked like medical notes. I found myself facing a small shrivelled woman who looked about ninety, wild grey hair and so many long whiskers on her face I wondered if she really was a woman. 'What medication do you need?' she asked. 'I don't need any,' I replied. 'Oh but you must need something, if only to make you sleep. You are Maud?' she asked, while shifting through the papers on the bed. 'No, I am Margaret, I arrived yesterday.' 'I was sure you were Maud,' she mumbled to herself. I asked if she would like me to help her find my notes. 'That might help,' she said. I found my notes. She looked at them but I felt sure she couldn't see well enough to read them. 'All my ladies need medication,' she said, as she wrote something on a pad. 'No need to wait. I will give this to Matron, and I will see you next week.' Not if I have my way. I will be gone from this mad house. Whatever medication she had prescribed, I would not be taking.

Matron was in the hall. 'I think I will go for a walk.' Matron stiffened.

'Not on your own; get your coat and Sister Anne will go with you.' Well at least it would get me out for a while, and Sister Anne was a lovely lady who had devoted her life to the church. She had entered a convent at the age of twenty, and she was now over fifty. Every morning she was up at five thirty for prayers. She had a certain amount of chores at the convent before helping the outside community, and arrived five mornings a week at the convalescence home. Her sense of peace and tranquillity, I am sure, was a great help to everyone, especially the ladies suffering with their nerves. Sister Anne told me Matron did not like the ladies going out on their own; some of them became confused and got lost or had falls.

The walk down to the sea perked me up, and I noticed a telephone box not far from St Teresa's. We were only allowed to use the phone in Matron's office at her discretion, and with her being present. We arrived back from our walk in time for lunch, followed by the compulsory rest period in our rooms, after which the ladies would assemble for tea and their various hobbies. Jean with her knitting; it appeared she always made fluffy lacy jumpers. Other ladies were knitting for their grandchildren. Cynthia read novels that Elizabeth did not approve of. She said it would be more beneficial to Cynthia if she did tapestry like her. The retired doctor liked to walk in the garden on her own.

I had decided to sneak out the next day after lunch; as soon as we went up for our rest, the staff had their lunch. I went up to my room, put on my coat, and crept downstairs, my heart beating so fast and loud I was sure someone would hear me, but I slipped out of the front door and into the avenue. I could not run but made my way to the telephone box as quick as I could. Julie was now working in a bank, and she says she had this strange call from me: 'Julie, this is Mum. I have to be quick because I have escaped to make this call. Would you get in touch with Dad and tell him to come and get me tonight? Tell him not to phone St Teresa's, just turn up as soon as he can. I must go.' Hoping to get back in, and that the door was not locked, I was in luck and I crept up the stairs. I longed to lie down and have a sleep, but was afraid I would not wake up for tea, so I lay on the bed until I heard the other ladies moving about and went down. No-one seemed to have missed me, and after tea I excused myself and went to my room.

Maud and Phyllis were already at the table when I went in for dinner. Everyone was very subdued, and Maud was crying. 'It's all right, dear, she has gone to a better place,' said Phyllis, patting Maud's hand trying to

The Convalescence Home

comfort her. One of the new ladies died this afternoon, only forty-three, she came last Friday, you must remember her, she always wore a long black dress, her hair in one thick plait. Phyllis informed me that she had spent a lot of time in her room with Sister Anne. Betty as usual complained about her dinner. She did not like the pate. 'You never know what they put in it.' She pushed it around her plate and nibbled on her toast. After dinner I went up to my room quietly, packed, and went down to the lounge. The ladies were watching a documentary about the royal family. Mildred, a quiet woman with piercing blue eyes, told me with great excitement that Lady Diana's old music teacher lived opposite St Teresa's and always went in and played the piano for them at Christmas. You will enjoy it if you are still here. At this point, Elizabeth told Mildred to stop talking as they were trying to watch the television. I thought it was a good time to excuse myself. I said I had a headache and was going to my room.

It was an awful night; the wind rattled the old sash windows, and lightning lit up the room. I could hear the sea crashing on the shore. I sat on the bed, watching out of the window the rain and lightning, and I hoped Roger would arrive soon. I was dreading Matron coming to check on me.

I heard the door bell ring, then twice more. I thought, that is Roger and they are not going to let him in. It was difficult to hear with the thunder rumbling and the rain lashing on the window. I was sitting on the bed when Matron came in. 'I am sorry you want to leave. I thought you wouldn't stay, you need somewhere with younger ladies. Your husband is downstairs. I will get him to come up and get your case.' It had been easier than I thought. Roger came into the room, hugged and kissed me, and said he had missed me. He wanted to know what had happened, but I said I would tell him in the car; I just wanted to go. Apparently Sister Anne had stayed on as some of the ladies were disturbed by the storm. I said my goodbyes to Matron and Sister Anne, and asked them to say goodbye to the ladies. We struggled to the car in the strong wind, and drove off. Roger said he was worried when he received Julie's message, but when he had rung the bell three times and Sister Anne opened the door, he had said to her, 'Good evening, it is Mr Knight,' and she replied, 'it is a dreadful night, isn't it.' He had then thought: this is not the place for Margie.

On the way home I told him about the other ladies and the doctor. He agreed I would be better off at home, and he hated not having me there. We had to call at Valerie-Joan's and Sid's house on the way home, as the next day Valerie-Joan and her Mum, my sister Nellie, had arranged to visit me at St Teresa's. We went into their sitting-room, and Sid said, 'I thought you were at the convalescence home?' 'I was,' I said, 'but I've run away.' Sid said he did not know what I would do next, but when I told them about my stay they agreed it was not for me.

It was wonderful to be home, and Roger said he hated sleeping on his own. Holding me tight, he said he was so pleased I was home, but I must promise not to overdo things. The next day I felt quite poorly, and was losing a lot of blood. I phoned the surgery, and Dr. Vaux said he would call and see me. He said he felt it was due to what had happened, so I was to rest; I told him about the doctor, and I think he found the whole episode quite amusing.

When I went back to the hospital for my follow-up appointment, I asked to see the almoner who made the arrangements for patients going to the convalescence home. I told her what had happened and she said Shelia had not stayed. She arrived to find I had left, and did not feel it was the right place for her. The almoner realised it was not for the younger woman and apologised. It was not long before I was back to work.

16

25 YEARS MARRIED AND A WEDDING

The year 1984 started with us celebrating our silver wedding anniversary. We decided to have a party. The Castle was doing Sunday lunches in the Fairfax Hall, so we booked for lunch. We wanted to have a blessing in Leeds Church, as there were times when I had been so ill that we did not think we would celebrate twenty-five years. During the time I was ill, prayers were regularly said in church for me. Jenny and Norman were a great help, and Norman, a lay reader in the church, came to sort out the service with us. It was a lovely surprise to find that the Bishop of Maidstone was to take some of the service. Up early on the Sunday morning, we picked up Sybil and took the cake into the Fairfax Hall. The tables looked really nice, and the ladies all had carnations. We collected Diane and made our way to the church; it was a lovely service. The Bishop blessed us, and then we had photos taken outside the church with the Bishop, splendid in his regalia. There were twenty-six of us, and we had a super lunch, followed by a tour of the Castle, finishing the day with tea at our house. When everyone had gone, Roger and I watched the Thorn Birds on television. We had had a great day.

Our anniversary was on the following Tuesday. It was another nice day with lots of cards and flowers, and we had dinner at home with the family. The next weekend, Valerie-Joan came with a super album of photos she had taken at the lunch; it was a lovely surprise.

After Roger had told me what the prognosis was about my illness, I thought of all the things I had not done. Ever since my Dad had stopped me going to art school, I longed to do something arty. On a shopping trip in town, I passed a shop that was advertising, 'learn to paint on china.' This was something I had not thought of doing. I had been saving my tip money from work, so I went in and saw Janet who owned the shop. She said I would need some white china, china paints, medium to mix them with, and after painting the china I would have to take it back for firing in her kiln. I could not wait to get home and start. Little did I know I would eventually get my City & Guilds, earn commissions, and have my own kiln. Every spare moment, I was trying to master mixing and painting.

Some of the girls I had worked with at the shop still kept in touch, and we would have a reunion every so often. I visited Sybil regularly, and my dear friend René and her husband Charlie were in our thoughts because Charlie had been diagnosed with throat cancer. René decided she wanted Charlie at home so she could nurse him herself. There was a room full of equipment that René had learnt to operate as Charlie could only have a liquid diet fed by using the machines. He was so thin and looked very ill, but remained cheerful. René did a wonderful job looking after him. Sybil, Pauline, Jackie, and I all met at René's, and the girls all made it a happy day for René and Charlie. Not long after our visit, Charlie died. Jackie was also to die of cancer.

The week after our anniversary, we were to get another surprise. Julie and her boyfriend, Kevin, came to tell us they wanted to get married. Julie wanted to have the reception in the Gate Tower at the Castle, and Richard, my manager, said there were two days free, one on the twenty-second of September, so they decided on that date. The rest of the year was taken up planning the wedding. I went with Julie to try on wedding dresses, and she eventually decided on a long white lace dress with a tiara and a short veil. As with all mums, when they see their daughter in a wedding dress, I felt very emotional and hoped she was going to be happy.

Richard had now started work at Shepherd Neame's brewery at Faversham, a town full of history. Richard had been given the chance to live in one of the brewery houses, a black and white timbered house. A near neighbour was Bob Geldolf, the pop star, and his wife, Paula Yates. Richard often saw them shopping in the town with their children.

In July, Vera, who was a supervisor at work, asked me if I would like to serve Princess Anne with tea as she was going to visit the Castle for a special children's day in her capacity as President of Save the Children fund. As usual on these occasions, there was a lot of police activity, and the rooms where we were to serve tea were checked by sniffer dogs. Then Vera and I stayed in there, and we could see the Princess through the window. There were stalls all around the courtyard, with volunteers from Save the Children fund, and the Princess made a point of having a word

25 Years Married and a Wedding

with them all. She walked through the Culpeper gardens, and I found myself asking her if she would like tea. 'Yes please,' she said, and thanked me. Once again, she made a point of speaking to the guests that had been invited to take tea. I don't think photographs do the Princess justice; she has a lovely complexion and beautiful hair. Then it was all over. She thanked Vera and I for the tea and said goodbye. Our exciting day had finished.

I was finding it difficult to get an outfit to wear to Julie's wedding, so Roger and I decided to go to the town of Tunbridge Wells and, quite by chance, found a designer workshop that made hand-worked silk bridal and special occasion dresses. We fell in love with a beautiful hyacinth blue dress; it cost a fortune but Roger said I should have it. I knew the sort of hat I wanted. I had seen Lady Diana wearing it, and we found one that went really well.

We booked a holiday in Italy for Julie and Kevin for their honeymoon. I did not write in my diary for the next two weeks. I think we were under too much stress, and were trying to block the whole thing out. Kevin was being very difficult about everything, and we were more and more worried about Julie getting married. He only had the cars to sort out, but it was two weeks before the wedding and still they had not been ordered. Roger said perhaps he did not have the money to pay for them, so we decided we would book them for him. He went berserk and did not speak to us until the day after the wedding. He also booked another car. The night before the wedding, Roger asked Julie if she wanted to go through with the wedding. His feelings are that, once you have made those vows in church, you should stand by them. It did not matter what people thought if she cancelled the wedding, but Julie said she wanted to go ahead.

We awoke to find it raining, but by the time we arrived back home from the hairdressers, the sun had come out. Julie's best friend Hilary, who she worked with, was chief bridesmaid. My niece, Heather's daughter Chloe, two little girls who Julie baby-sat for, and a little girl who was the daughter of a friend of Kevin's, all wore pink dresses with pink and white flowers in their hair, and carried baskets to match.

Two friends, Ethel and Thelma, were going to tidy the house after we all left, and get the buffet ready in the village hall for the evening. Roger went in the car with Julie, and I went with the bridesmaids. When we arrived at the church, Richard was waiting and asked me to walk in with him which was a nice thought. It was tense in church, especially having our photos taken with Kevin who was not speaking to any of us. Some of the guests were calling out to him to smile for the camera, but of course no-one knew he was not talking. We arrived at the Castle, and had drinks on the lawn in front of the Castle, and a lovely meal. The staff made it extra special for us, but it was many months later that the girls from work found out Kevin was not speaking to us. They said we would all make good actors because they did not realise anything was wrong, but we had tried to make it a good day for Julie. After the reception at the Castle, we all went to a local village hall for dancing and a buffet.

That night, Julie and Kevin stayed at a local hotel, and when they came home the next morning, he acted as if nothing was wrong and said the wedding was wonderful. We took them to the airport to go on their honeymoon. They decided to try for a baby soon after they were married, and some weeks later Julie told us we were going to have our first grandchild.

17

MODELLING AND A GRANDCHILD

At the start of 1985, it was our twenty-sixth wedding anniversary. Twenty-three of us went to the Castle for Sunday lunch. On Monday, I met Julie and we went to the hospital for her scan. When I saw the baby, I wanted to cry. It was moving about, really active; it was a wonderful experience.

We had a lot of snow, and the Castle looked wonderful. The moat was frozen, so the ducks and swans were sliding on the ice. I was working full-time because we were very busy. Sometimes I would get up, do the housework and washing, prepare dinner, then go to work for the day, pop home, cook dinner, and go back to work for the evening. I was getting fitter all the time, and managing to eat very small meals. We had a new manager at the Castle, Humphrey Shepard, a lovely man, tall and wide, red hair and a beard. He looked like Henry the VIII, so right for the Castle. I had a surprise when, in February, Humphrey asked me if I would accept the position of supervisor. Roger was pleased and said I should.

In March, I was very excited to receive a letter from *Woman's Realm*, asking me to go up to London for a feature in the magazine. The next morning, I had a telegram to say a photographer would come to the Castle to take some photos of me. When I arrived at work, the magazine had been in touch with the Castle, and they said the photographer would arrive that afternoon. The weather was not very nice, a bit damp, but this did not worry the photographer. We went into the grounds, and he said that, with such wonderful surroundings, we were sure to get some good shots. *Woman's Realm* phoned to tell me where the studio was in London.

Two days later, Roger took me to the railway station at seven thirty in the morning. I was to go to the Steve Campbell studio in Chelsea. On arrival, we had coffee and I was introduced to Dorothy the hairdresser, and Pattie the make-up artist. There were four of us: Sharon, a housewife with two young daughters, Ann, a headmistress, and Sandra who worked in a library. We had a wonderful time trying on lots of outfits. I chose a printed two-piece and red shoes, and then we had our hair and make-up done. While we had lunch, I looked at the photos taken at the castle. After lunch, it was time to do our modelling. We had lots of photos taken and, all too soon, it was all over and I was sharing a taxi with Sandra to go back to the station.

Back in Maidstone, as I walked out of the station, I saw Julie sitting on her bus. I tapped the window, but at first she did not recognise me with my new hair-style and make-up. Roger thought I looked great. I had had a super day, and we could not wait for the article to appear in the magazine. We were very excited when they rang to say it would be in the May issue. A week later, on the way home from work, Roger bought a copy and, as he was collecting me from work, brought it in for us all to see. He was very proud when the magazine sent me the photos that were in the article.

On the twentieth of June, Julie had our first grandchild, Joe. He was a lovely little boy, and we were all very excited. When Julie left the hospital nine days later, she asked me to have a week's holiday to look after her. Julie and Kevin had bought a house in a small village near us, so Roger dropped me off on the way to work. I felt quite awkward as things were obviously not going well with them. During the next three months, Julie and Joe came to our house at least three times a week. Kevin had a dog, which had had pups, and Julie said it was not hygienic having them in the kitchen with the baby, so could she stay?

David had been having a lot of problems with his back, and had seen a consultant who said he would need an operation.

In November, Tina from work married Anthony who worked in the gardens at the Castle and lived in our village. Tina lived in Lenham, a typical medieval village built around a square, surrounded by old timbered houses. The chemist's shop is called Saxon Warriors, since the discovery of skeletons of three sixth-century men with their weapons. The church with its Kentish tower is next to the square, and in the churchyard there is a tombstone of Mary Honeywood who died aged eighty-two in 1620, leaving no fewer than three hundred and sixty-seven descendants. Tina and Anthony were to be married in the church. The weather that day was not kind; it thundered, with lightning flashing across the sky, and it rained so heavily we could hardly see where we were going. It was so dark, it was if the day had turned to night. All the photos had to be taken in the

Modelling and a Grandchild

church, but the reception was in the Fairfax Hall and, by the time we arrived, the weather had cleared.

The following Sunday, Julie started to be sick and had a very bad pain in her left side. By nine o'clock that evening, the pain was so bad that Roger decided to take her to hospital. He arrived home at three thirty in the morning. The hospital was going to send her home, but when she stood up she was in so much pain she almost fainted. The doctors decided to keep her in, and we were to ring the next morning. When we rang, the staff nurse said they were keeping her in. The doctors thought it might be an ectopic pregnancy, but Julie knew she was not pregnant. Then they thought the colon had gone into spasm, and by Thursday it could be a cyst on her ovary. She was still in a lot of pain, unable to eat, and so weak she could not hold Joe.

When Friday arrived, Julie said they were going to send her home on Saturday. We did not think that was a good idea because she seemed worse instead of better. We were told to ring the next morning. Roger rang and was told she had gone for minor surgery, and that we could visit that evening. We were so worried. Arriving at the hospital, we were told that, as we were not her next of kin – her husband was – and even though we explained they were not living together, the nurses would not let us see her. They would only say she had had major surgery. At one stage, I had to sit down. I thought she might have cancer of the womb. Had she had a hysterectomy? All sorts of things went through my mind.

While we were talking to the nurses, Kevin came in. Roger, who is usually quiet and doesn't say a lot or get angry, told Kevin to go in and see the doctor and to come back and tell us what was going on. We seemed to wait an age, but at last he came out. Her fallopian tube had gone 300% round her ovary and had gone gangrene. It had all been removed, but it appears it was an awful mess and she was very lucky the doctors had decided to operate. This of course would mean she would only have a 50% chance of having any more children, but with marriage problems that looked unlikely at that stage. The good news was we now knew what the problem was, and when we saw her she looked so much better. I was still working, but only some evenings, so when Roger came home he would look after Joe while I went in to work. I found it quite hard work; Joe was a very active baby and did not sleep much, and when Julie came home she could not pick Joe up for a while. When she came out of hospital, she had decided not to go back to Kevin, and asked if Joe and her could live with us. For the next few years, it was a nightmare time for Julie and us. Things with Kevin became very bad, so bad I wonder we did not all have nervous breakdowns. However, Julie wishes me not to write about it in this book, so I respect her wishes.

David now had his own workshop repairing cars. He still had problems with his back and, at the end of 1985, three weeks before Christmas, David went into hospital to have an operation. As with all back operations, it was quite risky but it had got to the stage where his consultant felt he should have it done. He had a spinal decompression. He had hoped to be out for Christmas, but it was not allowed so we had our lunch and then took tea up to the hospital. We had a great time with the nurses and the other patients. I had thought he might have scoliosis like Julie, so I had been with him on one of his visits to the consultant, but he assured us it was not, thank goodness. David came home after Christmas and had to convalesce for quite some while. Although the operation was a success, every so often his back will go into a spasm and he cannot move. He is in a lot of pain, but with rest it recovers.

18

NEW HOME

At the end of February 1986, David came home and told us that a house, which Roger had always said he would like if it came up for sale, was on the market. A friend of David's parents was interested so, if we were, we should find out about it. I rang the estate agent, and they said there was a lot of interest. They were doing two days at the weekend for viewing, so I booked the Saturday. An old man had been living there on his own since his wife had died, and the house was not at all as we had expected. It needed a lot of money spent on it, and the kitchen was only an old lean-to. I also had a strange feeling when we entered the house, especially upstairs. The family which eventually bought it were friends of David and said they were sure it was haunted.

Roger was quite keen. He said we could buy a caravan to live in while the house was being renovated, but although I did not say so, I did not feel too happy about that. The next day, after lunch, Roger suggested going for a drive. We drove past the house, and he said perhaps we should have a drive around to see if there was any other property we liked before we decided. We saw a sign for new houses, left the car near the show house, and walked down what was to be the road. The houses appeared to be sold as they were built, but, although the next one was almost finished, it did not have a sold sign. We looked through the window, and Roger said, 'I like this house. I can see grandchildren sitting on the stairs in their dressing gowns, and a log fire in the fireplace.' We went back to the show house and said we were interested. The sales lady said it was for sale but we would have to complete the sale within six weeks. On the way home, Roger said we would contact the estate agent the next day to get things going, and hope we could sell the house in time. The agent did not think we would have a problem.

The next weekend I was at work, and when I arrived home, Roger said a young man had been to view the house. He seemed really interested, and as he was working at the local TV studios, it was nice and convenient for him as it would be only fifteen minutes drive to work. But I didn't think he would buy, as he was single and it was a three-bedroomed family house. In the next few days, we had two other families to view, and then the first young man came back and said he had decided to buy. We told him we wanted to complete in five weeks, and he said it would not be a problem. The new house was almost finished, and we had hoped to move in for Roger's birthday on the twelfth of June, but it was not until the twenty-seventh. In the meantime, Joe had his first birthday.

We were very excited about the move. David, Richard, and a friend of Richard's, helped Roger and me with the move. It was a very hot day, but I was very organised. It was decided I would stay with David at the old house and, as each room was cleared, we would clean up. All seemed to be going well, when David said he would go with the others to see how they were getting on in the new house. On returning, he informed me all was well; apparently there was furniture in the garage and garden. They had not done as I suggested and, as they moved furniture from each room in the old house, put it in the appropriate rooms in the new house. As I only had one day off from work, it seemed to take forever to get ourselves organised. I said if we ever moved again, we would have a removal firm.

The rest of the year was a nightmare for us with the problems Julie was having, and at one stage she had to live away from home. When she was able to come back, she went to live in a flat a short drive from us. Joe and her settled in well and made new friends.

In November, I had gone from work to the supermarket and saw one of my nieces. She said, 'how about Aunt Nellie getting married today?' I must have looked surprised because she said, 'didn't you know?' The next morning I had a letter to say she was getting married and they wanted a quite wedding, and then they were going away for a few days. A few days later, my sister Lili-Anne was at a function at work which I was supervising. Lili-Anne said, 'what about Nellie getting married?' I replied that I was pleased for her, but wished she had told me as I had found it quite hurtful being told by my niece, after the event, in a supermarket. The problem was that the letter she wrote to me had not arrived until the day after. The next time I visited Nellie, she was very angry with me. I don't know what Lili-Anne had told her I had said, but Nellie said it was nothing to do with me if she did not tell anyone, so I left in tears and for the first time we had fallen out. It worried me so much that, in the end, I went to see Nellie and explained I was not upset about her getting married; I was pleased for them both. She had looked after Dad for all those years after Mum died, and I know it was not easy. I had been upset because someone else had told me. After more tears we made up.

It was 1987, and we started the year with more marital problems for Julie. Then, in May, the day after my birthday, Nellie rang to say Lili-Anne was ill. Apparently she had been poorly for a while but had not told anyone. Barb had been to see her and was worried, so she had rung Nellie. They were going up to see her and wanted me to go as well. I was shocked to see her looking so ill, so we rang her doctor, and after a visit from him, Lili-Anne was taken into hospital. Two days later, we were told she had stomach cancer. This brought all my illness back. Would she have to go through all that treatment I had? For the next two weeks, Roger and I went most evenings to see her. I was worried that she did not seem to improve at all so we had a word with one of the nurses and I asked why she was not having any treatment such as chemo. She said they were going to start the next day. At the end of that week, the doctors had decided to stop the chemo as Lili-Anne was so ill it was not helping her.

That weekend, David and his girlfriend Nina got engaged so we had a party in the Culpeper rooms at the castle. It was warm and sunny, and we had drinks in the gardens. It was a lovely day, but Lili-Anne was on all our minds. Three days later, she died the day before David's birthday. I was so upset. I had always been close to her, spending the school holidays with her in Canterbury. We would write frequently to each other in the following years, and her letters were always full of fun. If she wrote something happy, she would write 'ha, ha,' and I could imaging her laughing. I still have her letters.

In July, Richard and his girlfriend, Sandy, got engaged. In August, we decided to go up to Yorkshire for a short holiday, and on the way home stop at Cheshire to meet Sandy's parents. We drove to Whitby and found a bed and breakfast nestling in a secluded hollow in a picturesque hamlet of ten houses and a village pub. Beckhole was right in the heart of the North Yorkshire National Park. Opposite our B&B, was a house for sale. It stood on the village green on which sheep were grazing, and where the locals played the French game of boules. The house, which was owned by an artist, was also being used for bed and breakfast, and it had a studio on the side with rooms over the top. We fell in love with it. We had thought about running a bed and breakfast, and this seemed ideal. We went to the estate agent in Whitby, and said we were interested.

For the last two days of our holiday, we arrived in Manchester. Richard had now moved up there to work for Boddinton's, the brewery, and he was staying with a friend, Ian, from university. When Richard had gone up there for one of his interviews, Ian had asked him to make up a foursome. Ian's girlfriend, Pam, had a sister called Sandy. Richard did not make a good impression. He had had chilli before they went out and, as he had spilt it on the only shirt he had with him, he had put on a jumper which was a thick Aran. The evening was very warm, so he sat in the car with perspiration dripping off his red face; not a very good impression for their first date. When Richard arrived back at Shepherd Neame, he told his friend that if he was offered the job in Manchester he would ask Sandy out.

We arrived at Ian's, and then went to meet Sandy's parents, Mary and Barry, where we had lunch with them.

We drove home, excited with the thoughts of another wedding, and hopefully moving and starting somewhere new. But as with plans such as that, Roger pointed out we would be a long way from the rest of the family, and I was still attending the hospital, so we decided to stay where we were. We did like the house and area we lived in, and it was only just over a year since we had bought our house.

In October, Roger left for work but came back within fifteen minutes and said he could not get onto the main road. There were fallen trees and devastation everywhere. We had slept through the worst hurricane for years. There were roofs off, huge trees down, and roads blocked. At the Castle, a lot of trees were lost but, luckily, there was not too much damage elsewhere on the estate.

It was December, and getting near to my check-up at the Westminster Hospital. I pretended to Roger that I was not worried, but as always I was. As usual, the clinic was on a Saturday. I was hoping to see the Professor, but he was not there so I saw his registrar. He thought it was amazing I had done so well, so that was a boost, but he did tell Roger there was still the possibility of the cancer returning. The hospital is near the Tate Gallery so we usually went to view the wonderful works of art they have there. They often have exhibitions, and we were lucky it was the children's author and artist, Beatrix Potter so we spent the afternoon there. We always found it relaxing going around the gallery after my check-up.

New Home

The year, 1988, started off really well. My Mum's favourite actor had been Richard Todd, and I was told I would be supervising his son's wedding. It was a thrill to meet him, and when I was chatting to him I thought how my Mum would have loved me to tell her all about it. The day went really well, but Richard Todd left early as he had to be at the theatre. When the bride and groom left they gave me some flowers.

One morning, at the end of January, I had a letter and a cheque from Lili-Anne's solicitor. I had a few tears; it was lovely of her, and she had left the same to Ted, Barb, and Nellie. The following weekend, Roger and I went to the little fishing town of Rye, where there are lots of art shops, because I wanted to buy a painting. I chose an oil painting of a country scene by a local artist which Lili-Anne would have liked.

In March, Julie was granted a divorce and we hoped it would be a new start for her and Joe.

Mrs Terry was a receptionist at the doctors' surgery. She was very kind to Roger and me when I was going each week for my chemo, so we had become friends and I had painted china for her. She asked me to see a friend of hers, as her dog had died and she would like a painting on a plate of him. I arrived at a well-kept bungalow and was invited in by a lady who reminded me of my Mum. I liked her instantly. Joan had been the local district nurse before she retired. She had married late in life, had no children, but came from a large family and was very close to them. The little bungalow was like a mini art gallery. Her husband and his father had a talent and a love of painting, and the walls were full of their work. Joan said she would like my advice about a large oil painting of children playing in an apple orchard with an old cart; it was delightful. Joan told me her father-in-law had painted it, and she asked me if I thought it was worth having it cleaned and, if so, could I recommend someone. I said it was definitely worth having it cleaned, and advised her of a local person. When the painting was finished, she invited me round to see the result. It had been transformed; the colours were as bright as the day it had been painted.

Joan and I became great friends, and she was always so bright and cheerful although she was not in the best of health. I would sometimes invite her to tea - she was a great conversationalist - and I did a lot of china painting for her which were gifts for her family and friends. On one occasion, she said she had a surprise for me, and gave me a package. Inside was a painting of a still life by her husband which she said she wanted me to have. I was thrilled, and it hangs in pride of place in our hall.

19

TWO WEDDINGS

Nina asked her Mum and me to go with her to choose her wedding dress. We both felt very emotional when Nina came out in the dress she had chosen; she looked lovely. Nina's mum, Mig, came to see us about the wedding arrangements. The reception was to be in the Gate Tower at the Castle, so we decided on a menu with Mig, and a few days later I bought my wedding outfit.

This wedding was again not to run smoothly. A week before the wedding, we discovered the banns had not been called properly, and in the end David and Nina had to go up to London, to Westminster, and collect the banns four days before the wedding. It was a very fraught time because, if they did not get the banns, they could not marry.

On the twenty-third of July, the day of the wedding, we awoke to find a dark grey morning, with the rain bucketing down. Roger and I were taking Julie and Joe, who was to be a page boy, to Mig's house to change with the bridesmaids, but on the way our car decided to break down on the main road. With the rain lashing down, Roger got out of the car to see what he could do, and a lorry passed, drenching him and his new suit. Then the wedding car with Nina, followed by the car with Mig and the bridesmaids, passed us on the way to church. Julie and I sat helpless in the car, until at last Roger managed to get it started. He turned the car around and we made our way to the church. Boughton Monchelsea church is situated on a hill overlooking a lovely park with deer, and all around the back of the church is the most wonderful old wisteria which when in bloom produces great droppings of purple flowers hanging in abundance.

We arrived at the church, but it was raining so hard the water was gushing down the road. At the entrance to the churchyard is a lych-gate, and waiting there was Nina and her Mum. We had to change Joe into his sailor suit outfit, and he looked really sweet, but Nina was upset because two of the bridesmaids were sick and unable to come. Also the vicar was sick, and the one standing in for him did a different service, standing people in different positions from those they had rehearsed. At last the service started. Roger's new suit was soaking; his hair dripping wet. When we emerged from the church, the rain had stopped and the sun was shining. When we arrived at the Castle, it had dried enough for us to have bucks fizz on the lawn. Joe, who now three was always getting up to mischief, decided to take off his sailor suit while running around the Castle lawn with a bare bottom, followed by Julie trying to catch him. It all turned out to be a lovely day, even with so many problems.

I had been so sad that we had not been able to invite our special friends, Trisha and Jim, to Julie's wedding, due to the trouble we were having with Kevin. This time, we not only had them but also John and Sue whom we had known since Roger stopped going to sea, and Roger worked with John when they both joined the Singer Sewing company. Then there was Diane who I worked with at the Castle, a dear friend, also my special friend Sybil, and of course other friends and family. The reception had its problems, however. My lovely friend, Ros, who was working, offered to look after the roast potatoes, but decided to go outside to see us arrive and forgot the potatoes. When the staff went back into the kitchen, they were ruined so more had to be fetched from another kitchen. The three-tier cake had started to sink, and Tina, who was supervising, had to dismantle it until we were due in to sit down. We wondered if anything else could happen, when we discovered Nina had given her Mum the marriage certificate to look after while the photographs were taken at the church. When Nina asked her Mum for it after our meal, she could not find it, so in the end Mig went back to the church and found it floating in the gutter outside the church. She must have dropped it as she left.

My diary records that the next day I was exhausted. Two days later, we were up at three o'clock in the morning to take David and Nina to the airport for their honeymoon. There had been another problem four days before the wedding when I had the day off from work to meet David and Nina. They were two and a half hours late as they had not been able to get their passports. We had told them they would need their birth certificates, but they had not bothered so they still had no passports. Fortunately they did get them sorted in time for the honeymoon.

Tina, my friend at work, told me she was expecting a baby in March,

Two Weddings

and I was so pleased because I knew how much she wanted to start a family.

The next sad occasion was attending the funeral of the teenager, Jason, Lili-Anne's grandson. Jason's mother was Margaret, and her family had a heart problem - something very rare - and she had lost other members of her family who all died very suddenly. Jason was on holiday with his brother, Mum, and Dad, my nephew Adrian. The boys were in the pool when Adrian and Margaret realised something was wrong; Jason had died the same as the other members of the family. Lili-Anne would have been devastated.

In October, we had a message to say Richard was in hospital; he had appendicitis. He was now living in Macclesfield where he had bought a house. I rang the hospital every day, and I was very worried being so far away. He then developed an infection so had to stay in hospital three days longer. We were able to go up to see him two weeks later, and we all went out to lunch with Sandy's mum and dad. We stayed for three days. On the way home, we called into my china supplier; it was so nice to have a look at the stock as normally I had to order by post.

Living in one of the Castle houses were Pat and Keith with their young family of five children. Keith was a carpenter, and Pat helped in the Fairfax Hall in the evenings. We were all so shocked when Kelvin, one of their boys, was diagnosed with cancer and had to have part of one of his legs amputated. He also had to have chemo which is so distressing for teenagers. The girls at work wanted to raise some money for him, so one of the ladies, Pat, a jolly person who was always chattering, said she would do a sponsored silence. It was a great success and we were able to buy Kelvin a television and a variety of presents. Kelvin recovered really well.

I was now working five days a week, still going up to London for the hospital check-ups, and having scans, X-rays, and endoscopes, and still going to Dr. Vaux for my B12 injection. Some days I was up at five o'clock for work, but there were days when I felt so tired that I think this made me more determined to get really fit.

The year, 1989, started off well. January the tenth was our pearl wedding anniversary; we had been married thirty years. We had a nice day, and it was also the Castle's staff dinner dance. Natalie, one of my managers, knew it was our anniversary and asked the band to play Phil Collins' 'A groovy kind of love'.

The following Sunday, we had an entertaining anniversary lunch at a local pub; we had taken all the family, plus our friends Diane and Sybil. It was like a comedy sketch. The waitress brought our main course before we had had our starter, and as she went back into the kitchen, we heard her say, 'They haven't had their bloody starters yet.' Then she could not remember who had ordered what for main course or dessert so had to take the order again. When it came to paying the bill, it seemed a lot more than we had worked out so we had to check through the bill with the waitress to discover we were being charged for the table next to us as well. We all enjoyed the day as we spent most of the lunch laughing. Richard and Sandy had come down from Macclesfield, so they took Julie and Joe back for a holiday at Richard's house which was a nice break for them.

I was waiting for an appointment for an endoscope, as I had been having a few problems, when I heard that Dr. Stevens, the doctor who found my stomach cancer and always did my endoscopes, had had a stroke. I was so upset; thank goodness he was to recover and return to the hospital. In the meantime I had my appointment; it was most unpleasant as the nurse forgot to spray my throat so it was very sore and uncomfortable to eat for a few days. The problem with my insides was a sore place, but with medication it should heal. I was told, if it did not, I was to go back, but it did eventually.

I phoned Tina who was very distressed; she thought she was losing the baby. I rang again the next day, and she had. I was so upset for her; life is so unfair sometimes.

In March, Sandy asked me if I would like to go with her, the bridesmaids, her mum, and Julie to choose her bridesmaids' dresses. We all had a great day in Canterbury, and the girls all looked lovely in the dresses they chose.

In April, Lord Aldington, who was now chairman of the Castle foundation, had invited some of the staff, including me, to dinner in the House of Lords. We left the Castle by coach, and drove to London where we were given a tour of the city before arriving at the House of Lords. We had drinks, and then went into dinner in the Chomondeley room where we saw the lovely views across the river Thames. The menu was devilled white bait, escalope of veal with lemon and orange sauce, mange tout, delmonico potatoes, baked Alaska, and coffee. It had been a delightful evening.

My forty-ninth birthday came round in May; it is now twelve years since my first operation, and Roger says we always have to celebrate my birthdays and anniversaries. I was diagnosed with stomach cancer in 1977, only thirty-seven years old, and the doctors told him I would be lucky to live three months, so we have to always make the most of every moment of time we have. I have been so lucky. When Richard marries in two months, I will have seen all our children married, and, twelve years ago when I was so ill, I never thought I would see them grow up, let alone marry and have children. So once again I was very spoilt on my birthday, with lots of presents and flowers.

In my china painting magazine, I saw that you could go on a china painting course in Sussex, which was not too far from us. I booked the course, but was a bit worried about driving there as I have no sense of direction. However, I was determined to succeed so, armed with maps and directions, I left home on the Sunday for the course which would start on Monday. By some miracle, I arrived at the house without getting lost. I was welcomed by Shelia Southwell, who was running the course, and introduced to the other ladies attending. It appeared I was the only one not staying in the house, and I would stay in bed and breakfast about ten minutes drive away. Shelia rang ahead to say I was on my way, and the husband said I could still go but his wife had been taken into hospital, so he would be there with his young daughter. I was not too happy about staying with his wife not there, but I did not have much choice. It was made worse by the other ladies saying they would not like staying on their own, so at night, as there were no locks on the bedroom door, I pushed a chair under the door handle. I felt guilty at the end of my stay as they were a very nice family.

There were ten of us on the course, and it was sheer bliss painting all day. This was the first time I had ever been away on my own. We all got on so well and everyone was eager to help; the other ladies had been on courses before so I learnt a lot. On the last evening, we had a special dinner. Two of the ladies were sisters and lived in Jeddah; they had brought Turkish coffee and dates, and a key ring for all of us. I had had a super time; it was very relaxing and I had gained so much from the course. One of the ladies, Mary, lived in Rochester which is not far from us so I drove her home. It was lovely to be home. Roger said he had missed me, and had bought me flowers.

The first Saturday in June, I was supervising a lovely wedding reception for an Indian couple. It was a super day. They wore traditional costume; the bride was stunning in green, red, and gold, and the bridegroom was very handsome. Most of the guests wore traditional dress, with the ladies in the most beautiful silk saris, and when the couple left to go on honeymoon, they drove off in a car covered in flowers. The bridegroom's mother gave me and the waitresses, silk cushions. I had met the mother when she was arranging the reception, and she had asked how many of us were looking after them as she wanted to give us a gift from their home. They were the beautifully embroidered silk cushions. It had been a wedding we would not forget; a lovely day.

I had been to visit Julie and Joe, and as I left I called to Joe, saying he had not kissed me. He ran to me and fell on the edge of the kerb but he did not make a fuss. Later on, Julie realised he had really hurt his arm, and at the hospital it was confirmed he had broken it. It was put in a plaster; this was three weeks before Richard and Sandy were getting married, and he was to be page boy.

On July the first, Richard and Sandy were married at St Michael's Church, Macclesfield. Roger and I, plus all the family and friends, had travelled up north the day before, all staying at various hotels and bed and breakfast houses. It was an awful journey; it took us seven and a half hours. We arrived at the bed and breakfast too late for dinner; we had to have what was left because their son had eaten our vegetables. We were about an hour's drive from the church in beautiful countryside, and we awoke to the most spectacular view from our room. The church is right in the middle of the town of Macclesfield. Sandy looked lovely, as did the bridesmaids, and Richard and the rest of the men, very handsome in their top hats and tails, including Joe who still had his arm in plaster. After the service, we all assembled outside the church for photographs and a chance to meet up with all the family. The reception was held at Capesthorne Hall, a lovely old house, and we were in the conservatory overlooking the beautiful gardens and lake. It was a very relaxing day after Julie and David's wedding, with all their problems. Next morning, we went to see Richard and Sandy go off on their honeymoon to Naxos in Greece. It had been a lovely wedding. Driving home took us even longer - nine hours, we were worn out - but I had been lucky enough to see all the children married.

I was supervising a function, and one of the waitresses had dropped some food on the floor. I slipped on it and fell against a chair, cracking some ribs which made breathing painful. The doctor said to rest as there was nothing he could do; just wait for them to heal.

Two Weddings

We had booked a short holiday in the New Forest, staying in bed and breakfast at Brockenhurst. Next day, we did a walk in a part of the forest called the Queen Bower; it was very windy and the leaves that were left on the trees were coming down in showers of browns, gold, and copper - it was like walking on a colourful carpet. We walked beside a stream with water tinged red-brown by the soil's iron content. On the way back it started to rain so we had dinner and relaxed with a glass of wine. We saw deer and forest ponies in their thick winter coats at Lyndhurst next day, and had lunch in an old inn. Then we drove to Beaulieu with its Motor Museum, and to Bucklers Hard and the Maritime Museum. We had had a relaxing break and it was time for the drive home. My ribs were healing, though painful when driving, but it was back to work after our break.

In September, we had some exciting news; David and Nina were expecting a baby.

In December, we were very busy at work with Christmas lunches and dinners. I had been to visit Sybil who was not at all well, also been out to lunch with Jan and Diane, and then it was time for my check-up at the Westminster Hospital. All went well but I must try not to lose more weight. I felt quite down because the Professor said he was retiring. It sounds silly, but I had always felt safe all the time I could see the Professor, so I did not think this was a good end to the year.

20

HOLIDAYS AND A NEW BABY

At the start of 1990, I had a nice letter from the Professor, who, after leaving the Westminster Hospital, went to Cambridge. And, in April, I decided to surprise Roger with a fishing holiday. I knew he had always wanted to fish the river Piddle in Dorset. We arrived at Briantspuddle, a tiny village near Tolpuddle which is famous for the Tolpuddle Martyrs. In 1834, the infant trades union movement was dealt a public blow at the trial of six agricultural workers, later to become known as the Tolpuddle Martyrs. They were tried in the courtroom of the old Shire Hall, now Tolpuddle memorial, and were sentenced to transportation for joining forces to request a wage increase for local farm workers. The river Piddle runs through the most beautiful countryside; Thomas Hardy country with lush water meadows and chalk downland. I fell in love with the whole area, and as we drove through the village it was full of thatched cottages and pretty gardens.

At the Tolpuddle trout fishery, we were given the key to our cottage, The Hollow, a delightful thatched cottage and one of the oldest in Briantspuddle - at least two hundred and fifty years old. The large cottage garden had views across the Piddle valley. After unpacking, and a cup of tea, we decided to explore the area. There was a tiny village shop and post office which seemed to have everything, and Roger was tempted by some local cheese. The next day, Roger was booked to go fishing so I stayed at the cottage. I had taken my china painting with me, so I sat at the window, painting. After a while, I don't know what it was, but I felt as if I were not on my own. I suppose a cottage that old must have the presence of all the people who lived there. Roger came back for lunch, and we sat in the garden under a lovely old apple tree. After lunch, Roger went back to his fishing, and I sat knitting for the new baby. The next day, we went for a walk through the pine forest. Roger said the pine smells were lovely, and this is when I miss not being able to smell. Another day, we went to Cerne Abbas with its famous giant carved in the chalk hillside, and also went to the swannery at Abbotsbury. My favourite visit was to Thomas Hardy's cottage; driving through the wonderful countryside made Thomas Hardy's novels come alive. On the way home, we stopped at Shaftesbury which is situated on the edge of a 700 ft plateau. Its most famous street, cobbled Gold Hill, plunges down the hillside. Thomas Hardy used the original town name, Shaston, when featuring it in his novels. We also went to Marnhull, which he called Marlott, in his wonderful novel, *Tess of the D'Ubervilles*. We really enjoyed this holiday, and the rest of the year went quickly.

We were all waiting for David and Nina's first baby to be born. Nina was very into aerobics and had even taken her exams to become an aerobics teacher, while pregnant, so she was very fit. The baby was due on the twentieth of May, and as that was Mig's, Nina's mum's, birthday, we hoped the baby would be born then, but it arrived at twelve thirty p.m. on the twenty fourth, weighing seven pounds. We had to wait until the afternoon to visit. David would not tell us the sex of the baby until we went into the ward, but as soon as we went in I knew we had a grandson because he had a blue hat on. He was a lovely little boy to be named Luke. Nina was sitting up in bed with her make-up and earrings on, and did not look as if she had just had a baby. I think her aerobics had really helped her.

I was supervising weddings most weekends, and during the weekdays we had a variety from the traditional to the outrageous. One I really enjoyed looking after, was a couple in the music business, Hark and Paru-Paru. The theme of the wedding was black and red, and even the cake was iced in black and red. The bride wore a very short dress with a long train, and rode beside the moat on a flower-decked horse. After the meal in the Fairfax Hall, the bridegroom and some of the guests who were musicians formed a band to play heavy rock music for the guests. It sounded as if we had the Rolling Stones; they were brilliant and it had been a great day.

It reminded me of when I was first working at the Castle; it was near to Christmas, and my manager, Humphrey Shepard, asked me if I would look after some children while their parents attended a lunch in the Fairfax Hall. We were to be across the courtyard in the Culpeper rooms, and Peter, a musician who played at our evening functions, was going to dress up as

Father Christmas. We did not know who the people coming to lunch were until half an hour before they arrived, when we were told it was Paul and Linda McCartney. Apparently they had arranged a lunch with friends for charity, so there were a lot of stars from the music business, and three of the children I was looking after were Paul and Linda's. A very exciting day.

During the summer, all the family try and go out for the day, so in August we drove to Minster-in-Sheppey. The Leas and cliff tops are perfect for walks, and we picnic on the grass sloping down to the beach. On arrival, we set out the rugs and food and drink. Joe loves investigating the rock pools with granddad; Luke is now two months old, a gorgeous little boy who hardly ever cries, and seems so contented. He lay in his pram as good as gold all day; it is great to have a day all together.

At the end of the month, we had an open-air jazz concert at the castle. Roger and I were on our way to the evening performance, when we stopped at the phone box to call David and Nina. David answered the phone in a panic; he said they were leaving for the hospital because Nina had dropped the baby on his head. He did not explain what exactly had happened, so as you can imagine we were really fraught. We decided we would go straight to the hospital instead of going to the concert. Arriving at the hospital, we found them, and to our great relief, Luke was all right, but the hospital had decided to keep him in over night just in case he had any reaction. Nina had not actually dropped him on his head as David had said. He had been in his little bouncing chair on the work surface while Nina prepared dinner, and he had bounced so much he had bounced off, but not on his head. Of course it had frightened them both, and they panicked, but thank goodness he was fine.

In October, it was Luke's christening. The service was at Farleigh church which is near the river Medway, and after we had the christening party, once again in the Culpeper rooms at the Castle, the sun shone and we were able to have drinks in the lovely gardens before our meal. It was another great day, with the staff looking after us so well.

In November, I supervised a literary dinner; one of the speakers was the author, Joanna Trollope, and another was Robert Morley, the actor. He was a brilliant speaker, very entertaining, and it was a good evening.

Once again we are in December, and my check-up at the Westminster Hospital went really well. I had the usual tests, and the doctors are amazed I am doing so well.

Another busy year, 1991. In between going to work, we were having Joe and Luke, whilst also trying to get all my china painting orders completed. I went for my endoscope; no problems except I had a very sore throat for a few days, in fact almost lost my voice. Roger said I sounded quite sexy!

Rose, our next door neighbour, had told Roger that her husband, Alf, was ill. Although we would have a chat, I did not see her much because of my working hours, so I had never told her I had had cancer. However, Roger told her and she asked if I could have a chat with Alf, which I did. They are a lovely family, and not long after Alf was taken into hospital, we were devastated at the end of September when Rose told us he had died. I had to go to work that day to supervise a wedding, which I really did not want to do, but could not spoil the bride and groom's day. I just kept thinking about Rose and her family.

Everywhere, people were touched by the story of Jackie Mann who had been taken hostage on the twelfth of May 1989 in Beirut. He was the oldest Western hostage held captive in Lebanon, and a former Battle of Britain Spitfire pilot. Not once in two and half years was he allowed to see a human face, and he was chained in a bare room with only a decaying mattress. His wife, Sunnie, on her own in a city ruled by terror, had no way of knowing if her husband was dead or alive. Living with constant shelling, no gas or electricity, and destitute, she showed great courage. On the twenty-fourth of September 1991, he was released. I cried, as I am sure people all over the world did, watching the news, as I saw a frail, unkempt man who had had no comb or toothbrush, no shoes or socks, had not had a shave, but was still showing such courage. Eventually they went to live in Cyprus.

In October, we were looking forward to our holiday. Roger wanted to go to Austria so we booked a coach holiday to St Johann in the Tyrolean Alps. Julie took us to the coach pick-up. As soon as I was on the coach, I was asleep. I was so tired. The wedding I had been supervising the day before did not finish until one o'clock in the morning, so it was two thirty before I arrived home. The coach took us to the ferry at Dover. We had a nice meal on board, and soon arrived in Calais, France, where we drove through the night into Belgium, along the autobahns of Germany. The next morning, we continued into Austria and arrived for lunch. We loved the hotel; it was typical Austrian style with flowers everywhere, and we

Holidays and a New Baby

had a balcony with views of the mountains. St Johann is a small town at the foot of the Wilder Kaiser Mountains. We had a day excursion to Innsbruck where we saw the golden roof, the Hofburg Imperial Palace, and the Maria-Theresienstrasse, the famous street with its wonderful mountain vista at each end. Another day, we went to Achensee, one of the most beautiful lakes in the Tyrol. At dinner we shared a table with Eve who lived in America. She was with one of her daughters, Debbie, a lovely looking girl, and some days we all hired cycles and had some enjoyable rides up in the mountains.

Roger and I decided we would do one of the mountain walks up the Kitzbuller Horn. It was a lovely clear sunny day; at 2,600ft we stopped at a café and had hot chocolate, and at 5,525ft there was what looked like a traditional Austrian-style building. We were surprised to find this was a pub, but unfortunately closed. Having walked all that way, we would have enjoyed a drink, but had to be content with sitting outside eating our packed lunch. We passed the winning post for the famous mountain bike race which was on the day after we were leaving, but how anyone could ride a bike up there is amazing. We walked up to 6,100 ft and decided we should start back. On the lower slopes were flower-decked wooden houses where golden cows, with bells around their necks, grazed. Arriving back at the hotel, we learnt that some of the other guests had been walking, but none had managed to go as high as us, so we were tired but quite pleased with ourselves, especially as they were younger than us. One evening we went to a Tyrolean night in Wiesnschwang. Another day was spent at Kitzbuhel, famous for its winter sports; it is a fashionable expensive resort, and a ride in the cable car gave us the most wonderful views. At the end of the holiday, we stopped at Oberammergau which is famous for its Passion plays held once every ten years. We loved Austria and thought it would be lovely to spend a Christmas there. Too soon we were back at the docks on our way home.

It was time for my check-up at the Westminster, and one of the doctors asked if we could have a chat as he had been doing some research on stomach cancer. He said I was the only patient, of those who had similar operations, who had survived so long. I have been so lucky.

22

THE GREMLINS ARE BACK

On July the twenty-seventh 1992, Roger and I started our holiday. I had an appointment for a breast mammogram which I thought was at Larkfield, a short drive up the motorway from home, but when we arrived there was no sign of the mobile unit. I checked the appointment letter to find it was at Grove Green which is only five minutes from home. Roger was a bit cross and said I should have read the letter properly as it was important not to miss my appointment. This was the first time I had been for a mammogram, and the strange thing was that for a few weeks I had been thinking I should have had one when I was fifty; now I was fifty-two. I seem to have tests such as liver scans and endoscopes and various other tests, but no-one had suggested a mammogram. When I had been to Dr. Vaux for my B12 injection, I mentioned that I had not had one and he asked if I had a problem. 'No,' I replied, but little did I know that the gremlins were lurking there. He told me I should soon get a letter to go for a mammogram as there was a mobile van in the area, but if I did not hear he would get me an appointment.

A few days later I had a letter. Even though I had made a mistake with the location of the unit, I arrived for my appointment on time, and it was only a few seconds and it was all over.

I didn't think any more about it. The next day, we went to France, had lunch in Calais, and walked around the town before a relaxing journey on the boat home. On the last day of our holiday, we took Joe and Luke to Port Lympne Zoo. We had a great day. Luke was so excited and thought the chimps were wonderful. One of them spat water over him, and he couldn't stop talking about them. It was a long day. We arrived home and had tea, gave the boys a bath, and took them home; I was worn out.

August 5th.
What a shock. I picked up the post to find a letter from Preston Hall hospital saying I needed more tests. I felt numb; surely I haven't got breast cancer!

August 10th.
I arrived at Preston Hall breast clinic. The nurses were very nice; the radiographer said something had come up on the scan so they needed to do more. After taking the first ones, I had to wait in the little waiting room until, after what seemed ages, I was called back in. 'We need to do more,' the nurse said. I was soon back in the waiting room, only to be called again. This time they wanted to do another scan and enlarge it, so I was back in the waiting room. When called again, the nurse showed me the enlargement, and there was what I dreaded. It looked just like Professor Ellis had told me when I had my stomach removed; a bit like a flower head with the seeds scattered around the edge. In between having the mammograms, I told the nurse I did have a previous history of cancer, plus there was a family history. I was taken in to see the doctor, a tall slim woman who was saying they had found something and it would have to be removed. She had made an appointment for me to see a Mr Jones in two day's time. She then said perhaps she should examine me. 'Oh look, we have a lump,' she said, prodding me under my left breast. 'Haven't you noticed this?' she asked. 'No,' I replied, thinking if I had I would have been straight to Dr. Vaux. I was in a state of shock when I felt the lump. Why hadn't I found it? I think it was because when I examined myself I had not felt *under* my breast. I needed an ultra scan, the doctor was saying. 'This will have to be done by a male doctor,' she informed me. I did not care if there were 10 male doctors as long as it was done.

The lump showed up clearly on the scan, and the lady doctor was saying it would be all right to leave it. 'No,' said the male doctor. The radiographer looked concerned and asked to look at the scan again. The lady doctor was saying leave it six months, and the male doctor said he wasn't sure about that, but she was insistent and told me I could get dressed and come back in six months. She would cancel the appointment with Mr Jones. I left in a state of confusion, and sat in the car thinking that the doctors at the Westminster Hospital always told me all lumps were to be investigated. I WANT IT OUT. I felt mentally exhausted. When I arrived home, Roger came in from work, and the family came to see how I had got on. After explaining what had happened, they said I should not leave

it, and should go and see Dr. Vaux. The next day I made an appointment.
August 11th.
I have decided to keep a daily diary.
I cannot stop thinking about it.
August 14th.
I went to see Dr. Vaux and told him I was confused about what had happened. After examining me, he said he was not happy and would ring the hospital. He told me to ring him back that evening, and when I rang back he said he was still not happy, so he would get in touch with Mr Jones.

The next day I was too busy to think about it too much. I am booked to go on a china painting course at the end of the week, so hopefully it will take my mind off it a bit. I am so looking forward to the course.

Roger drove us up to Yorkshire. He dropped me off at Westfield House, owned by Celia Shute and her family, where they run the courses. I am so excited because Celia is the tutor on this course and I so admire her work. Roger leaves to go on a fishing trip, and will be staying near by. Celia greets me and shows me to my room, and I meet the other ladies on the course. One is Marion; it is her first trip away since having her family, and it reminds me of my first course, doing something on my own. We get on well and fine, lots to chat about late into the night after dinner. It is a lovely group of ladies, and the next three days fly by, but I had learnt so much and cannot wait to be able to do another course. Roger returns to collect me; he had enjoyed his fishing.

Back home, I receive an appointment to see Mr Jones.
September 9th.
This is the day I see Mr Jones. Before I go for my appointment, I am going to visit Sybil as it is her birthday. She is now in a nursing home and, on my last few visits, it took her a time to recognise me. Poor Sybil. This shrivelled little old lady, propped up in a chair and sleeping most of the time, doesn't seem to know who anyone is. She would have hated to be like this; she was always so smart and intelligent. After I left, I sat in the car feeling so sad. She always called me her other daughter.

I arrived at the clinic, where there are about thirty people waiting, and I looked around at the ladies, some with husbands or partners, others with perhaps daughters or friends, and some like me who prefer to be on their own. There are older ladies, trendy younger ones, smart professional looking ladies, and we could all have the nasty little gremlin in us. We are told by some doctors it is what we eat, or our lifestyle, but looking at everyone here, I would think we all have different lifestyles. At the end of the room is the children's clinic. I feel sad when I start to think about the grandchildren because I do so want to see them grow up.

At last I am called into see Mr Jones, the consultant. I like him, and feel confident, mainly because he says he had had lunch with Dr. Stevens and had been discussing my case. He asked me questions about my previous operations, treatments, and family history. He wanted to examine me, so I lay on the bed. He feels the lump straight away, and says I am a very lucky lady. Had this been left, not so lucky. He did not know what the lady doctor had been thinking, to say leave it six months. In six months… and he waved his arms as if gone. He is telling me he is sure the lump is malignant, and has gone into the lymph glands. He will remove them and the lump, and follow this with chemotherapy and radiotherapy. SHIT! I think this is one occasion when I needed to swear, but to get it out is the main thing.

Mr Jones then sends in the breast care nurse, Pam Wright. She is a lovely lady who has a great calming presence. We have a chat, and I am to go in for the operation next Wednesday.

Roger said to phone him as soon as I have seen Mr Jones. I don't want to tell him on the phone, but he will worry if he doesn't hear from me. I use the pay phone in the foyer, but it is difficult to talk with people all around, waiting. The receptionist at Roger's works called him to the phone. 'How did you get on?' he asked. 'Mr Jones is sure it is malignant and gone into the lymph glands. He will remove the lump and glands, follow it up with chemo and radiotherapy,' I said. He didn't answer. 'Are you still there?' I asked. 'You have got that all wrong; you wouldn't have more chemo and radiotherapy,' he answered. For the moment I felt confused. Had Mr Jones told me that? Yes, he did say it. Roger is still saying I must have got it wrong, but there are people waiting to use the phone so I tell Roger I will see him at home and explain everything.

I sat in the car, trying to get myself together before driving home. I drove onto our drive to find Roger getting out of his car. He had left work as soon as I had phoned him, and he came and held me and kissed me, but neither of us spoke. I would have cried if I had. It was too much for me to see him so upset. 'I had so hoped you would not have to have more chemo,' he said. 'I know, but it worked before,' I replied. Later the children came, and it was difficult having to tell them.

The awful thing was that, when I told some of the ladies at work what had happened with the lady doctor saying it was all right to leave it, they said if she had told them that, they would have thought everything was all right and not done any more about it.

September 11th.

I went to see Diane. I don't feel I can tell her on the phone that it seems I have cancer again.

We will not know for sure until Mr Jones operates and takes biopsies. After she had made us a cup of tea, she asked if everything was all right. I told her I had to go into hospital, and she hugs me and we have a few tears, but I tell her the gremlins won't get me yet. I left Diane and went to work. It was a hard evening, and I felt tired. Pauline and I have worked together for some time, and I am very fond of her. She can be very blunt, but is very caring and emotional. I take her into a corner at the end of the function and tell her I am going into hospital. She hugs me and cries, and I tell her not to get upset as she will make me cry too.

Driving home, I do cry. I have such caring friends, and they seem so upset. Roger looks worried when I get in, and I knew it would be hard telling Diane and Pauline; in fact, it had been a difficult day. I had rung Nellie and Valerie-Joan, and they said they would ring the rest of the family. I also rang Trisha, and I am sure it was harder for them to know what to say to me. I said I would ring as soon as I knew when I would be going into hospital.

September 12th.

We had just finished dinner when David, Nina, and Luke came with some wonderful news. Nina is having another baby. They were going to wait a bit before they told us, but thought the news would cheer us up before I go into hospital and give me something to look forward to. We opened some champagne to celebrate.

September 14th.

It is Sunday, and we decided to go out for lunch at the Bull, near Bewl Bridge Reservoir. It is a pleasant old pub and we enjoy our lunch. We drove down to the reservoir and, after parking the car, walked along the water's edge, watching the antics of the noisy geese and ducks, and the fishermen hoping for that large trout. Roger sometimes comes here fishing. It was a relaxing day, but I must admit my mind would wander, and I would think about the future. I hope I am not going to die.

September 15th.

Well, I am back in hospital; not the Westminster, but Maidstone. I still cannot believe the gremlins are back, but Mr Jones said he is 99% sure.

I have a little room to myself; it is very nice, with a television. A student doctor comes for a chat, then the house doctor, and next the anaesthetist, a jolly man who says I look ten years younger than I am. He probably tells all the ladies that, but it makes me feel good anyway.

The operation will take about an hour, and I am the second patient to go down. The lump will be removed, and the tissue under it, and the lymph glands under the arm. I asked the doctor if it is likely I would have a mastectomy, but he said only if the cancer had spread more than they think, and he can only tell when they do the operation. With my previous history, I am resigned that might happen. It will be a bonus, if not.

September 16th.

It is strange how things work out. When I was at the Westminster Hospital, Mr Jones was at one time Professor Ellis's registrar. Little did I think, in twelve years, he would be the surgeon operating on me for breast cancer.

Yesterday, I had an E.C.G. Pearl, my nurse, took my blood pressure and had the usual problem trying to find a vein for my blood. I feel sick now and not so brave. I do not want to die and leave Roger, the children, and the grandchildren, and not see the baby that David and Nina are expecting. I slept quite well, on and off, and nurse Pearl brought me a cup of tea at six o'clock.

By six thirty, I had had a bath. At seven thirty I was given some Gaviscon to line my insides in case I feel sick after the operation, then my pre-med. The nurse is holding my hand as I am wheeled into the operating theatre. Mr Jones arrives, pulls back the sheet and says, 'let's get rid of this.' Thank goodness they soon find a vein, and the masked faces quickly fade away.

I slept until four thirty when Roger came in with flowers; it tears me apart to see him so worried. Julie and Nina came in, and my niece, Heather, sent a beautiful basket of flowers. I kept drifting off to sleep. I tried to keep awake but the anaesthetic had not worn off. Roger said he wished he did not have to leave me, and could give me a cuddle.

Had my drip taken out.

September 17th.

Had quite a good night; woke early, had some pain killers. Mr Jones's registrar came round with the house man, and said I had to stay in five days. Then they would take out the drains, and I could go home. The registrar said the lump was malignant, but I would have to wait for the results of the lymph glands. I asked if I had had a mastectomy, and he replied no, a lumpectomy and the lymph glands under my arm. I will see Dr. Phillips at the Westminster to sort out the chemo as he did before. I had a few tears when they had gone. Louise the staff nurse stayed with me. I told her I was upset because I had to tell Roger. She said she would ring him if I wanted, but I said I would wait until he came in this evening. I do not like him knowing on the phone.

I had lots of visitors. David came first; he had been up to Scotland. My sisters, Nellie and Barb, with her husband Ted, then my nieces, Heather and Valerie-Joan, and her husband, Sid, followed by Nina and her brother's girlfriend, Jo, and Julie. It was difficult to talk to Roger when he came, with everyone there, and I longed to be on our own. At last, we had a few minutes after everyone had gone. He asked if I had any news, and I told him it was malignant, but I had not had a mastectomy. He was upset but took it quite well. He told me later that he hated going home on his own.

I was worn out with so many visitors. Nurse Pearl said I had too many, and I must rest. Heather said she would come and wash my hair on Saturday, but it is difficult as my arm is in a sling and I have to keep it like that until the stitches come out.

September 18th.

Had an awful night; I hardly slept at all. There was a dreadful storm, and my arm ached when I lay down, so I sat up in the armchair and at last went to sleep in the early hours of the morning. One of the nurses awoke me with a cup of tea. My arm felt swollen and it hurts where I had the operation; also feeling sick. Had some pain killers, some Gaviscon, and had the drain changed. When the doctor did his rounds, I told him I was not feeling so well. He said it was to be expected and I was to try and rest. The nurse told me off and said I had had too many visitors yesterday.

I slept most of the morning and afternoon.

All the same visitors came in the evening, plus my brother Ted and his wife Joyce. Gladys from work popped in. She was visiting a friend in another ward so thought she would have a quick word which was nice of her. Richard and Sandy brought Diane, Julie, Joe, David, Nina, and Luke. It was lovely to see them all, but once again I did not seem to get any time with Roger, plus by eight o'clock I was completely worn out and just wanted to sleep. Roger's colleagues sent a gorgeous basket of flowers, and Mark from work brought fruit and cards from the Castle staff.

September 19th.

Had a much better night. Woke at three o'clock, and then slept until six thirty. I feel so much better; not so sick. The man in the room next door came in for a chat. He said, 'I don't get many visitors but you seem to get lots.' 'I hope they haven't disturbed you. I have a large family, and we are always supportive of each other,' I replied. 'No, I enjoy watching and listening.' He then asked what I was in for, so without going into too many details, I said, 'cancer.' 'I don't think I would be as cheerful as you if that were me,' he said. Heather came to do my hair. She brought her friend Brenda, who worked at the hospital, and she wanted to check I was being looked after properly. I assured her I was. My sister Barb came with them. I still didn't get any time on my own with Roger as he came with Richard and Sandy, and was going to their house for dinner. My niece Michelle, and her husband Paul, came with David and Nina. Once again I am worn out when they have all gone. Nurse Pearl came to check me and said my temperature was up. She said I am still having too many visitors, and I must try to rest. I explain I have a large family and, of course, they are all concerned. She said perhaps they could spread out their visits.

September 20th.

Sunday, and I felt poorly first thing this morning, then had a nice surprise. Valerie-Joan arrived saying she thought it was visitors all day on Sunday. The nurse said not until two o'clock but she could come in. She was feeling a bit down, but felt better after we had a good chat. There were always so many visitors we had not had the opportunity for a proper talk. She cut up my lunch for me as it is awkward with one hand. The rest of the family came at two o'clock. Nurse Sandy asked if I would mind moving into the ward as there was a patient coming in who needed a room on his own. We all went into the day room while the nurses sorted out the beds. Mark brought Katie from work; I would have liked more time to talk to them. When everyone had gone, I moved into the ward where there were four nice old ladies already there.

September 21st.

I had a good night's sleep; hope I can go home today. As always when the consultant is doing his rounds, the ward is made shipshape. Mr Jones arrives with his band of students, doctors, and nurses. It reminds me of my time at the Westminster when Professor Ellis did his rounds. He says I can go home when the drains have been taken out.

Later I am given some painkillers for when the drain is taken out. I felt a bit worried about it, but it came out quite easily; I did not realise it would be so long. The nurse said, 'Oh look, there is another drain.' When I looked, there was a plastic tube sticking out about half an inch. Staff nurse Sally was not happy about leaving it in, as I was going home, in case of infection, so I had to wait to see a doctor. He said, 'take it out,' so out it came. The doctor also told me the cancer had started to go into the ducts, but the results tomorrow would show if it had gone into the lymph glands. They will tell me when the stitches are removed in two day's time. So at last I can go home. Roger left work early to collect me, and said he couldn't wait to have me home. I had enjoyed my short stay with the four old ladies on the ward, and the nurses had all looked after me so well.

When we arrived home, Trisha came round, so she stayed while Roger went to do the shopping. Trisha and Jim's daughter, Lisa, is getting married in October, so I'm glad I have got my operation over with, as we have an invitation to the wedding. I am looking forward to it.

September 22nd.

Got up when Roger went to work. It's very difficult to have a bath trying not to use my arm or get it wet, and doing my hair was very awkward; all this took so long. Julie came; she vacuumed and did some washing. We had lunch and she washed my hair, and was blow drying it when Michelle, Ros C. and Pat from work came with a 'get well' balloon. Rose from next door also popped in to see how I was. Julie left to collect Joe from school, telling me not to do anything silly. Richard, Sandy, and Nina, with Luke, arrived; he is a dear little boy. I wonder if Nina will have another boy, or will we have a granddaughter? Roger arrived home early. He said he could not wait to get home. I long for a proper cuddle but it is difficult with my arm.

September 23rd.

Once again, it takes a month of Sundays to bath and try to do my hair. I had such a nice letter from Yvonne, a girl at work, who I have only known a short while. It is so good of her to write.

Back at the hospital to have my stitches out, and to hear the rest of the results. Had hoped for good news but it is not to be. Pam the breast care nurse came into the cubicle with the doctor, so I felt it would not be good.

The gremlins have gone into the lymph glands, so it is back to the Westminster hospital for the chemotherapy, followed by thirty-five sessions of radiotherapy, five days a week for seven weeks. There is a mini-bus which takes the ladies to the hospital, and it will cost £42.50 a week. What a shock. The nurse had problems getting the stitches out under my arm. The trouble is it caves in where the lymph glands have been removed. They are right up under my arm, but she thinks she has got them all. I feel a bit down when I get home. Roger was upset again when I told him the results, but I reassured him I would be all right.

Now the stitches are out, I asked Roger if he would like to see where I had the operation. I carefully remove the dressing and he is amazed; he can hardly see it. The cut is under my left breast, and although the breast is a bit smaller now, once it has healed it will hardly be noticeable. The cut under the arm went right up into the armpit. Roger thought Mr Jones had done an excellent job.

September 24th.

Had a letter from Mr Jackson, our general manager at the Castle. It's so good of him to take the trouble to write. He also said I could have a Leeds Castle sampler to make which was very kind. Heather and Pauline from work came, and Heather brought me some books and tapes. David came with Luke as it is Nina's aerobics evening. When everyone has gone, I feel worn out.

September 25th.

Had a quite morning, writing lots of letters. Pat brought a gorgeous basket of flowers from work. Nina's mum, Mig, came with flowers, and Trisha sent beautiful carnations. The room is full of cards and flowers. I feel so lucky to have such great friends and family. Katie and Kay called in. It seemed a long day. I wish I had more energy; felt very tired but couldn't get to sleep.

September 26th.

Saturday, and Roger had to work. It was a busy morning; Julie and Joe came and did some housework and washed my hair as my arm is still strapped up. She then picked up her friend Hilary, with her children Katie and Matthew. Hilary and Kathy, another friend, both worked with Julie before they were married and used to come for dinner with us then. Hilary was also Julie's chief bridesmaid when she was married so it was lovely to see her. Roger and I had a nice quiet evening on our own. Still finding it hard to sleep.

September 27th.
Sunday, and Roger had to work. I cooked lunch with great difficulty with one arm. Richard, Sandy, David, Nina, and Luke came for tea. Shirley hobbled round - she had hurt her foot at work – and brought me a lovely dried flower she had made. Could not get to sleep again; started to get morbid thinking I have only got so long to live.

September 28th.
Richard's birthday, and I cannot believe it was thirty-two years ago when I had him. Ros S. called round to see how I am. Julie did some jobs for me. My boss, Andrew, came and we had a nice chat. Started my exercises, but quite painful.

September 29th.
Felt very down today. My arm is painful, and the exercises made it worse instead of better. Decided I should make a new will and Roger said he will sort it out for me.

September 30th.
Michelle called to see how I was. After she had gone, another young friend came with her little girl who decided to wreck the house. She squashed her sandwich all over the coffee table, and tipped up furniture. I felt something was sure to get broken. When Barb and Ted came, after Pippa had gone, they said what a badly behaved child she was. Julie came to take me to see my GP, Dr. Vaux. He said to exercise little and often. I felt he did not want to talk about the treatment, and I found myself starting to shake and feel nervous. He checked the wound and said it had not quite healed, but it was early days.

When we were back home, I asked Julie if she would like to see where the operation was, and she was quite amazed. Like Roger, she had thought it would show a lot more.

October 1st.
Did not sleep well again. I think it is because, as soon as I turn on my side, it wakes me. Roger said he wished we could have a proper cuddle. I did manage to go back to sleep after Roger had gone to work. Pottered about, and managed to hang out the washing with one hand. A quiet day.

October 2nd.
Hectic today. Mig came and we looked at old school photos. When we first met Mig, and David and Nina were getting married, we realised Mig and I had lived in Bearsted, had gone to the same school, and knew of each other's families, so we enjoyed looking at the old photos.

Rose called round to say have a nice holiday. Before all this happened, we had booked to go to Venice. I explained to Mr Jones, my surgeon, and he said it would do me good to go.

Lynda, my manager from work, came with a letter to say I had a bonus - a lovely surprise. The exercises are still painful but I must persevere. Had a letter from Judy Murray who is in the sales office at the castle. It was a lovely long letter, entitled a newsletter from catering and sales department. Judy is a super lady, always happy although she has had some personal health problems in the past, and so dedicated to her job. I have looked after some of her personal functions which I have really enjoyed, meeting her husband John and her Mum. I know how busy she is at work; she said she wrote it during her lunch break, and I very much appreciated it.

Roger is worried about going on holiday, and feels my arm doesn't seem to have improved much. We make love in a fashion, but it is very awkward as the grunts and groans are not of ecstasy but from the pain in my arm.

October 3rd.

I went to have my hair done, and told Lisa, my hairdresser, that, because of my treatment, I would not see her for a while – don't need a blow dry on a bald head!

Have been looking forward to today; Trisha and Jim's daughter, Lisa, is getting married. It is a horrible wet and windy day, so dark and wet, that the photo had to be taken in the church. It reminds me of my friend Tina's wedding when the weather was the same. Luke gave Lisa a horseshoe. A really nice day; it was lovely to chat with some of Trisha's friends, such as Marie and her husband who I knew, but I was beginning to feel tired. It had been a long day for my first outing since the operation.

22

VENICE AND MORE TREATMENT

October 4th.
We start our holiday today. Nina came with Luke, and a book for me. Then Richard and Sandy came to take us to the coach station. We left early which was lucky because, when we arrived, the coach was there already, so we made an early start. I am so excited; I love travelling, and especially as we are going to Venice.

When we arrive at Dover the sea is very rough, and quite frightening. The coach drove onto the ferry although we were told there may be a delay in leaving. It was difficult to stand up as the boat was rolling about, and many of the passengers were feeling ill. At one stage, we were in the restaurant when a trolley that had not been secured went flying across the restaurant, and crashed breaking all the china on it. The boat got on its way eventually but, arriving in France, we had to keep circling the harbour as a boat was trying to get out. At last the Captain broadcast that we were able to get into port, one and a half hours late.

It was a long drive through France into Switzerland, with a stop for breakfast. We arrived in Venice, had a bath and change, and went for a walk to look across the lagoon towards the city; it was wonderful. Back in the hotel, we had a very good dinner. I was feeling tired, and my arm was aching, but cannot wait for tomorrow to go to the city.

October 5th.
We went by launch over to the city of Venice; it really is the most wonderful place. Spent the day walking around; the architecture takes my breath away. We visited St Mark's Square, had coffee while the orchestra played, and went on to a glass factory and a place where they make beautiful masks. Then back across the lagoon to our hotel for dinner. After dinner, we went back for a moonlight gondola trip; there were six gondolas

with music, and the gondoliers singing. It was spectacular and so romantic along the little canals which passed the most wonderful buildings. We then walked back through the city and over the lagoon to the hotel.

October 6th.

We had the whole day in the city, walking around the back-streets. Went to the Doge's Palace; the statues and the paintings were fabulous, and then walked over the Bridge of Sighs. Had pizza, ice cream, and cappuccino overlooking the lagoon. Bought some presents, and then went back to the hotel on the water bus. After dinner, we walked to the beach and found some lovely shells.

October 7th.

I would have liked to have gone over to the city once more, but there was not time as we were going on a boat trip to Murrno to see the famous glass being made; it was very expensive. Also a bit disappointing as we did not get a chance to see much of the island. The next island was Tontel; really lovely, and only forty people live there now. We would have liked more time to look around. We went into the little church to light a candle and say a little prayer; it made me feel sad and I had a few tears on my own. Then we were on to the next island, Burno, which is famous for its lace. The old ladies sit outside making beautiful lace table cloths. All too soon, we were back on the boat, but a nice trip back to the hotel. We had made friends with a couple, Pat and Sue, who had got married the week before we came, so they were on their honeymoon. We sat with them for dinner each evening.

October 8th.

We left the hotel after breakfast for our long trip home. The weather was still good; we had been so lucky. On the ferry, I looked back at the city, and the sun was shining on the beautiful old buildings. It was like a Canaletto painting. One of our fellow travellers talked all the time, but I just wanted to sit and look and remember everything. Will I get a chance to see it again! Back on the coach, we drove to Vipoeena in Italy, had a quick look around, and then drove through Tuscany. Wonderful countryside; I love the colours of the flowers, the vineyards, and the villas. There had been a lot of flooding before our holiday, and we could still see some signs of it.

Then it was on through Austria, and a change of scene with the mountains, until we were back in France, and flat countryside. That is what I like about coach travel; you get to see so much. The return ferry

Mum and Dad's wedding, 1939.

Me, aged 15 months, with Mum and Sukie the dog at Scragged Oak.

My sisters, Phyllis with daughter Joan, and Lili-Anne, Dad holding me, Barb, and Mum (the hillbillies), at Scragged Oak, 1940.

Me, aged one.

Reluctant bridesmaid at my brother Ted's wedding, 1942.

Me with Valerie-Joan at Gidds Hill.

Dressing up when staying with Lili-Anne at Canterbury.

Richard and Sandy's wedding, 1989.

Ready for work, aged 17.

My handsome Roger, aged 17.

Three sisters - Nellie, me, and Barb, at our engagement party.

My brother, Ted.

Our engagement party, 1958, with Mum and Dad.

Our wedding day, 10th January 1959.

My little Martin Special.

With my sister, Lili-Anne.

Two special nieces -
Valerie-Joan and Heather.

Sister Barb as the May Queen

Roger with Richard (no, he didn't
come out of my belly button).

Our children, David, Richard, and Julie.

David, aged three, with Catty, Mummy's darling.

Three little angels! Richard, niece Michelle, and Julie.

Before I was diagnosed with stomach cancer, 1977.

Proud Mum and Dad at Richard's graduation.

A family day out - Sandy, Richard, Nina, Julie, Joe, Luke, David, and Roger.

David and Nina, 1988.

Three curly girls, Julie, Nina, and Sandy.

Our two handsome boys, Richard and David.

With best friend Trisha at her daughter's wedding.
My first outing after the breast cancer operation.

Venice before I started my chemo, 1992.

The start of my chemo, 1992.

Family party with niece, Jean, having not seen her for over twenty years.

Taken for the *Star* newspaper when I nominated Roger as Star Dad 1993.

Photograph by Peter Martin

Lovely holiday in Palaiokastritsa, Greece, after finishing chemo.

At last, some hair.

With Robert Kilroy-Silk after appearing on his programme.

The hydro ladies, Gladys, Maureen, Eileen, Sadie, and me, 1997.

Accepting a cheque for Breast Cancer Care from Linda and Janice.

Beautiful floral display, prepared by Maura, the florist at Leeds Castle, for Lord and Lady Thomson's retirement.

With two special people at Leeds Castle - Lord and Lady Thomson.

The most scary thing I have ever done - abseiling for charity down the library tower at Springfield, the tallest building in Maidstone.

Shirley's garden party - Sharon, Viv, Yvonne, Shirley, Anona, Gail, and me.

Looking posh in the Castle drawing room before dinner on New Year's Eve, with Roger, Michelle, and Trevor.

A special evening, introducing Roger to Princess Alexandra.

My surprise 60th birthday with Michelle, and Gail (holding cake) who organised it at her house.

My leaving party at Leeds Castle, with Roger.

Photograph by Peter Martin

Granddaughter Claudia's christening. Marcus, me holding Claudia, Roger, and Julie.

Our eldest grandson, Joe, ready to go to the ball.

I love this photo - Roger, the proud Grandad with Joe and Luke.

Roger with our special girl, Fleur.

Ros's birthday - Ros C, Ros S, Shirley, Gail, and Anona.

Luke.

Lucia.

Claudia and Alex.

Roger celebrates his 65th birthday with our lovely grandchildren, Lucia, Alex, Luke and Claudia.

was different from our journey over; we had a really smooth trip. Back at Dover, we said goodbye to Pat and Sue, and promised to keep in touch. The coach driver dropped us off near to home, so we rang Richard and he picked us up. That evening we had dinner with Richard and Sandy, and David and Nina came as well.

October 12th.

Ros C came to see me this morning and we had a nice chat. Made some chutney and pickled beetroot; had a good day. When Roger came home we decided to have a drink because, when I start the chemo, I won't be able to. Roger suggested a brandy but that was not wise. Fifteen minutes later, I was in agony; my insides did not like it at all.

October 13th.

Not a good day. It is getting near to going to the Westminster, and I feel quite down. I felt like sleeping all day, and was pleased I did not have any visitors. By the time Roger came home, I had brightened up. I did not want him to know I was worrying.

October 14th.

Decided to go into town to do some shopping; my first time since coming out of hospital. It is Julie's birthday on Saturday, and if I have to stay in hospital tomorrow, as the doctor said I might, I will not get another chance to get her present. I still cannot drive, so caught a bus into town. Trying to carry everything in one hand is not easy, and by the time I arrived home I was exhausted.

October 15th.

This morning I felt very wound up. I did not want to go to the Westminster Hospital. Roger suggested packing my bag as I might have to stay in. David called round. After he had gone, I packed and felt a bit better, and just as we were going, Michelle came with a card from one of the ladies at work, Amanda. We had a good run up to London. At last we were called in to see Dr. Philips who I last saw when I had chemo for my stomach cancer. He took a lot of trouble chatting about my past history, and said I had done so well after all that. He felt chemo plus radiotherapy, and also to take Tamoxifen, was the right treatment, but before they start he would like me to have a bone scan and body scans. They will do all the scans on one day, and then decide how much chemo to give me. I am to start the Tamoxifen tonight.

Included in my medical notes is a letter from Dr. Phillips to Mr Jones and Dr. Vaux, sent after this visit. Thank you very much for asking me to see this delightful lady with stage two, grade two intraduct and infiltrating carcinoma of the left breast with two axillary nodes positive. In the late 1970s, she had chemotherapy and a partial gastrectomy for carcinoma of the stomach, followed by a total gastrectomy a couple of years later for recurrence, and she has remained well since. She takes Gaviscon as required, Prempak since a hysterectomy twelve years ago under the care of Humphrey Roberts here at Westminster, iron supplements and B12 injections. She did have considerable sickness and hair loss with the chemotherapy, but she is extremely well-adjusted about the prospect of having further treatment, and I explained to her the current regimes are better tolerated, and we do have much better ways of controlling sickness. She has been very happy on Prempak and I thought she could continue this along with the Tamoifen since there is now a vogue for combining the two. I have arranged a chest X-ray, bone scan, and liver ultrasound, then suggest six courses of adjuvant chemotherapy prior radiation and we will keep you fully informed.

In the next letter, Dr. Phillips, Professor Coombes, and Dr. Cottrill had discussed my case and felt the previous chemotherapy would exclude me from trials of adjuvant chemotherapy, so I would have another regime followed by radical radiotherapy to the breast.

October 16th.

Got up late, felt grotty, but did housework and washing. Rose popped in; her little dog had died and she was so upset. Roger came home early. He had been to the castle and had a chat with Andrew, my boss, to explain it would be a while before I would be back to work. On the way home, he picked up Joe, and then Richard and Sandy called in. Julie came later and collected Joe.

October 17th.

Awoke feeling sick again. I am sure it is all due to thinking about the treatment. I decided to make myself feel better so I did housework and cooking, and made Julie a birthday cake. She and Joe came after school for tea; it was Julie's thirty-first birthday, and we had a nice evening.

October 18th.

We had a nice lunch on Sunday. Richard, Sandy, David, Nina, and Luke came, and we went for a walk along the river. The autumn is ending but there are still blackberries in the hedgerows, an abundance of various berries, hazel nuts, acorns, and chestnuts, but few wild flowers. They all stayed for tea.

Venice and More Treatment

October 19th.

Julie took me to see Dr. Vaux for my B12 injection, and we had a chat about my treatment. I said I was still concerned about my arm, for a start I cannot get it up very far. Missed Kay; she had put a note through the door. I would have liked to have seen her.

David came in to say Nina is in hospital; she has lost the baby and is staying in to have a D/C. I feel so upset for them. We had all been so happy when they came to tell us we were to have another grandchild.

October 20th.

Michelle came this morning for coffee and to tell me of news from the castle. Rang David to see how Nina was now she is home. We were just going to bed when David came to see if I would have Luke tomorrow.

October 21st.

Nellie and Valerie-Joan came. Mig, Nina's mum, brought Luke. When Nellie and Valerie-Joan had gone, I was feeling sick again so thought we would have some fresh air, and took Luke for a walk to feed the ducks. He is a good little boy - no trouble to have – and when Mig came to pick him up, he was very tired. I had loved having him.

October 22nd.

Barb and Ted came, and Rose called in. I would like to do some china painting but cannot seem to get motivated.

October 23rd.

Had a day on my own, without visitors. Julie brought Joe for the evening. I am worried about Roger; I know how he is worrying about me having the chemo. We had a chat, and I told him Dr. Phillips had said they can help with the sickness more now, and if it helps me fight the cancer it is worth having it. I think it is worse for our loved ones.

October 24th.

Saturday, Roger had to work in the morning, so I did my jobs, then after lunch we went shopping and had a quiet evening in. I feel in limbo at the moment.

October 25th.

David, Nina, and Luke came for lunch. I would have liked to have gone for a walk but it rained all day and Nina is still not feeling herself. I think once she can start her aerobics and get fit again, she will be her old self.

October 26th.

Up early, as Julie said we would go out for the day, but she did not arrive until this afternoon. She had been doing mother-in-law's housework.

Joe was very hyperactive as usual when he has been up there, so we decided not to go out. Kay called in for a chat.

October 27th.

Julie came to take me into town. I thought we would take Joe to the museum, but it was not a good idea; he ran around so we came out. We all got soaking wet as it was pouring with rain. Back home, I had a shower and changed. My niece Heather came to take me to her dolls' house teacher to see her collection of dolls' houses. They were all over her house; they were wonderful. When we arrived home, there was a note from Kay to say Kate had gone into labour last night.

October 28th.

No news of Kate in the morning; hope she is all right. Kay and Kate are sharing a house at the moment, just down the road from us. Kay called in on her way to work to say Kate had had a little boy last night, and all was well. So pleased for her and her partner, Sam. My brother Ted came, also Nellie and Valerie-Joan, and we had lunch. Ted stayed until Roger came home from work. I wanted to go to the hospital to see Kate, so I got ready quickly. Kate was pleased to see us. The baby is gorgeous. Sam, Kate's partner, is Chinese, so the baby has black hair and his Dad's almond eyes. I took some photos, so hope they come out well. On the way home, we dropped off a birthday present for my friend Sylvia who works at the Castle; she is a lovely lady. What a busy day; I feel worn out again.

October 29th.

Up early to go to the Westminster Hospital. I had my chest X-ray first, then the liver scan. I do not feel very confident about that because the doctor seemed to keep going back to one area. Next, I went for the injection for the bone scan. I knew we would have trouble finding a good vein, but on the third attempt, with the help of another doctor, he got it. We then had to wait two hours and drink as much as I could, so we went to the Tate Gallery for an hour, then back to the car so Roger could have his packed lunch. I was not allowed to eat, and I find drinking at least two litres very difficult. At last it was time for the scan. This took almost an hour. I asked the doctor what we were looking for, and he said, 'hot spots'. I could not see any, so hope I am all right. As we left, he said, 'good luck'. I did not know if that was a good sign or not; I have to wait a week for the results. Saw the nurse I had last time. She made me an appointment for next week, and gave me more Tamoxifen. I will be a nervous wreck by next week. The traffic was awful coming home. After dinner I had to go to

Venice and More Treatment

bed, I was so tired. The operation seems to have left me with no energy.

October 30th.

Did not have any visitors. I need some time on my own. Julie and Joe came early afternoon, and we decided to watch a video of my niece Valerie-Joan's son's wedding. I put it on, and then said to Julie I would make a cup of tea, thinking I had turned it off, but I hadn't, and had videoed a film over some of it. I was distraught. What if Valerie-Joan did not have another one? I will have to go and tell her.

October 31st.

Roger and I went shopping, and he bought me a new jumper. While having a coffee, he said he can't wait for me to start the treatment and get it over with. It is such a worry for him.

November 1st.

Winter is starting. We have had some cold frosty mornings. It is Sunday, so we decided to go out for lunch at the Bull at Bewl. On the way, we stopped at Valerie-Joan's to apologise about the video. I have been so worried about it, but she just laughed and said no need to worry, they had lots of copies, so all that worrying was for nothing. It had turned out to be a lovely bright sunny day, so when we arrived at the pub it was very busy, although we managed to get a table and enjoyed our lunch. Nina had asked us to tea, and Richard and Sandy also, so we did not go for our usual walk as it is getting dark earlier now. We had a nice evening, but everyone wants to know who is going to the hospital with me next week. I keep saying I want to go on my own.

November 2nd.

Julie came to see if I wanted to go shopping, but it was cold and raining and I did not want to catch a cold, so declined the offer. Heather, my dear friend from work, came and we had a nice chat. Stanley, her husband, picked her up not long after Trisha arrived. She had brought some gorgeous flowers. When Julie had left, she said, if Dad was not taking me, she or Sandy would. They are not letting me go on my own. I want to be on my own because, if it is bad news, I cope better.

November 3rd.

Michelle and Ros S came, then Rose. I found making conversation hard work; having to wait a week for the results is driving me mad. I told Roger to say he is taking me, but Julie came again and she had been talking to Roger. She and Richard say I am not to go on my own. Julie is coming, and Sandy will collect Joe from school. I know how worried they all are, and I feel mean not wanting them to come.

November 4th.

Valerie-Joan and Nellie come for lunch; they both have birthdays this week, so I made a birthday sponge for them. After they had gone, I walked down to the pond as I needed some fresh air. It was cold and dry. Some of the trees still have their leaves, lovely bronze, yellow, and chocolate brown. I had hoped to see the kingfisher, but no luck, although there were plenty of ducks for whom I had taken bread. They make a lot of noise, competing with the coots and moorhens to get the food. The little sparrows and a blackbird came for the dropped crumbs. Felt refreshed on the walk back home; thank goodness tomorrow is my hospital day.

November 5th.

Today is the day. I was up early and waiting for Julie. She was late, and I was getting really worried we would miss our coach, when she arrived with her neighbour Connie. Apparently Julie's car would not start. We managed to catch the coach. When we arrived at Victoria station, I could not remember which way to go (I have no sense of direction) so we ended up at the Westminster children's hospital. A hospital patient bus drew up, so Julie asked the driver the way and he said he would take us. After all that we arrived early for my appointment.

At last I was called in and told to undress. I was perspiring so much, I had to use a tissue to wipe under my arms. The doctor came in and said they were going to check the scans and X-rays. I waited twenty minutes, with the doctors and nurses popping in to see that I was all right, and at last I was called in to see Dr. Phillips. He said the scans were clear, but because there may be microscopic bits going around, and with my previous history, I was to have six months chemo and seven weeks radiotherapy, plus the Tamoxifen. I could not believe it was six months chemo. I thought I might have six weeks. I felt shocked. I am to start with injections plus tablets. They expect me to lose my hair and be quite sick, plus I am to have lots of tests that I did not have last time. I also had to take home a large container for spending a penny in for when I go up next time.

At last I was finished. Julie seemed upset about the amount of chemo I am to have. We walked back to the coach station. The traffic on the way home was dreadful, so we did not get home until nine thirty. We rang Sandy from the bus station, and she came and picked us up. Sandy and Richard had taken Joe down to Roger. Joe had been waiting to have his fireworks as it is the fifth of November. It was so late, Roger let a few off and then we decided it would be better to have the rest tomorrow. I couldn't wait to tell Roger the results, and that they looked good, and then how much treatment. Joe overheard me telling Roger, and said, 'I hope you are not going to lose your hair like Mummy's friend, Jane.'

November 6th.

Quiet day at home. I still feel shocked at how much chemo I am to have.

November 7th.

Roger and I went Christmas shopping. I want to get it all before I start the treatment. We had a nice lunch in the wine bar, but I paid for it later, having to spend most of the evening in the bathroom.

November 8th.

A nice day at home. Julie and Joe came just as we were going to have lunch, so I made enough for us all. After lunch, we went for a walk down to the pond for Joe to feed the ducks, then a quiet evening on our own.

November 9th.

Julie invited us to dinner. She came to pick me up. When Kay and Ros C. arrived, they stayed a little while, but we had to collect Joe from school. We had a nice dinner.

November 10th.

Thought I would make my Christmas cake and puddings. Michelle came as I was putting the cake in the oven, and we had a chat about work. I cannot wait to be fit and back there. Mavis, from next door, called with a plant.

November 13th.

Have had a few quiet days when I have been able to china paint. Julie and Joe came, and then Kate and Sam brought their new baby. Julie was so pleased she was here to see him; he looks like a miniature of his dad - olive skin, black hair, and almond eyes. He is gorgeous.

November 14th.

Saturday, and Roger and I went to do more Christmas shopping. It was cold and wet, so we had lunch in the wine bar. On the way home, we called round to see Richard and Sandy. Julie had left Joe with them for us to pick up as she was going to a friend's family party. Joe stayed the night, and Julie came for lunch. After they had gone, Richard, Sandy, David, Nina, and Luke came for tea. Luke stayed with us while David and Nina went for a meal. Luke was a good boy as usual, but I felt worn out.

November 16th.

Julie took me to see Trisha, and brought me home. I do miss not being able to drive the car and, of course, once I start the chemo, I will not be able to drive because some of the other drugs make me sleepy. Roger came home and said one of his colleagues at work who has cancer has only two weeks to live. I think this was on my mind when I went to bed as I had an awful night. If I was not in the bathroom having diarrhoea, I was dreaming and then waking up all hot.

November 17th.

Julie picked me up and I finished my Christmas shopping. We went and looked at wigs. I hate wearing them because they are so uncomfortable, but I did get the stretchy turban I had been looking for. Joe wanted to stay the night, and we all had a good night's sleep.

November 18th.

Today I went for my first chemo. The hospital had arranged for a volunteer driver to pick me up, so I had to be ready for seven thirty because we have other patients to pick up on the way. We arrived at ten thirty. I had to go to the Kenneth Newton Suite, the day chemotherapy unit where I first met Samantha, the receptionist. She sent me to have my blood taken. Next I met Dr. Cottrill whom I really liked. He checks my blood count and decides whether I can have the chemo. My count is good, so I can. He then writes the prescription for the injection, which I take to the pharmacy to be made up and then take to the chemo unit. Whilst waiting for it to arrive, I sat in the waiting room. There was a young girl and a boy waiting, both of whom had lost their hair. I also had a chat with a lady from Sevenoaks, a town near to us; she had had two sessions of chemo, and said she felt fine, no sickness or hair loss, and was still going to work, so that was encouraging. I was called in and introduced to the nurses who work on the unit. They are Staff nurses Tracy, Clare, and Gill. I had an instant rapport with them; everyone is so caring. I am to have injections and tablets. The injections arrive from the pharmacy. Gill made me comfortable on the bed, then once again my veins played up and I had to put my hands in hot water. At last she managed to get a vein, and we could start. Some of the patients were quite distressed, but the nurses were so good with everyone, giving them encouragement. At last I was finished, and left at three thirty. When the driver came for me and another patient from another ward, the nurses said I would probably feel sleepy as the anti-sickness had this effect. In fact, I did sleep most of the way home.

Venice and More Treatment

Roger came home early; he said he had worried all day and wished he could have come with me. I said I was feeling all right at the moment; perhaps I will not be sick.

November 19th.

Awoke feeling grotty; it seems to be working quite quickly. The unit gave me a Protocol for drug management. The tablet chemo I am to take is Cyclophamide – side-effects nausea and vomiting, hair loss, reduced blood count, menstrual irregularities, infertility, and bladder irritation. It's important to drink at least two litres of fluid a day, more if possible, and to empty the bladder regularly. One of the drugs which is injected into the vein by drip, has other side-effects including nausea, diarrhoea, reduced blood count, and a sore mouth. The other injected drug also has these effects, plus sore watery eyes and a horrible metal taste. Folinic acid tablets were prescribed to try and prevent a sore mouth, and these were taken twenty-four hours after the chemo, then every six hours. It is important to take them regularly, so you have to set your alarm clock for during the night. Other drugs were ondansetron which is used for nausea, dexamethasone, a corticosteroid, which will probably make me have chubby cheeks. The first morning, I had all the side-effects except the sore mouth which did not start until the third day when I also started to get mouth ulcers.

November 20th.

Do not feel like getting up. Just retching all the time, so had to take more anti-sickness pills. So glad I did not have any visitors. Had Joe while Julie went shopping; he seemed to sense I was not feeling my best and was a good boy. Once again I start thinking I am going to beat this. I am not going to miss out on seeing my grandchildren grow up, so I must not think about it. I read in the newspaper that Marti Cane, the singer, is back on chemo.

November 21st.

Again felt like staying in bed, but didn't. Cannot spend the next six months in bed. Decided to take the maximum number of sickness pills. Had a letter from Judy Murray, giving me an update on all the news from the Castle, which I do appreciate. A colleague of Roger's came over to see if he would take him and his wife to the farm shop. I felt awful; I could not stop retching and had to keep going to the bathroom. The wife would keep on talking. It sounds rather rude of me, but I just wished they would go. Even while making them a cup of tea, I had to stop to go to the bathroom. I felt quite embarrassed.

November 22nd.

Did not feel so bad this morning. Still taking the maximum anti-sickness pills. They are helping, but still having quite a few spells in the bathroom. Julie and Joe stayed for lunch, then David, Nina, and Luke came later. I am pleased Nina seems much brighter; losing a baby, even at such an early stage in pregnancy, is devastating.

November 23rd.

Julie came to take me to Dr. Vaux for my B12 injection. We had a chat about the treatment, and he asked how I was. He seemed quite upset that I was having chemo again, and said he thought I had finished with all that last time. I said, 'It will be worth it in the end.'

Nellie and Valerie-Joan came for lunch, but I do not feel like eating much. After they had gone, I was reading a magazine and there was an article about a woman with breast cancer who had died, then I put the television on, and in one of the soaps a young girl died of cancer. I suddenly felt depressed and had a good cry, but pulled myself together before Roger came home. I did not want him to see me upset.

November 24th.

Got up, had a shower and washed my hair. Retched all the time and felt I could not get going. Still trying to remember to take all the pills and drink two litres. It is just as difficult for me to drink a lot, as to eat a lot. Eventually sat and did the ironing, then lay on the bed as I was feeling hot, but shivering at the same time. Ended up in the bathroom being sick. David was coming for dinner, so got up and prepared a roast.

November 25th.

For the second chemo, the volunteer driver picked me up at seven thirty; it is hard getting up so early when I feel such a grot. I was the only patient he had to take today, and we had a good run up to the hospital. Booked in with Sam. The doctor had usual problem trying to get blood out of me, but succeeded eventually. I waited until it had been tested; the blood count was good. Today I had to see Dr. Phillips; he read my notes and said, 'what could he say after all this time, since I had the chemo for the stomach cancer and now I have breast cancer, he had decided to put up the dose of the chemo pills. Then I saw Dr. Ramsey, the lady doctor, who wrote the prescription for me to take to the pharmacy. I am so impressed with how the unit is run. Dr. Cottrill, who I saw last time, came over and asked me how I had been getting on. They all seem to care so much.

Venice and More Treatment

I take a packed lunch because patients should not leave the unit once they have signed in and, as I cannot eat much, I usually take a Marmite sandwich. There are plenty of drinks available. While I was waiting for my chemo, I was chatting to a couple. It was their first visit to the unit, and the wife was very angry. She explained that her husband had had his operation six months ago, but because he had been messed about at the hospital he was attending, he had been trying to get an appointment to start his treatment here. However, his notes kept getting lost. It appears he had the same type of cancer as the singer, Marti Cane, his wife said. She felt angry that famous people seemed to get treatment straight away, and we ordinary people got left behind. I said I thought they had been unlucky and had had a bad experience. Back home, Roger said that's a good title for your book, *The Story of an Ordinary Woman*. At last I was called in to have my treatment. Gill, my nurse, said I would start feeling even more grotty and would lose my hair. She also said it was a good idea to stay in bed the first couple of days after the chemo, rather than trying to soldier on feeling awful. I told her I was having strange dreams, and she thought it was because I was worrying. While I was making my next appointment, I saw the couple again and wished them luck. The driver collected me. He is very thoughtful, and always has paper cups and water, plus cushions, so I am comfortable if I want to sleep on the way home, which I do. I was home quite early, about three thirty, so was able to sort out dinner before Roger arrived. I like to get in first because he worries until I get home.

November 26th.

Quiet day. Stayed in bed until ten o'clock, and spent most of the day feeling sick and having diarrhoea, but remembered all my pills. David came after work to look at Roger's car. He brought Luke with him, and although he slept all the evening, I did get the chance to have a cuddle with him.

November 27th.

Washed my hair and it came out in chunks. It seems I will lose it quite quickly; nurse Gill said I would. Michelle came with a lovely surprise; the girls at work had bought me a beautiful gold necklace. They had decided to give it to me when I was on my treatment, to cheer me up. After Michelle had gone, I was overcome with emotion, and had a cry; they are all so thoughtful.

November 28th.

Roger had to work, and did the shopping on the way home. We had a nice quite evening. I had had a good day; not too much time in the bathroom.

November 29th.

Start of the day, not too good, but as the day goes on, feel better. It is Sunday, and David, Nina, and Luke came for tea.

November 30th.

Trisha came today. I was sick in the morning, but improved as the day went on. Enjoyed the afternoon with Trisha. After she had gone I wrote my Christmas cards and letters. If I feel the same tomorrow, Julie said perhaps we can go into town.

December 1st.

Up early. Took extra sickness pills and felt quite good. Julie came, and we went into town. We walked and walked, and when we arrived home I was exhausted. Julie left to collect Joe from school. My mouth was so sore. I had been stupid; we had not stopped for a drink, and I had not taken any of my pills. Tried to eat some dinner, then spent the rest of the evening in and out of the bathroom, retching and having diarrhoea. At last I went to bed with a hot water bottle as I am shaking with cold, although Roger says it is warm. I don't want to think about the next six months.

December 2nd.

I felt awful all day, and just wanted to lie down. Forced myself to cook dinner and do some housework. I realise the problem was not drinking yesterday, and not taking my pills at the correct time. Now I have this metal taste, and ulcers in my mouth, and sore and runny eyes. Rose called in and said I did not look so good.

December 3rd.

Felt better today; my mouth is not so sore. Jan brought Diane. Jan had been to a health farm and had an awful time. I think I will need a health farm when this is all over. We exchanged our Christmas gifts.

December 4th.

Felt so much better today, I was inspired to paint a leopard. I want to do it as a present for Roger. It was after watching a TV programme about the wildlife artist, Wolfgan; his paintings were wonderful. Did the first stage and put it on to fire.

December 5th.

Nice day. David came round, and said he felt better as he had had a chat with his doctor about me, and he had explained about the treatment I am having. Still retching and in the bathroom a lot.

Venice and More Treatment

December 6th.

Sunday, so after lunch Roger and I went out and gathered holly and ivy. It was a nice cold crisp day, and lots of berries on the holly. Back home, we put up the decorations. It's a bit early but I may not feel so good after my next chemo. The nurses did say I would feel more poorly. On my grotty days, I wonder if I will have another Christmas, so I want to make the most of this one. I am enjoying this week, with no chemo, so trying to get as much done as possible. Still having problems with moving my arm, and the shoulder is quite painful.

December 7th.

Pauline came round. I felt so sorry for her. She is to have a hysterectomy; her smear test was not good again. I shall be thinking about her. Did more of my painting.

December 8th.

I cannot believe how good I am feeling. I still get the odd retching and diarrhoea spells, so I hope it lasts. Julie called in and I did more painting.

December 9th.

Andrew, my boss, had invited me to the supervisor's dinner at the Fairfax Hall. I was so excited to be going. After so much of my hair fell out the last time I washed it, I hoped not too much would come out before I went to the dinner. I washed it gently, and not too much came out, so managed to disguise it. Also took extra sickness pills. Only once during the evening did I have to go to the toilets to be sick, so no-one knew. It was great to see all the staff again, and I had a lovely evening. It was thoughtful of Andrew to ask me.

December 10th.

I felt very down today. I had a letter from René to say my dear friend Sybil had died last Saturday, and her funeral is tomorrow.

December 11th.

Julie drove me to Sybil's funeral. René and Helen, Sybil's very good friends were there, and it was good to see Sybil's children Roger, Nicholas, and Jane, and Sybil's brother and sisters. I did not stay long after the service as Julie was waiting to take me home. René and Helen were upset to hear I had had another operation and more chemo. I shall miss Sybil; she was such a lovely lady. By the time we arrived back home, it was time for Julie to collect Joe from school. As I had done the housework and prepared dinner before Julie came this morning, I thought I would read the newspaper. I love reading, but, when on chemo, I find

I cannot concentrate. Sure enough, after one page I have to stop.

December 13th.

I thought it was the carol service at Otham church, and had looked forward to it all week. I love church music and the chanting. It was a frosty evening when we walked to the church, but I had got it wrong, the service is next week. Nina, Luke, Richard, and Sandy came, but they all went home early so Roger and I had a quiet evening. I had felt good today.

December 15th.

I had a letter from my lovely Professor Ellis. He said he was sorry to hear I had had another operation, and also said the breast cancer was not related to the stomach cancer. Mr Jones had told me this, and Dr. Phillips. The Professor said I was in good hands with Mr Jones and Dr. Phillips; also that I was a tough girl and would once again knock it on the head. This letter really boosted me up.

Also had a letter from Pauline who is going into hospital tomorrow. I will be thinking about her; she is so nervous.

Felt quite good today; better now I have a routine with my anti-sickness pills and drinking more, but tomorrow is chemo again. I wish I did not have to go. Went to bed early as I have to be ready again at seven thirty in the morning. I am still looking quite healthy; I have not lost a lot of weight, probably due to the steroids, but my hair is very thin. The nurses cannot believe how quickly it started to come out.

Having breast cancer is quite different to having stomach cancer. I suppose it is because, with the stomach operation, no-one can see it. Apart from people at work, who do not know I have had it removed, sometimes saying, 'no wonder you are slim, you don't eat enough,' I wish I could eat properly. But having the breast cancer, for some women, is hard to cope with; also their husbands sometimes find it hard. Roger said he just wanted me well; it did not matter if I lost my breast, although if I had had a mastectomy, I think I would have had a reconstruction if it was possible.

December 16th.

My driver, Neil, was on time as always; we picked up a lady whose husband always comes with her. I feel so sorry for her because, as soon as we start moving, she is sick. The driver always has paper sick bowls, and half-way he stops for her to have a drink which he also brings. We arrive at the hospital, and I sign in, and straight away I am called in to have my blood taken for testing. Blood is made up of three different kinds of cells: red cells which carry oxygen, white cells which fight infection, and platelets which clot the blood. Chemotherapy tends to kill all three kinds.

I saw Dr. Ramsey who is also registrar to Dr. Phillips. She wanted to see what movement I had in my arm; she did not feel there was any improvement, and I told her the shoulder was still painful. She thought I should have an X-ray, so sent me to have it done. The X-ray department is across the other side of the hospital. After having the X-ray, and on my way back to the unit, I rang Pauline who is in St Thomas's hospital. The sister on her ward said I could speak to her. Pauline was in a bad mood and said she didn't know how I put up with all the operations; the poor girl is so frightened.

Went back to Dr. Ramsey with the X-rays, and she said the problem was due to the operation and having my arm strapped up. We must try and get some movement for when I have the radiotherapy. My blood count was fine so she wrote up my chemo prescription, but was worried that I was still retching so much. This time I have to have all the chemo by injection; hopefully I will not be so sick, but the rest of my hair will come out. I would rather that than be sick so much. I know my hair will grow again once I finish the treatment. I also asked if I could have extra anti-sickness today as I want to go to Joe's school nativity play in the village this evening. She said I could, so I took the prescription to the pharmacy as usual, and then went to wait in the unit.

While waiting, there were three ladies also waiting for treatment. They said they were tolerating the chemo really well; none had lost their hair, and they did not seem to have much sickness, but everyone is an individual and having different drug protocol. At last my chemo arrived, and the usual hassle of trying to get a vein, but as always my nurse Gill succeeded. Then the usual procedure followed, flushing out the veins, and then the chemo and anti-sickness etc. Neil, my driver, was waiting to take me home, and the other lady was also ready. My next appointment is two days before Christmas. I slept all the way home, and arrived a few minutes before Richard and Sandy came to take me to the church. We all enjoyed the nativity play; the children were so sweet.

When we arrived back at Julie's, we had a phone call from David. Luke had had an accident. He had been at the farm with Nina, in a large shed, and there was a gas fire with a guard around it, but Luke was on his little bike when he fell against the guard, and his trousers caught alight, burning his leg. He was in East Grinstead hospital, so I asked Richard if we could go home as Roger would want to go to the hospital when he knew what had happened. When we arrived home it was nine o'clock, and Roger said, as it would take an hour to get there, we had better wait until the morning. What a year it has been.

December 17th.

The only good thing with the burn was that Luke was not in pain because it had damaged the nerves. He stayed in hospital overnight, and they called in to see us on the way home. At first the doctors thought he would need to have skin graft, but thank goodness he has not. Nina said he had been so good and had not made a fuss at all. He has to go to the hospital every day to have the dressing changed; I wish I was driving so I could take them.

Nellie and Valerie-Joan came and we exchanged Christmas presents. Apart from the usual sickness and diarrhoea, I had quite a good day. Roger and I wrapped the rest of the Christmas presents; it is feeling very Christmassy.

December 18th.

I did not want to get up, so I stayed in bed until nine o'clock, and then spent the next half an hour in the bathroom retching up the foul-tasting gold liquid, and having diarrhoea. I wonder where it all comes from, seeing that I am eating so little. My mouth is so sore, I am having problems eating and drinking. When I washed my hair, nearly all of it came out; there is very little left. It is quite distressing to see it coming out. I hope I can cope with the next five months.

December 20th.

Sunday, and it was the church carol service. Roger asked if I was sure I wanted go as I had been so grotty all day. I was looking forward to it, so I wrapped up warm and wore my turban as the weather has turned very cold and I do not want to get a chill. The doctors tell me to try and not get any germs as I have very little resistance. Richard and Sandy came as well, and we saw Trisha and Jim at the service; they came back for a drink with us.

December 21st.

Julie took me for my B12 injection; she left Joe at the doctors with me while she went shopping. I wanted to walk back home; I feel I am shut in so much. It was cold but sunny, and the fresh air helps my sickness, so Joe and I walked home past the pond. We had taken some bread to feed the pair of swans and noisy ducks, and then we walked along the footpath by the stream; Joe wanted to see if he could spot any trout.

Venice and More Treatment

December 22nd.

Julie took me down to the Castle; I wanted to see the girls before Christmas. Took extra anti-sickness pills and had a good day. I had hoped to see Judy but she was out to lunch. Not many girls in so that was disappointing, but did see my boss Andrew who invited Roger and me for a drink after Christmas. I did the last firing on my painting of the leopard.

December 23rd.

I really have to psyche myself up on the morning of my chemo. I think it is because I will have two good days, then it's back to being grotty. George, my other driver, picked me up. We had to find a house in the village of Farley, to pick up a lady; it took an hour and half to find the house, and then a neighbour told us she had gone into hospital. No-one had thought of letting the driver know. We still managed to get to the Westminster hospital on time. After signing in etc., I saw Dr. Ramsey who said I was not looking so well. I told her I am so sick, and the retching is not very pleasant. She said I should have told her I was like this when I had chemo. She said they now are more advanced now with all the drugs, so she decided to try another anti-sickness drug which cost sixteen pounds a pill, and I am to take three a day. I hope it will help. I slept nearly all the way home. The traffic was bad as usual, so we were late getting home. I like to get in before Roger because he worries if I am late.

December 24th.

David and Nina took me on a surprise visit to the wig shop to choose a wig. Later, Roger said I am to let them buy me one because it is David's way of coping; he hates me losing my hair.

My sister Barb, her husband Ted, and my niece Heather, came as they were leaving. My lovely friend Ros C came to wish us a happy Christmas, and we had a long chat. Phyllis, another of the ladies from work, came. She gave me a hug and kiss, and then said she could not stay long as her daughter was at a home with a bad cold. After she had gone, Roger said, 'I hope you do not get any germs.' It was another dry crisp evening, so we wrapped up warmly and walked to church at midnight. We sat at the back of the church. Roger said then if I felt sick we could leave quietly, but we did not have to. Back home, Roger said he was looking forward to the New Year, and the end of my chemo.

December 25th.

Christmas Day, and awoke feeling quite good. We opened our main presents in bed, and I had a lovely surprise. Roger had bought me a word

Memoirs of an Ordinary Woman

processor to get started on my book. Roger was pleased with the painting of the leopard. Went to Richard and Sandy for lunch; my new sickness pills seem to be working. Had a lovely lunch, and then started feeling sick, so spent most of the afternoon in the bathroom retching and bringing up the foul-tasting gold liquid, and the usual diarrhoea. I longed to go to bed. I did lie on the sofa and had a sleep. Julie, Joe, David, Nina and Luke joined us for tea. Went home after tea back into the bathroom will it never end and at last went to bed.

December 26th.

Boxing Day, and awoke with a sore throat and runny nose. I was hot to touch, but felt so cold. I cooked lunch but could not eat it, so Roger lit the fire and I lay on the sofa. The hospital said if I had any infection to ring. Roger wanted me to, but I did not want to ring on Boxing Day; hoped I would feel better tomorrow.

December 30th.

I felt so ill the last three days, I haven't been able to write. My throat is so sore and now I've lost my voice. Roger is still saying I should ring the hospital, but for one thing I don't feel like going to London, and for another, I do not know what they would do. David and Nina came in with Luke. He is still going to the hospital; poor little fellow. He has not made a fuss at all.

December 31st.

My cold was awful today; just felt like sitting about. I did write thank you letters, and did a few jobs. I would like some fresh air, but still have a temperature and feel so cold, so it would not be wise to go out. It is New Year's Eve. If I was well, I would have been working; I have always supervised the New Year dinner. I hope I feel better than this next year, and I'm back to work.

January 1st.

At last, I feel better today. I do hope that next year I will have finished my treatment, and get fit and back to work. I feel it has been an awful Christmas and New Year for Roger. David, Nina, Luke, Julie, and Joe came, so we all wrapped up warm and went for a walk; it was lovely to get out, although it was quite damp and a bit misty. As usual we walked to the pond for the boys to feed the ducks and, as we walked along the river, there were masses of catkins, and even some primroses. There were flocks of rooks and starlings in the fields. Back home we sat by the fire and had tea and crumpets. I am worried that David is having trouble with his stomach.

Venice and More Treatment

January 2nd.
John and Sue came. We had a pasta supper; it was good to see them again. I thought it had been too good to be true; the last two days I thought at last the sickness pills are working, but I was back in the bathroom after John and Sue had gone.

January 3rd.
Richard and Sandy came for lunch, and we then went to Andrew's for drinks. It was good to see friends from work, Lynda, Kay, Graham, and Michelle. Afterwards, we went to David and Nina for tea. We had had a good day.

January 10th.
Our thirty-fourth wedding anniversary. We are so lucky to have had so many good and happy times with our family. Feeling good, no sore mouth, and not too sick. I still have to remember to take all my pills and try and drink as much as I can. Two more days, and chemo again.

January 13th.
Neil, my driver, picked me up; I was the only patient. As usual, signed in with Sam, had my blood taken. I dread it as it is such a job to get a vein. Saw Dr. Ramsey; told her how ill I felt at Christmas. She was rather cross and said if it happens again I must ring the unit because I could mess up my blood count. And I must try to keep clear of people with anything infectious. She was concerned that I still cannot get my arm up, and decided to change my anti-sickness pills again; the new ones I will take four times a day for three days - expensive at fifteen pounds a pill. While having my chemo, Staff Nurse Clare said the chemo did not like me and was giving me a hard time. She said it was unfortunate because, with all the new drugs, so many patients tolerate it so much better now, and the doctors can control the side-effects which means they can go to work and carry on life as normal. She told me once again to stay in bed and rest as each treatment builds up, and this time I would feel poorly, but hopefully the new anti-sickness pills will help. I slept all the way home. Roger was looking out of the window, waiting for me.

January 16th.
I have felt too ill to write since my last chemo. I make myself do some jobs, and prepare dinner, but I do not feel like eating at all, and have to make myself have something, and drink as much as I can. The new anti-sickness has worked; I am not being so sick, but I do look and feel awful. I have just a few strands of hair left; I've lost weight, and my complexion

looks grey. Got up this morning, did housework, had a shower and had to lie down. I suddenly get so tired I can hardly move. Can you believe it? I have won a competition for a make-over. I think they'll take one look at me and have a fright!

January 17th.

My sister Barb, niece Michelle, and her little girl Emily, came. When I opened the door, they looked shocked. I do feel I look awful, and it was obvious they thought so too. After they had gone, my niece Heather came and said she was going to cut my few wispy bits of hair off. I do not know why I was hanging on to them; it looked so much better when they were cut off.

Julie called in; she had brought me another turban as I am going to the hospital tomorrow, and I do feel the cold with no hair.

I feel so frustrated that I am not painting or reading, but I just cannot concentrate. I try to read the newspaper, but have to give up. Anyway, as soon as I sit down, I go to sleep; that's the side-effect of the anti-sickness. That is one good thing; I do not have trouble sleeping.

January 18th.

I had to force myself out of bed. Neil, my driver, arrived at seven thirty. We picked up the lady and her husband; she is sick on the way up so Neil stops to give her a drink. I booked in and went to Haematology to have my blood taken; as usual the veins played up, but successful at last. I waited for the results to take to Dr. Ramsey. The blood count was fine, so back to the chemo unit. The nurses were amazed I had lost all my hair; they said it didn't usually go so quickly. Joesa, a Spanish man, was having his treatment at the same time as me. We always have a chat; he hates losing his hair, and wears a baseball cap. We both have trouble with our veins, but at last we are both successful and the procedure begins. A nurse sits with us all the time and chats. We were quite late, and did not get home until six thirty, so it is a long day. Roger was home and once again said he was worried, but pleased I was now home.

January 21st.

I feel down today. The actress Audrey Hepburn died yesterday of cancer, and this starts me thinking about how long I have got. Rose called round and said I was not looking too good, but in fact I have had quite a good day; not so sick. My new pills do help.

January 24th.

The last three days have felt like nothing on earth. I seem to have all the side-effects; my mouth is so sore and full of ulcers, I really do not feel like eating, but when I do, I am then in the bathroom. It is as if it is going in one end and out the other. I am so hot, the perspiration drips off me, but at the same time I am cold and shivering. The one good thing is that I am not retching so much; being sick is not so bad, but the retching pulls my insides which already feel raw. My other problem is my arm which I still cannot raise, and the shoulder is very painful when doing the exercises.

January 25th.

Felt better this morning; did housework and prepared dinner. Then the retching started with the foul-tasting gold liquid; took some anti-sickness, and after a while it seemed to control it. Then I had a lovely surprise. There was a knock at the door and, to be quite honest, I hate opening the door because I look so awful, but there stood Humphrey, my previous manager at the Castle who, as I have said before, looks like Henry VIII. I could see he was taken aback by my appearance, but he gave me a hug, and after a while he told me he had called at the Castle and asked the girls where I was. They said I had had another operation and was having some treatment. He said no-one had said how ill I looked and that I had lost my hair, so when I opened the door to him it was such a shock. I could tell he felt quite emotional. I explained I was near the end of my treatment, and that this is the worse time as the chemo builds up. Once I stop, it takes a while to get it out of my system, but my hair will start to grow as soon as I stop. There was still the radiotherapy, but that did not have side-effects like the chemo. This time next year I will be my old self again and back to work. I am not sure he believed me; I was so pleased to see him. Later, Pauline called in for a chat about her operation; she has now come to terms with having the hysterectomy and is feeling better about the whole thing.

January 26th.

Julie picked me up and took me for my B12 injection with Dr. Vaux. I told him I had been feeling rather grotty, and he said that hopefully it would soon be over. I asked him if he thought the doctors would decide to carry on longer with the chemo, but he did not really know. It was usually six months and then the radiotherapy, so I hope this is so. Thank goodness I was having a good day. Ros S had asked me to lunch with some of the girls, and we had left it that I would go if I was not too sick. Had a really nice lunch and saw Pauline, Shirley and Michelle. We had a joke about whether my head was cold without hair. I said it was. Pauline had picked me up, but I wanted to walk back as Ros only lives five minutes down the road. I put on my turban to walk home, saying it was new Joan Collins look, as the actress sometimes wears one like it. It was lovely to get out in the fresh air. I miss my walks most of all.

January 29th.

Roger was up early; his friend Keith was coming for breakfast, and then they were going fishing. Julie and Joe came to pick me up to go to the garden centre. When I got in the car, Joe said he didn't like my hat. I asked him if he wanted me to go without it, but he said no. He did not want to see me without hair; it reminded him of Julie's friend, Jane, who was also on chemo and had lost her hair.

January 30th.

Pam Wright, the breast care nurse, had invited me to the breast cancer support group that she held at the hospital once a month. We had coffee, and a chat from Pam who said she is going to try and get some speakers in the future. I had hoped another friend, Judy Woodman from work, who is having treatment, would be there, but Pam said she is having a hard time at the moment. I must write her a note when I get home. I enjoyed the meeting; it was good to share our feelings and details about our treatments. I was the only one there who had lost my hair, and when I mentioned this to Pam, she said lots of the ladies do not lose their hair; for some it gets thin, but others do not have sickness and are able to carry on as normal and go to work. With me it was the regime of chemo that I was having due to my previous history.

John and Sue had invited us to dinner, and we were pleased to see Liz and Dave. Roger had worked with Dave back in the sixties with John. I do not know how I managed to get through dinner. I had taken extra anti-sickness etc., and got through the evening without being sick or having to rush to the bathroom, but as soon as we arrived home, it all started. I was so whacked out, I sat on the toilet trying to keep awake. It was the most I had done in a day, for weeks.

February 2nd.

Julie came and asked if we would like to go for dinner. Nina was here with Luke, and we had been to feed the ducks. He said he wanted to come to Julie's for dinner as he likes her dinners; he is such a dear little boy. Nina had to get back as she was meeting her Mum. We had a lovely dinner, and then Julie said she had some bad news; her friend Jane, who had been having chemo, had been to see her and said the doctors were stopping her

Venice and More Treatment

treatment as it was not working and they couldn't do any more for her. Julie was very upset; Jane is only twenty-five. If I could swap places with her I would, although I suppose that is unfair of me to say that because of Roger and the family. I have had a good life, and she was getting married but has called it off. Life can be so unfair sometimes.

February 10th.

Hospital day, and Neil, my driver, picked me up the usual time. There were no other pick-ups, and we arrived in good time. Saw Dr. Cottrill; my blood count was good so went ahead with my chemo prescription. I said the sickness pills helped, so I am staying on them. I went to the unit; my veins are so bad now, it is the worse part trying to find a good one. It was staff nurse Gill and, as always, with great patience, she succeeded in the end. I slept most of the way home.

February 13th.

The last two days have felt like nothing on earth. Got up each morning, had a shower, then went back to bed. Got up in the afternoon, did some jobs, and prepared dinner. But today felt so much better; Julie, Nina, and Luke arrived. Luke came in carrying a bag, and holding it up he said, 'We have got your wig.' I stood in front of the mirror at the bottom of the stairs and put it on. Luke laughed so much he laid on the floor. We all ended up laughing, but, as grotty as I felt, it made me feel better to realise that, to Luke, I looked funny because he had accepted seeing me with no hair.

Heather from work also called in; she said the ladies had made a collection, and she had written a poem to go with it:

> Margaret Knight, we think you are great,
> And want to celebrate in your fight for life,
> Roger you've got a plucky wife!
> So just to show our love for you,
> We've gathered up a bob or two for something you both can share
> And let you know we really care.
> On what to buy? Don't be nonplussed,
> Just spend it on the National Trust.

Once again, I am so emotional, and cried. Everyone has given us so much support, and been so generous. When Roger came home he was very touched by it.

He went to do the shopping, and called to see my lovely old lady friend

Joan. She has an orchid plant that she manages to get to flower every year, and she had sent me one of her precious stems of these beautiful flowers. It had been a full, great day.

February 14th.

Valentine's Day, and it is Sunday. Roger is at home, and cooked a special lunch. We thought we would have champagne. I tried to eat some lunch, but was promptly in the bathroom retching. David and Luke came; David hoped I liked the wig although Luke thought it so funny. We went to feed the ducks; thought the fresh air would help my sickness. After tea, I spent the rest of the evening in the bathroom having diarrhoea. I sometimes wonder if my body will ever get back to normal.

February 16th.

We suggested Julie got a part-time job as she has no social life, so she has started helping in a hotel bar one day or evening a week. I will look after Joe as he is on holiday this week, so she is working daytime. It was such a lovely bright day, I said to Joe, 'let's wrap up warm and go for a walk.' We took Joe's fishing hook and some bread, and walked down to the pond. I was sitting on a bench when I thought I could hear someone calling my name, and then I saw Diane. She had had an urge to see me as she had been worried about me, so she caught a bus to the village and walked to our house. After getting a bit lost, she asked a postman the way and eventually found our house (she had always been brought by car before). Then, when she did get there and found I wasn't in, she saw Rose next door who told her she had seen me go off with Joe and that we were probably down by the pond. She was so pleased to have found me. We went home and had some lunch, when Michelle came and very kindly said she would go home and change for work, come back and pick Diane up and take her home. Then my brother Ted and his wife Joyce arrived. Julie collected Joe and they all left. When Roger arrived home, and we had had dinner, I said I cannot believe how much I have done today. By two o'clock in the morning, I was back in the bathroom retching up more foul gold liquid, and having diarrhoea. My eyes were watery and sore, and at three thirty I went to bed exhausted.

February 17th.

I don't know how I managed to get up at six o'clock, but I had to as it is chemo day. Neil picked me up just after seven thirty; not too much traffic. Saw Dr. Cottrill who told me the chances of the cancer coming back are quite high, but hopefully the chemo will do the trick. (I did not tell Roger this). My blood count was good; I have been very lucky with the count, so went to the unit for my chemo. Saw the wig man, and told him I now had a wig. Had a chat with Joesa about how we had been since our last chemo. Staff nurse Gill called me in for our usual struggle to find a vein, but after putting my hands in hot water, she found one. At last it was all over; arrived home at six forty-five; only four more chemo sessions to go.

February 18th.

Thank goodness, no visitors. Stayed in bed most of the day, and when I did get up to do a few jobs and prepare dinner, I felt grotty, but not too sick.

February 19th.

Julie came with Joe. I would have like to have stayed in bed, but Julie and Nina were being models for a hairdresser. Mid-morning, I told Joe I wanted to go back to bed so he played around me; he is so good when I have him. I got up and prepared dinner. Roger came home; he said I did not look at all well and should go to bed, but I waited until Julie and Joe went. I couldn't wait to lie down.

February 20th.

Saturday, so Roger's at home. I wanted to go shopping with him, but had been sick and had diarrhoea since the early hours. Roger said he felt I was better off at home. I hate him having to see me like this.

February 21st.

Had a really nice day in on our own. I like the family coming, but we do not get much time on our own so had a nice lunch and a little walk up past the church. We picked some catkins, and saw a few clumps of snowdrops, but resisted the temptation to pick any. I thought the day had been too good to be true, and spent most of the evening in the bathroom.

February 22nd.

Felt so awful again. Julie and Nina came; Julie has had her car stolen. We were going to Valerie-Joan's, but we didn't go as I felt too poorly, plus I had to keep going to the bathroom. Some days it is a nightmare.

February 23rd.

The last few days have felt so awful. I did try to make an effort to do some housework and cooking; the sickness not so bad, but I seem to have diarrhoea all the time, plus today there was blood in it. I am sure there is not a problem; just that I am going so much. Had the horrible metal taste in my mouth, and it is so sore with ulcers it is a problem to eat. By the afternoon I'm feeling better. Nice surprise; Kate came with the baby who has a name now, Oscar. They came to say goodbye as they are going to Hong Kong. Sam, Kate's partner, has already gone, and they will live with Sam's family until they find somewhere of their own.

Felt sad when I heard Bobby Moore, the footballer, had died; he was one of our generation's great players.

Roger came home early, and said he had been worrying about me all day. He is so good, and looks after me. It is so hard for the family. Everyone has been so kind, visiting and writing, and also, if anyone has any germs, they phone or write as they know I can catch sore throats and colds etc. so easily as my immune system is low.

Had a nice weekend. Sandy's Mum and Dad were staying with them so they called in. Sandy's Dad, Barrie, is looking really well; he has been ill with heart problems.

Today has been grot again; had so much diarrhoea, and I am still passing blood. My mouth is bad again with the ulcers, so Roger made an appointment with Dr. Vaux. Just as we were leaving, Jan and Diane arrived, but they waited while we went to the doctor. He gave me some mouthwash and told me to drink as much as I can; he felt the blood was, as I thought, due to the diarrhoea I had, but I was to mention it at the hospital.

Jan had her photos from her holiday in Egypt. It looked wonderful and, feeling as I do, I wondered if I would ever be well enough to go there. I do hope so.

February 25th.

Ros S called round, but did not come in as she had a sore throat. She had made me one of her delicious lemon cakes. Trisha came with flowers; she had booked a weekend away. Then Michelle came; she had been to Castle Howard and had a lovely weekend. I hope we can have a holiday when this is all over. After Michelle had gone, Nina, Mig, and Luke arrived; he looked so grown up in his playgroup sweat shirt. He had made a bird cake; he is such a little darling, and his leg is healing well.

March 1st.

Had a letter from Judy Woodman to say she has been told she is in the clear once more, which is marvellous, but she said that mentally she has found it a bigger struggle than the first time. The treatment has left her feeling at rock bottom and very tired, but she is back at work for the mornings. She said the daffodils and snowdrops are all coming out in the Castle grounds. I shall miss seeing them as it is always like a carpet of yellow and white. Judy and I said we felt that having cancer made us enjoy and appreciate the little things in life so much more.

March 7th.

The last few days had felt pretty grim. Roger said, if I was feeling okay, we would go out for the day as I haven't had a day out since September. So yesterday I made sure I drank plenty of water, and I had extra sickness pills this morning. We decided to go to the seaside town of Hastings, as I felt like a walk along the beach. I'm also looking forward to walking round the old town. It was a glorious sunny day, and the drive down was lovely with green buds and primroses along the banks of the woods. We were lucky enough to see a jay fly in front of us. Arriving in Hastings, we could not find anywhere to park as so many people had had the same idea as us, so we drove on to Rye, another lovely old Cinque Ports town with lots of winding streets, old book shops, and arts and crafts. We had lunch in one of the old pubs, and then bought some lovely fresh fish to take home. We had a really nice day, and the sea air had a good effect on me.

March 9th.

Julie and Nina said they were taking me into town as I haven't been in since Christmas. I bought a hat as a change from my turban. Had lunch, then saw my sister Nellie; she did not recognise me. She said she is worried about me because I look so ill, and should I be out? I had a really nice day. I have been feeling good the last few days, and have not had any blood in my toilet which is a relief. I am dreading tomorrow as it is chemo; just as I get the side-effects under control, it starts again. But I must be brave this month; then only one more to go and I hope it will be finished.

March 10th.

Chemo day, and Roger is up and ready for work. Before I leave, he gives me a cuddle and says he wishes I didn't have to go. He hates me going on my own, and wishes he could come with me, but it will soon be over and worth it in the end. Neil, my driver, arrives on time as always. We have to pick up a lady from the other side of town who is waiting when we arrive, and we have a good journey to the hospital. None of the other patients that we pick up are on chemo. It would be nice to have some to chat to about the treatment. Dr. Cottrill was running late as he was the only doctor on duty, but still takes as much care as always. I told him about the blood in my toilet, but he did not think it was anything to worry about as it had stopped. He thought it was because I am having so much diarrhoea, but to keep an eye on it this week, and if it still happens I will have some tests done. The main problem is having no stomach, so eating is not easy. Anyway, what with the combination of drugs, he felt I had coped well just to get through these last few weeks. My blood count was good so went to wait at the unit for my chemo to arrive from the pharmacy. There was a boy and girl in their late teens waiting for treatment; it is so sad being so young, but they seem to cope really well. They were chatting to each other about what problems they were having, coping with school and trying to keep up their work ready for exams, when some days they felt too sick to do anything. I have such admiration for them.

Today it was staff nurse Tracy; she said once again I would probably feel grot again as it is building up, so try and stay in bed for a couple of days after the treatment to get as much rest as I can. It was a long day; we arrived back home just after seven o'clock, and I had slept most of the way home until we dropped off the other lady. Roger was waiting as usual.

March 15th.

Have taken nurse Tracey's advice and stayed in bed. Well, I get up and have a shower, do some jobs, and get dinner ready, but by this time I feel exhausted so I go back and have a lie down. My arm is still not moving much although I do my exercises every day, but it is not helping my shoulder.

March 17th.

Chemo day again, and I could not get a driver so Roger took me which was nice. Saw Dr. Cottrill; told him the diarrhoea was better, and no blood, so that was good. Although I have lost weight, I look quite chubby in my cheeks due to the steroids. My blood count was good; thank goodness, because if it was not, I would not have been able to have my chemo. I do so want to get it over with. So far I have been so lucky; it has been good each time. Saw staff nurse Gill; as always, the veins were difficult so I had my hands in hot water for a while, and that helps. We were home by six o'clock. Roger said he liked taking me as he always found it hard to concentrate when he is at work and I have gone for my treatment.

March 18th.

Had a bad day.

March 21st.

Felt awful this morning; tried to stay in bed, but spent most of the time retching up the foul-tasting gold liquid. My mouth is bad again. I had a shower, and thought I would lie down for a bit, when there was a knock

Venice and More Treatment

on the door. By the time I had got downstairs and opened the door, the man was about to walk away. He introduced himself as Peter Edwards from our local newspaper, the Star. I do not know what he must have thought of this very thin, grey-faced lady with no hair in a white dressing gown. The Star had been running an article called Star Mum. Well, I had written to nominate Roger as a Star Dad. Peter was easy to talk to, and we chatted away. He asked me about when I was first ill, and about Roger and the family, and he then said he would like to have some photos taken. He said the photographer would come on Sunday, and could the family be there as well? I was going to keep it a secret from Roger that I had written the letter, but as the photographer was coming. I could not.

March 21st.

Mothers' Day, and all the family came for lunch. Really hoped I would have a good day, so drank as much as I could and took extra sickness pills. The photographer came at three o'clock; he was also a Peter. It was a lovely sunny day and our front garden was full of daffodils, so he thought it a good idea to take the photo outside. When he arrived, I did not have my turban on but asked him if I could put it on as the photos were outside. He told me sometime later that, when he first saw me with my shiny bald head, he thought he would have problems with it shining in the sunlight, so he was pleased for me to wear it. We had a great time with Peter. Luke took a liking to him, and he took some super photos of us all. He then stayed and had tea with us. I had an early night as I was so worn out, but it had been a nice day.

March 22nd.

I felt exhausted today; my mouth was a bit better, and not too much sickness and diarrhoea. Stayed up all day, but went to bed early.

March 23rd.

I feel such a grot, and wish I didn't.

March 24th.

Julie has her car back, so wanted us to go for dinner. She picked me up after Joe came out of school. I was ready when she arrived, but I don't know what happened; I found myself on the floor, and had knocked over a vase of flowers, so I think I must have fainted. I had managed to sort myself out before Julie came in. We had a pleasant evening; Roger came straight from work.

March 25th.

I was in the bathroom, sitting on the toilet, with my head hanging over the sink, retching, when Roger came in and said we had made the front page of the *Star* newspaper. Peter had written a lovely article about us with a photo of Roger and me with Luke and Joe. We had a lot of response from the article, with people ringing and writing to say it was lovely. Roger was really chuffed with it. He has been worried these last few weeks about what is going to happen at work. The company has been taken over, and there have been some redundancies. They have been told that most of the staff will go, not all at once, but over a period of time.

March 26th.

Decided I would walk to the library along the footpath by the stream. Saw lots of green buds, but no kingfisher unfortunately. Coming out of the library, I saw Julie who had driven up to find me, so had a lift back. I must admit I felt worn out, but lovely to be in the fresh air.

March 29th.

The last few days, I have felt good most of the time.

April 1st.

A letter from Judy Murray, keeping me informed on all the office news and gossip. She had been to a leaving party for Peter, the man who had looked after the birds at the Castle for many years, and, while there, Rita the seamstress, who had seen our photo and article in the *Star* newspaper, said I looked fetching in my turban hat. It is great of Judy to take the time to write. I like to write letters because I think there is nothing nicer than receiving a letter.

April 3rd.

Thought it had been too good to be true. It was back to the sickness and diarrhoea.

April 7th.

At last, after today one more chemo. Neil picked me up. I was his only patient today, so we arrived early and did not have to wait too long. Signed in with Sam, and then went to Haematology to have my blood taken. I was saying to myself, 'please make my blood count good'. It was Dr. Ramsey who said the count was good, but she was concerned about my shoulder as it is still painful and the movement severely restricted. She decided to write to Dr. Vaux to see if he would arrange some physiotherapy. While waiting for my chemo, I sat with Joesa, the Spanish man, and he said that next week would be his last. It was staff nurse Gill on duty, and I was disappointed as she will not be on next week. She gave me a big hug and said she hoped all went well. I gave Neil a bottle of wine as Roger is taking me up next week because it will be the last one. Neil was pleased, and I told him how much I appreciated how caring he was, not only to me but to all the patients.

April 8th.

Stayed in bed most of the day, but got up when Roger came home. I just feel so grotty; the nurses told me this, and after next chemo, it will be even worse because it has built up over the weeks.

April 12th.

I have just felt like nothing on earth the last few days; all I seem to get done is to have a shower, do a few jobs, and prepare dinner, and then I have to lie down if I am not in the bathroom. I am so pleased Roger is at work as he worries so when he sees me retching and looking so awful. I just keep telling myself it is nearly over. Well, only one more day, then my last chemo.

April 14th.

Red letter day, I hope; my one worry is that the doctors will decide to carry on with the chemo, as it happened once before, so I'm trying not to think about that. Roger drove me up to the hospital; he had wanted to come as it is the last one. Thank goodness my blood count was fine; saw both Dr. Ramsey and Dr. Cottrill, and had a long chat with them. They said they would not carry on with the chemo. I could have hugged them, but they said, for the next two or three weeks, I would not feel very good, then gradually I would start feeling myself again. Gave them some wine for looking after me so well, then had to wait five hours before I had my chemo. They had problems in the pharmacy. Saw Joesa, and we wished each other good luck. Staff nurses Tracey and Clare were on duty. They said: no more hands in hot water trying to get veins after today; I do not want to see any more needles. Gave Sam and the nurses some wine to thank them; they are all so brilliant. Nursing on the chemo unit is very stressful; I admire them so much, and they all gave me lots of hugs, and said to go in and see them if I was back at the hospital anytime and hoped all went well for me. I wanted to run out of the hospital to get to the car. I cannot believe today was the last one. Roger is so pleased; it has been so hard for him. We sat in the car and he held me, kissing me; neither of us could speak.

April 15th.

Stayed in bed this morning; felt so sick, and retching so much it exhausted me. I cannot believe the chemo has finished.

April 16th.

Stayed in bed this morning, got up, then after dinner I was so sick I went back to bed. David, Nina, and Luke came during the evening. Luke sat on my bed, holding something. Nina said, 'we have a present for you.' I opened the long slim package, and asked what it was. Nina said it was a pregnancy test (I had never seen one before), then I realised she was telling me they were having a baby; we were over the moon.

April 17th.

Nice surprise; my lovely friend Janet came. She now lives in Newbury, so I do not see her very often. We had a lot to catch up on. Roger went fishing, but didn't catch anything. It had been a good day - only sick during the evening.

April 19th.

Went to see Dr. Vaux for my B12 injection. He was pleased to hear I had finished my course of chemo, and sorted out my physiotherapy for me. I am to have the first session next week; hopefully I will be getting over some of the side-effects of the chemo, although the doctors did say it would be a while before I felt back to normal.

April 21st.

Had another nice letter from Judy Woodman; she had been given the all-clear again, and was so relieved. She had been having some pain in her back, but she is working full-time. She still feels very tired, but her doctor said that was to be expected. She had seen the article in the newspaper and thought it was lovely, and that our husbands really are unsung heroes. I will definitely second that.

April 28th.

Had my first physiotherapy with Lynn. She said we had a lot of work to do to get the arm above my head for the radiotherapy. It was very painful, as the shoulder is not moving. Lynn asked if Roger can help with the exercises when he is home. After next week, the oncology unit is to have a physiotherapist, as so many ladies who have breast surgery need physio. Lynn has set me some exercises, and I will have to go to the department at least twice a week. I will go again the day after to morrow.

May 1st.

I have not had time to write since last week because it has been so exciting. We are going on holiday to Greece. Last week, while at the hospital waiting to have my physio, Roger came and found me. He had been made redundant, but he said it was a relief as it had been going on for so long, and he knew it would happen in the end. He will be with me for the rest of my treatment, and feels, if he had to be made redundant, now is a good time. I know what a strain my illness has been for him, on top of not knowing when he would be made redundant.

Roger feels a holiday will be good for us both. Last week, I asked Julie if she would take me to the Castle. It was lovely to see everyone; it is funny how different people react to how you look. I went into the kitchen to see the chefs. One of them, Giles, said he loved my haircut, but Peter, our head chef, was so overcome when he saw me, that after giving me a hug he had to walk away. As it is warmer, I do not wear my turban, and I think the bald head was quite a shock for them; also I have lost my eyebrows and lashes which make quite a difference. There were lots of hugs and kisses, and everyone seemed pleased to see me.

A company which runs retirement courses has been coming to the Castle for a number of years, and I have always enjoyed looking after them. I had a good rapport with Mr and Mrs Smith, who own the company, Mrs Scott-Knight, Mr Barbour, and Gill who are tutors. I went to the Gate Tower to see the girls who were working, and Mr Smith came out to see me. He asked how my family was coping, and I told him Roger had been made redundant. He said we should go to their office in Faversham, and they would give him advice about money and getting another position. He said I had helped them over the years, so he would give us some help which we thought was very generous of him.

Since I was diagnosed, I have been overwhelmed with how caring everyone has been, and not a day seems to pass when I do not get a visit, a card, or letter, from someone; my brother and sisters, and their families, and nieces. Heather, Janet, Anne, Jan, Diane, Judy Murray, Judy Woodman, and Yvonne all write regularly, and Trisha, Rose, Michelle, Ros.C, Pauline, and Ros.S visit regularly, and of course my own family. I do appreciate it.

23

GREECE, THEN RADIOTHERAPY

I was so excited when we flew out to Corfu in Greece at one o'clock in the morning. We arrived at the hotel in Palaiokastritsa at six o'clock in the morning. The hotel is super, and it is very hot. There are only three hotels, some villas, and one shop that sells everything, and, during the day down by the beach, a few stalls selling handmade gifts, and a jewellery shop - not at all commercialised. It is lovely; there are so few people here as it is May and the start of the season, and I am feeling so much better already. I still have my sick spells but that is to be expected.

The next day we decided to walk down to one of the coves where there are a few taverns, and we had lunch sitting on the veranda. After dinner, we walked to the beach; it was lovely in the moonlight, and on the way back along the roadside were fireflies. It was magical; just like fairies flying around. Next day, it was still very hot so we decided to walk up the mountain, mostly through woods, so it was nice and cool. The doctors told me not to sit in the sun so soon after finishing my treatment. As we neared the top, we saw wonderful wild flowers and huge cacti. Roger collects cacti so he was most interested. At one point up the track, an old woman in traditional long black dress and head covering, passed us with her well-laden donkey. She seemed to come out of a sea of wild flowers. At the top, we found an old village, and it was as if time had stood still. It was siesta time, so the place was deserted. We wandered around winding streets of houses with paint pealing, but which at one time had been soft pinks, yellow, and white with terracotta roofs and wonderful old doors and windows - an artist's dream.

We emerged from the village to the most stunning view over the bay; we could not believe how high we were. Our map indicated there was a road back down so we followed the route and, overlooking the bay, was a taverna which was a welcome sight. We stopped for a snack and drink, and a couple from the hotel joined us. They had walked a much easier route, but said they would walk back with us. I had had a lovely day, but was worn out. I had not done so much exercise in months, and I am still taking anti-sickness pills. Today, after dinner, I had a bad spell; I think I had done too much, but apart from that I have been feeling really good. At least I have no trouble sleeping.

The following day, we went on a boat trip to Paxoi. As we approached the island, it was like a painting: a cluster of houses, sparkling white with terracotta roofs built up in the hillside, and the busy harbour with its fishing and sailing boats, and tavernas where we had lunch. The island produces olives and almonds, and grows vines. It was another hot day, so back at the hotel we had a relaxing evening.

After breakfast, the next day, we caught the little old bus into Corfu. The land is well-watered and fertile with fig, orange, and lemon trees found in profusion, and olives, and the tall elegant cypresses are everywhere, as are the vineyards. We wandered around the busy streets of the town, went into the museum, had coffee in one of the many open-air cafés, and a picnic lunch in one of the pretty gardens.

May ninth, and my birthday; the best I have had. In the morning, Roger bought me a silver necklace and earrings. We had coffee by the beach, then lunch in one of the tavernas on a balcony overlooking the sea. I had the largest prawns ever, and a delicious Greek dessert. Halfway through lunch, Roger said I would have to put my turban on as my head was getting the sun. I had brought a white one which was more summery. After lunch, we went to one of the little beaches; we had it all to our selves. Apparently, in the high season, Palaiokastritsa is very popular for boat trips coming from Corfu for the day, so we were lucky to go at the quiet time of the year.

On our last day, we decided to walk to the monastery. The road up to it was lined with trees that kept us out of the heat, and we stopped to look at the little roadside shrines with icons, and candles always burning. The monastery had a lovely air of calm, and beautiful terraced gardens, where we saw the priests with their flowing black robes and long white beards. As always, I lit a candle in the church. I felt a bit sad, but we had had a super time, and I had been really well. There had of course been frequent trips to the bathroom, and on one walk I stood at the side of the road retching, but thank goodness we were on our own. Roger is looking brown

Greece, Then Radiotherapy

and well, and he is more relaxed. The holiday has been good for him, and I hope we will be able to come back again. All too soon we were packed, and the coach came to take us to the airport for a night flight home.

The day after we arrived home, we were up early as I had to have an endoscope. It was back to the problem of finding a good vein, but after warming me up, the doctor managed to get one. All went well on the day, but for the next three days I had a sore throat and almost lost my voice. I am still having problems with the sickness.

Then a special weekend; Valerie-Joan wanted to have a family party and, as they have a large games room, she said she would hold it there. We were all going to cook something. My brother and sisters and all their families were invited. My eldest sister Phyllis's daughter, Jean, used to come and stay during the summer holidays when we were young. Phyllis was pregnant with Jean when mum was pregnant with me so we are more or less the same age. After we both left school and started work, Jean no longer came to stay and I had not seen her for over twenty years. When she walked in the room, she had not changed a bit; she has a look of Marilyn Munroe. She ran and hugged me. We were so emotional, neither of us could speak, and we all ended up in tears of joy. It was a lovely evening. I was a bit of a shock for some of the family, particularly Jean, who had not seen me since my treatment. I was looking so much better too - I had lost that awful grey complexion – and I had a nice tan from our holiday. I had been careful in the sun because, so soon after chemo, the skin can burn so easily. But the biggest shock was seeing me with no hair.

I started my physio again with Ruth, the oncology physio, who is a lovely lady. I am to have a session every other day as I must get more movement for the radiotherapy.

We went to Faversham to have a meeting with Mr Smith who is giving Roger advice as promised. The staff at the offices made us very welcome and gave Roger a lot of help with how to do his CV, finances etc. I am looking forward to going back to work, and looking after Mr Smith's company again.

June twelfth, and Roger's birthday. I wanted to take him somewhere special. His gran's old family home, Kits Coty House, is now a restaurant so I booked a table and we had a lovely evening. We have a small caravan so we decided to tow it to a site not far from home, a beautiful setting up on the downs. On the Sunday, the family all came and we had a BBQ. Everyone had a great time; there was a swimming pool, so Joe, David, and Luke all went swimming. Roger said it had been one of his best birthdays, and it was good to see him relaxing.

The physio is going well, but painful. Ruth has now given Roger instructions on how to do the exercises, so, as well as going to the hospital, I have to do them four times a day at home. We had Joe and Luke for the day. They thought it great fun to see Nanny lying on the floor, and Granddad looking as if he was trying to pull my arm out of its socket, and me shouting, 'oh, that hurts.' Every so often they say, 'when are you going to pull Nanny's arm so we can watch?' Children can be very sadistic. On one occasion, I was lying on the floor in the lounge, with Roger straddled across me, doing the exercises, and of course it made me groan - lots of ohs and ows. We laughed when we realised that anyone looking in the window would have thought we were doing other things.

I had to go back to the hospital for a bone scan before I start the radiotherapy planning. I am feeling so much better, hardly any sickness, and my hair has started to grow, although it is so fine I still look bald. It all seems to be going on forever. I wonder when I will get to go back to work.

July, and what an awful start to the month. Julie rang me. She was so upset because she had had a phone call from her friend Jane's mum to say she had died. I could not stop thinking about her; she was only twenty-five. Life is so unfair sometimes.

Jane's funeral was held in the lovely old church at Chart Sutton. The church was full; Jane had been very popular. It was a dreadful day. After the service, we went to look at the flowers, and Jane's Mum, Dad, brother, and boyfriend spoke to everyone as they left. Jane was very like Julie before she was ill, with dark hair, slim, and always laughing, and when Julie spoke to Jane's Dad, he said, 'whenever I see you, I will think of my Jane.' I think Julie became more mature after that day; it made her realise what death meant. It always makes me cry when I think of that day, and sometimes, writing this book, I have found it very hard.

I went to see Dr. Keen the consultant in the oncology department. I had asked Dr. Cottrill at the Westminster if I could have my radiotherapy at the new oncology unit at Maidstone hospital. He said he would have to check with Dr. Phillips, who agreed, but said he would like me to have a follow-up at their clinic. Dr. Keen, a very pleasant gentle man, had hoped to arrange the planning for my radiotherapy, but I could not get my arm up enough. This was so disappointing and meant more physio.

At last, the planning for the radiotherapy, but still I could not get the arm right up so it was decided to put my arm behind my head; I could just about do that. The areas to be treated are marked so that the treatment can be given accurately, and this takes quite a while. Tiny blue dots are tattooed on this area so that each session is measured correctly. It is the area where the tumour was in the breast, and also under the arm because some of the lymph nodes were malignant. It all seemed to take so long, and when it was finished my arm had gone completely dead. The nurses had to massage it so they could get it back down. But thank goodness it was done.

On Tuesday third of August, I went to start the radiotherapy, and waited all morning. The machine had broken down so we did not start until Thursday; the whole procedure is very quick but the setting up of the machine, and getting the patient in the correct position, takes a little time. At my second session, I asked if they had the results of my scan; it showed no problems, and my blood count was good. The only side-effect I have is tiredness, but I am told this is to be expected.

I went out with Jan and Diane for Jan's birthday. It was lovely to go out, and we had lunch in a pub near the village green. Afterwards, we left to go to a craft centre for tea, but we had only driven about five minutes before I had to use the toilet. Jan turned around and drove me back to the pub. I am still having the diarrhoea and sickness, although not so frequently, and I still look bald. These are the reasons I am not going out much, and it is so humiliating, when you are out with people, to have to keep going to the toilet, but we had a nice day.

At the end of August, the great Pavarotti was to stage an open-air concert at the Castle, and everyone was very excited. Again, I wished I was back at work, but as a surprise Roger bought some tickets. It was quite a long walk from the car park into the grounds, and the radiotherapy was now making me very tired. Dr. Keen said this happens when you have chemo as well, and with all the physio on top, so by the time we arrived at the concert area I was worn out. We had arrived in plenty of time so I could sit and rest before the concert started. I spotted Mr and Mrs Smith, and some of the other people from their company. When I went up to them, Mrs Smith did not recognise me at first because, although I had seen Mr Smith when we went to their offices, I had not seen Mrs Smith. She was so pleased to see me. The weather was kind, and it was an evening to remember.

At last, I finished the radiotherapy. I had no problems - the only side-effect was tiredness - and I think this is due to having to go to the hospital every weekday, and the travelling involved. It is now September, and today I went to Mr Jones's clinic. I saw his registrar, and what a shock it was when he examined me. He said he had found enlarged glands under my other arm, and that I would need an operation to remove them. I was totally shattered by this. Julie and Joe had taken me to the clinic, and when I came out we stood in the corridor and Julie asked what was wrong. Although I tried so hard not to get upset in front of them, I just cried and said now I have to have another operation. I did not want to have to tell Roger, but when he came home he knew something was wrong. He was so upset; it is such a setback. Tomorrow, I have my check-up with Dr. Phillips at the Westminster.

The lovely Dr Phillips examined me and said he was not sure if there was a problem. Sometimes the glands appear enlarged, but he would like me to see Mr Jones and made an appointment for next week.

Well, after a week of worrying, I have at last seen Mr Jones who said, 'yes, there is a lymph gland,' but he felt it is not a problem so will leave it for the moment. I have been trying very hard not to think about the gland but of course every so often when I shower I have to see if I can still feel it.

I had a lovely day with Nina who was doing her morning at play school with Luke. All the mums have to do one morning, so Nina asked me if I would like to go along. I really enjoyed helping.

I went to the support group where I am starting to get to know some of the ladies; a pleasant morning.

It was time for my appointment with Dr Keen. He said he could feel the glands, but Mr Jones was the expert so we would go along with him. He is sure that, if Mr Jones was at all worried, he would take them out. He checked that I was taking the Tamoxifen and H.R.T., and was pleased with my progress. I am still feeling a physical wreck, but Dr Keen said I must be patient as the chemo was hard on my body, as well as having the radiotherapy. I just want to feel really fit again.

I have decided to do some adult education classes as I am to be at home for a while. I saw in the brochure that my former art teacher, Mr Herbert, whom I have seen on and off over the years, was running a china painting class, so I thought I would surprise him and join. When I arrived, Mr Herbert did not recognise me at first with my skinhead-look, but when he realised who I was, he was really pleased to see me. Most of the ladies had been in his group for a number of years, but there were two other new

Greece, Then Radiotherapy

ladies. One of these was Jean, a very pleasant lady, who I discovered lived at the top of my road. As I am now back driving, I offered to take her each week.

I have also joined a writing group. I was very apprehensive the first evening, and felt a bit out of my depth when we all introduced ourselves. Because so many people had said I should write my story, and I have always kept diaries and letters, I had started to write my memoirs, and was hoping the group would help me. I was the only one at the group doing this; the others wrote novels, short stories, and poetry. Then I nearly had a panic attack when we all had to read from our work. The tutor, it seemed, could be rather harsh with his comments, so I was very nervous. Perhaps he saw I was, because he was very complimentary and gave me constructive advice, so this gave me confidence. I am looking forward to going next week.

The next week was rather busy. It was Julie's birthday, so all the family came for lunch on Sunday. Next day, Jan and Diane took me to Chartwell, home of Winston Churchill, and we had a very interesting day. I enjoyed seeing his studio, house, and lovely gardens with lots of miniature cyclamens under the trees.

There was great excitement when a television company rang to invite me on their programme. They booked a hotel for Roger and me near their studios in Norwich, a lovely city. When we arrived, we were given tea, and then before dinner, we were introduced to some of the other people who were to be on the programme which was about hair loss. I thought it would be mainly people who were on, or had been on, chemo, not knowing anything about a condition called alopecia which can cause a small patchy loss, but in some cases, complete loss of hair; very distressing. There were ladies from all walks of life, but one case I found upsetting, while having dinner, was that of a little girl of about eleven, completely bald. Roger said that little girl must be on chemo, but we were to discover later that she had lost all her hair at the age of four. She had alopecia, but she was a happy, pretty girl, and very confident.

After breakfast the next morning, we were all taken to the studio by taxies, and given coffee and biscuits while the researchers had a chat with us. At last it was time to go into the studio. We sat in a semi-circle, and the lady interviewer started talking to a young nurse, then a lady we had sat with at dinner. She then came to me - I did not feel at all nervous – and I told how the first time I had chemo, no-one told me I would lose my hair, and during the week I had at home before I started the treatment, I had read an article about a young girl on chemo, and how she had lost her hair. I told her I was horrified and how, when I went back to the hospital, no-one wanted to talk to me about it. And I said how much better I had coped this time, as so much more is explained to patients now. Then she spoke to the little girl we had seen last night, and she told how other children could be cruel at school sometimes, and that she did not like wearing a wig, as all the other speakers had said, because they are so uncomfortable. But she was a very brave little girl whose ambition was to be a hairdresser. After the programme finished, we were taken back to the lounge for more coffee. The researchers thanked us for coming, and taxies took us back to the hotel. I went into the ladies' cloakroom, and one of the hotel staff said, 'I have just seen you on *The Time The Place*. You came across very well.' We had to ask the family to video the programme for us as it went out live. We had a quick look around Norwich, and then started for home. We would have liked longer, as it is a lovely city, and it had been an exciting day, but it was a long journey home.

At the beginning of November, I went to see Dr. Vaux for my B12 injection. He said he thought I was looking much better. I do feel on the mend now.

Had some sad news. Roger's auntie Eva had died. She was a lovely lady, and we were both very fond of her.

It is now a year since I went to the Westminster Hospital for my results and assessment. I went with Nina for her anti-natal check-up at the hospital, and we had a scare when the doctor said she had to go back tomorrow for a scan as the results were not good. Thank goodness, the next day, the scan showed there were no problems. The baby is due in the middle of December, so we cannot wait; we are all very excited.

November was a good month. I'm still doing my classes, and they are going well. Also did a day course, making rag rugs like my Mum used to make. The tutor started by telling us the history of rag rugs, and then demonstrated how to make them. I enjoyed the day and felt inspired to make one.

There is nothing nicer than a walk in the snow, so when, in the middle of the month, we awoke to a fairyland, we wrapped up warm, including Joe who had stayed the night, and walked up past Otham church. It is in fact on the outskirts of the village - of the church mentioned in the Domesday Book, nothing remains – but the present church is the oldest

Greece, Then Radiotherapy

building in the village. We continued up the lane past Gore Court, a very large hall house. On a few occasions, the local history society held their meetings there. Roger and I were members, and I can remember a huge fireplace with logs burning, but it was still very cold. In recent years, the house was for a while used as a school. The house and grounds also featured in the film *Kind Hearts and Coronets*. As we passed the house, we walked under, what our grandchildren call, the tunnel, because the trees meet overhead, then on past the White Horse pub. I am told there are records of an ale house since 1752. Into the hamlet, and many lovely old houses still remain. One of these is Stoneacre, now the property of the National Trust, which is opened to the public some days. The history meetings were also held here. It seems there has been a house here since 1293. It stands in its own little valley, and is my favourite house in the hamlet. We pass Madam Taylors, a Manor house much altered over the years, and in fact very little of the house remains that was there in 1543. It overlooks the village green and, on the other side, are Tudor Cottage and Elizabethan Lodge which were originally one house, part of which was the village post office and shop. Opposite here is what was the village school, now a private house. We turned off the road and finished our walk on the footpath across the fields, leaving our footprints in the crisp white snow.

At the end of November, I was invited to the yearly assembly at the Castle. Various members of staff give a talk on their particular role at the Castle, and the chief executive and general manager also give talks. At the end, members of staff who have worked over fifteen years, or are retiring, are made presentations. It was over fifteen years since I had started, so I had been invited to receive my inscribed wine goblet and champagne. I did hope, as I went up to collect it, that I would be fit soon to start back to work.

The snow had cleared when we went to Auntie Eva's funeral; her husband had died some years ago. One of her daughters, Margaret, lives with her family in America. Ian, the only son, and his children, were there, and another daughter, Janet, who is married to Roy, Roger's friend at school and also his best man when we married, and then there were the twins, Susan and Eileen, and their husbands and children. A sad occasion, but lovely to see them all again.

At the beginning of December, I saw Dr Vaux for my injection and he said it was not a good idea to go back to work just yet.

On the fifteenth, we had a message to say Nina had had the baby, so

Roger, Julie, Joe, Richard, Sandy, Nina's mum, Mig, Dave, her brother Neil, and girlfriend Jo, all arrived at visiting time. David met us and said they would not let us in until it was visiting time. We all wanted to know whether the baby was a boy or girl, but David said we would have to wait until we went in. At last we were allowed in to find we had a lovely granddaughter, Lucia. Nina was sitting up in bed, looking her usual glamorous self with her make-up and earrings on, and said she felt fine. The next day, we looked after Luke while David went to collect Nina and Lucia from the hospital. As always when we have a new baby in the family, there was great excitement.

Roger and I were both looking forward to Christmas, especially after last year when the chemo made me feel so grotty. On the Sunday before Christmas, it was a nice crisp frost when we went gathering wood, holly, and ivy. We spent the afternoon decorating the house and tree, and finished wrapping presents. On Christmas Eve, we went to midnight service at the church, cold and frosty with a velvet sky and stars so bright. As always the church was full. I feel it is Christmas once we have been to church.

Christmas Day was hectic with all the family. It was lovely having a new baby. Lucia is good, very contented like Luke was. It was great to feel well and really enjoy the day. We went to Julie for New Year's Eve, while she went to work at the hotel. Once again, I think of all the New Years I have worked, and I cannot wait to feel fully fit again. I am trying not to be impatient, and hope the New Year brings Roger a job.

24

1994

January tenth was our thirty-fifth wedding anniversary. We had a nice day, so I hope this is a good start to the year. I've started a new term for my painting and writing classes, and I now feel more relaxed with the writing; the group has given me confidence.

The end of January, and my check-up with Dr Keen at oncology; I felt a bit uptight so Roger came with me. Dr Keen thought I was looking well, but could still feel the nodes under my good arm. He said we would go along with Mr Jones and keep an eye on them, but he wanted me to have some X-rays before I see him next time. I am still worried about the nodes but must try to not think about them.

Time for my B12 injection, and had a chat with Dr Vaux about going back to work. He said to wait until I go back in six weeks for my next injection, and then start by going perhaps one day a week. I went to see my manager, Andrew, to talk about going back, and he said it was fine for me to start going for one day.

Lucia is now six weeks old, and my friend Trisha had not seen her, so I picked Lucia up and brought her home. Nina was taking Luke out as it is nice for him to have some time on his own with Nina. Trisha thought Lucia a sweet little girl and she was very good. After we had taken Lucia home that evening, we had some bad news; Roger's friend, Bill, who had been ill for a while, had died. Roger and I were so upset; Bill was a lovely man. Roger had taken him and another friend out on a boat fishing last year, and Bill never stopped talking about their day, he had enjoyed it so much.

I am still going to the monthly Breast Support meetings. I enjoy the talks and meeting the other ladies. When I arrived home, I read the newspaper and the main article was that Jackie Onassis had died. She had been the wife of American President John F. Kennedy, who had been assassinated, and she had then married Aristotle Onassis who also died. I had admired her courage when John F. Kennedy was shot, and she was a great leader of fashion; the news upset me.

Today was Bill's funeral. When we got up, it had snowed overnight and was a bright crisp morning. After the service, Pat, Bill's wife, asked us back to the house. Roger was pleased to see many of his colleagues from his old work place where Bill had worked too.

About once a month, we had a managers' meeting at work. Andrew invited me to join them this month, and afterwards to a meal at a local pub. He takes us out once a year as a thank you, so it was nice to be invited.

I now have some hair that looks like a very short hair-style, and I have had lots of complimentary remarks. I only have problems with the sickness and diarrhoea when I eat something my body doesn't like, but it has always been like that, and I feel like my old self again.

It's the first week in March, and my first day back at work. I was worried I would not get up in time as I had an early start - up at five thirty to leave at six thirty. I drove into the grounds of the Castle through the park. The view was stunning: before me lay the Castle surrounded by the shimmering moat, and the spring flowers, a golden carpet of daffodils on the banks of the water and through the trees, and not another human in sight, only the various water fowl, geese, and swans, both black and white gliding around the moat. It was great to be alive and back to work. My body did not like me going back; the next day I could hardly move, but I will get used to it. The next week, I did an evening and that was not quite such long hours. It is a difficult situation because, as Roger is unemployed, I cannot earn any money or else it is taken out of his unemployment money, so I am actually working and not being paid. It is a sort of therapy really, to get fit again.

On Mothering Sunday, Roger and I went up to my Mum and Dad's graves to put some flowers on, and we also went to my sister, Nellie. I take her flowers because she was a sort of mum when Mum died, and because she looked after Dad for so long. The family all came for tea, and it is now a year since Peter came to take our photographs for the newspaper. What a lot has happened in that year. A lot of good things, like: Roger being with me while having my treatment, Luke recovering from his burn, and having another grandchild.

1994

I had my injection with Dr Vaux, and told him I was working. He said he hoped I was not overdoing things.

I am still having physio. Ruth the oncology physiotherapist thought it a good idea if the ladies who had had their lymph glands removed when having breast surgery, and were having trouble with movement like me, would benefit from going to the hydrotherapy pool. I picked up Jean, one of the other ladies who lives near me. I was a bit apprehensive as I cannot swim, and have to admit to being frightened of the water. When I was at junior school, we went to the local baths for lessons. I was doing quite well, and gaining confidence, when we all had to stand on the edge of the pool and jump in. Well, I was not ready for this, so did not want to jump, but the teacher pushed me in. Well, that was the end of me going swimming; it terrified me.

I told Ruth I was worried about going in the water, but she said not to worry as I would be holding on to the bar. I walked slowly down the steps into the water, and it was immediately relaxing, so lovely and warm. After we finished the exercises, Ruth said we could have a swim and, for those of us who couldn't, she produced a variety of apparatus to help us float, so I felt quite pleased with myself, and perhaps, sometime, I will learn to swim having gained the confidence to get in the water. We are to have a session once a week. My first exhausted me but Ruth told us to expect that.

This has been a busy month; we have had Joe, Luke, and Lucia (who is a little poppet) quite a lot. Sometimes when Nina brings Lucia, she does what she used to do with Luke; she will bring her in her car seat, ring the front door bell, and when I open it there is Lucia sitting in her seat on her own as if she has been left. Nina is hiding around the corner.

I am still going to my classes. Tony, our tutor at the writing class, told us he may not do next term. I do hope he does; he gives such encouragement. I have nearly finished a painting of a leopard, and hope to give it to the oncology department as they seem to have a lot of bare walls.

Work is going well, and I am back in the swing of it, although it still makes me tired.

At the beginning of April, I had to go for my endoscopy as usual. Dr Stevens did it and told me he is going to retire. I will not feel so confident with someone else; it was Dr. Stevens who found my stomach cancer, and as with Dr Vaux and Professor Ellis, I owe my life to them. I did not seem to have any problems. He told Roger and me that, in future, he will refer me to Mr Jones. Dr Stevens told me to make sure I always have my check-ups. Two weeks later, and I have my breast check-up at Mr Jones's clinic. I saw his registrar who said he could still feel the lymph nodes under my arm, so back in three months unless I notice them changing.

Had a letter from Judy Woodman; her remission had not lasted long. She had been back in hospital for an operation to remove lymph glands, and is now on chemo. She had the operation on a Friday, crashed out over the weekend, and managed to go to work on Monday, feeling very frail. She now has help in the house, and said she couldn't cope with work if she didn't. She is in bed by seven o'clock, and hopes I can pop into the Gatehouse office to see her when I am working.

At the end of April, we had a week's holiday in Weymouth. We started early, and it was warm and sunny as we drove to the New Forest; everywhere was fresh and green. Spring is a lovely time to drive through the forest. We stopped to have our lunch and watch the deer, and we saw a kestrel swooping up and down; then a heron flew in. We could have sat watching the wildlife all day, but had to find the caravan park where we were to stay. Arriving late afternoon, we found we had a lovely new caravan, suitable for four people, so we had plenty of room. We got up early and drove into Weymouth; it was sunny again so we went to the quay and saw the fishing boats unloading. After lunch, we drove to Poole to look around the china shops and factories, and bought some china for my china painting. China painters can never resist buying white china.

We drove to Lulworth Cove; stunning scenery but it started to rain quite hard so we decided not to go for a walk. I hope we can come back some time. Next day it started a bit misty. We wanted to do a walk along the river Piddle, so we parked at the church at Piddletrenthide. It was supposed to be an eight-mile walk along the river, we thought, but after a while the river runs out. We stopped at a pub and had a drink before resuming our walk, but although we did not see a lot of wildlife, we were privileged to see a buzzard and a badger which was great. After stopping for our packed lunch, we walked on, but could not find any more signs. After another two miles, we eventually saw Piddletrenthide Church; it had been an enjoyable day.

The following day, we visited the lovely village of Abbotsbury, full of thatched houses, and went to the Swannery and gardens. Another day was spent in Dorchester, and then we packed, ready to leave next day. We

1994

were up early as it was the last day and we wanted to make the most of it. We drove to Durdle Door and parked overlooking the bay, then walked along the beach and along the clifftop to Lulworth Cove. It was warm and sunny, and there was yellow gorse, cowslips, and violets everywhere. We stopped for a cup of tea in the Cove tea shop, and it was a long walk back up the cliff, but the views were spectacular. We drove home through the New Forest, but on the way we had driven off the road and were opposite what looked like a woodman's cottage, when suddenly two white rabbits hopped out of the garden followed by a rather anxious lady. Roger called out, 'would you like some help?' 'Yes please,' she replied. Roger took out his large fishing net and slowly followed the rabbits. After about five minutes he had caught them and put them back safely in their hutch. The poor woman could not thank Roger enough. Apparently, she was looking after them for a friend whose child would have been devastated if she had lost them. It was an uneventful drive home - another good holiday.

I went to the Breast Support group where the talk was about becoming a volunteer for Breast Cancer Care. I told the ladies I was interested, so they took my details and said they would be in touch.

It's May, and my fifty-fourth birthday. We had a nice day, with the family coming. Yesterday, as it was Sunday, after lunch we all walked along the footpaths to the village green, where there was cricket being played, then back through the bluebell woods; it was a beautiful sight.

A few days later, Jan and Diane took me to lunch at Biddenden; it is a typical Wealden village, and was important as a centre of the Weald's cloth-making industry. Most local people would say its fame is because of the two twelfth-century residents, Eliza and Mary Chulkhurst, Siamese twins joined at the shoulders and hips who lived and took an active part in village life for thirty-four years. To this day, every Easter the sisters are remembered by their bequest of bread and cheese to the local poor. Today, special biscuits are baked with representation of the twins stamped on them. After lunch, we went to the Pinetum at Bedgebury Forest, and although it was a dull damp day, we had a lovely walk.

June, and it's Roger's fifty-fifth birthday, and also Lucia is to be christened. The service was in a tiny church at Coxheath, and then we drove to the Culpeper rooms at the Castle. The French doors lead out to the beautiful Culpeper gardens where we had drinks on the terrace and a super lunch. We walked around the grounds, and had a tour of the castle, then back for tea and cake. Roger said it had been such a nice birthday, and Lucia had been as good as gold all day.

A week later, Roger and I were going to the wedding, in the evening, of one of the chefs at work, but during the afternoon Julie rang and asked if we could have Joe for about half an hour. I said we could, but not to forget we were going to a wedding. They arrived, Julie, Joe, and Marcus who had been a friend of Julie's after meeting him through David. They both looked pleased with themselves, and then Marcus brought out a bottle of champagne. He told us he had asked Julie to marry him, and she had accepted and was wearing a diamond ring. They wanted to get married in September or October. We were pleased, especially after what Julie had been through in her first marriage. Joe was happy and wanted to call Marcus Dad. The next day we met Marcus's parents, sister, brother-in-law, and niece.

At the end of the month, I was at Preston Hall hospital for a mammogram. I have been worried about this, and was more worried after talking to the radiologist. I explained about my previous history, and the fact that the lymph glands were swollen under my good arm, but she laughed and said, 'I thought you had a problem with your ankle.' I did not know what she was talking about, and lost confidence in her then. She did the first set of X-rays and then asked me to wait while the doctor looked at them. After what seemed an age, she called me back; the doctor was not happy with them so they would have to do some more. After another wait, she said I could go, and ring next week.

I went for my injection the following week, and asked Dr Vaux if he had the results; he had not. Once again, he said he hoped I was not doing too many hours at work. It was my day for the hydro-pool which is next to the breast unit at Preston Hall, so after my session I went to the unit and asked if they had my results. I received a very negative response; the lady at the desk looked at some notes, 'Oh, have you had surgery?' 'Yes,' I replied. 'Oh, they are all right then,' was her answer. That did not really put my mind to rest, so I will have to wait until I go to the clinic.

At the beginning of June, I supervised a function at work for a group of Americans. The speaker, who had been Sir Winston Churchill's secretary, gave a most interesting talk.

I had a super evening at Staplehurst library when one of my favourite authors, Pamela Oldfield, was giving a talk. I love her books, as most are set in Kent, so when reading her stories I can visualise the towns or villages. I most enjoyed the books about a hop-picking saga as they brought a lot of memories back. She was a pleasant lady who gave a most interesting talk, and lots of advice to some of us who wanted to write.

At the end of June, our neighbour Rose's daughter, Lynne, was getting married. Rose asked Roger and me if we would stay and look after the house while they were at church, and serve the drinks as the guests arrived back. Lynne wanted to have the reception in the garden, so a small marquee was put over the patio doors for the food, and tables and chairs were set out in the garden. The bar was in the garage, and Roger served the drinks. It was a very hot day, and it was one of the nicest weddings I have been to; it was like an old country wedding. The next day, Rose invited us round to lunch to thank us for helping.

In August, my niece Valerie-Joan, and her husband Sid, wanted to move somewhere smaller now that their family was no longer at home. The house I had been born in, Scragged Oak Farmhouse, was up for sale. I cannot remember living there, and had always longed to look inside. Valerie-Joan was interested in buying the house, so she made arrangements to view it. I asked if I could go with her and her mum, my sister Nellie. I wanted to know if I would get any feelings of having lived there. The house was built in the late 16th century - I am told 1665 - timber framed beneath a Kent peg-tiled cat slide roof. The solid wood front door was believed to have come from a French monastery. We arrived and parked in the drive, and Valerie-Joan told Nellie not to mention we once lived there. I loved the house; it had such a warm feeling. The kitchen had a stable door, and the sitting and dining rooms, plus the main bedroom, all had inglenook fireplaces, whilst the other bedrooms had pretty cast-iron ones. The whole house had a wealth of exposed beams. Outside, the garden had a pond, a small orchard of miniature fruit trees, and a pretty cottage garden, and to the side of the house was what had been the original stables. The disappointment was that I could not remember living there at all. I was hoping something would jog my memory, but it didn't. There was now a garage over the well where the water pump had been, which was where Mum would draw water from the well, and of course they only had oil lamps. Although Valerie-Joan liked the house, she felt it was too far out in the country, so did not buy it. It is very lonely, and in winter often gets cut off if there is heavy snow.

I had been feeling very stressed about my next hospital appointment, so was a bit upset that Roger had forgotten it. We arrived at the clinic. When I was called in, it was Mr Jones's registrar, and after examining me, he said he felt the enlarged glands and thought they should come out. In a way I felt relieved as I had worried since first being told. The doctor said I should go in for the operation by the end of the month. I feel it is such a setback having to have another operation so soon, but better to be safe than sorry, and I want to get it sorted out before the wedding.

At the beginning of September, a young lady reporter from the *Maidstone Star* newspaper came to interview me as a follow-up to the article that had appeared in the newspaper the year before. It said I was writing a book on my experiences of having cancer and how it had changed my life. We once again had a lot of reaction to the article; one of the ladies, who used to work in our local library, for whom I had done china painting, contacted me, and another lady who had worked at the castle until she retired. Everyone who wrote wanted to buy the book, but it was still not finished.

I had been accepted to go on a course to train as a volunteer for Breast Cancer Care with Sadie whom I met at the support group. We travelled up to London by train for the three-day course. I enjoyed the training and we were with a nice group of ladies. When a client rings the help line at Breast Cancer Care, they are matched with a suitable volunteer who rings the client. Many women who have breast cancer find it helpful to talk to someone who has shared a similar experience. Contact with a volunteer who is leading a 'normal' life can offer great encouragement and hope. All volunteers are at least two years post-diagnosis and treatment. They will also visit clients in hospital before or after surgery, and visit them in their own homes.

I received an appointment to see Mr Jones. After examining me, he said he was sure there was not a problem; it was just that the glands were enlarged. He did not want to do another operation, and I was not to worry about it. I would see Dr Keen next, and then Mr Jones, and in the meantime to check myself, and if there were any problems they would see me. I was so pleased not to have another operation, especially so near to Julie's wedding which is in two weeks, although I must admit I am still worried about the glands. However, I am going to do as Mr Jones said, and not think about it. I want to enjoy the wedding, and only wish my hair had grown a bit more. At least I do have a little; I am not completely bald, and I have bought a hat to go with my outfit which will help.

The weather had not been very good this last week, but today it has changed. We are all very excited; today Julie and Marcus are getting

1994

married. The flowers arrived and were lovely. Czarsie, Marcus's niece, was a bridesmaid, also little Lucia who will be one in December. Joe, who was best man, looked very smart in a suit. The wedding was at Tunbridge Wells, and my sisters, nieces, and friends came to the ceremony. Then, just the parents, Marcus's sister and husband, Richard, Sandy, David, Nina, Luke, Joe, and the two bridesmaids went to the Castle for lunch. We had a meal in the Culpeper rooms where we had Lucia's christening. The table looked really nice; I had learnt some calligraphy so had done the place names and menus. I had also painted all the ladies a china shoe, and each had flowers which matched the menus and place names which I painted with water colours. We had a lovely meal, and then Joe made a speech which he had written himself, so of course we all found it emotional. It was a great day, and the ladies at work looked after us so well as usual. The next evening, there was a party for the rest of the family and friends. Marcus's parents had a barn next to their house, which had been renovated, so it was held there and we all had a super time.

When I was diagnosed with the breast cancer, there were times when I did not think I would be so lucky again. It has been brilliant seeing all the children get married. Each time one of them told us they wanted to, I just hoped and prayed I would still be here to see them, and to have grandchildren has been the icing on the cake.

A few weeks later, I was visiting my sister Nellie when our brother Ted called in. While chatting, he said, 'I am sure Dad was not the father of one of our sisters.' I did not take a lot of notice of this, and Nellie carried on making us a cup of tea and made no comment, but months later, an incident to do with this was to occur that could have caused an upheaval in the family.

It is nearly the end of the year, and lots of good things have happened. At the end of September, Roger was offered a position where Richard works, which was great news.

I have also been to Breast Cancer Care for my training as a volunteer with Sadie. We really enjoyed the course, but I have to do some written work before I know if I have been accepted.

Julie and Marcus had hoped to start a family as soon as they were married and, in October, she became pregnant, so once again we are all very excited. In November, I have been really busy going to work, doing my writing and painting classes, and looking after Luke and Lucia when Nina is doing her aerobics. David still has his car repair workshop near

Julie, so most days on my way to work I pop him in cakes and sandwiches. I also go into Julie, as she has been quite sick, to do her ironing (which she hates doing), and Joe stays with us on a Friday night as Julie continues to work at the hotel.

At the beginning of December, I had a phone call from the health editor of *Woman* magazine; they wanted to write an article about me having cancer. We were all very excited, and I had to send some photos of before I had cancer, during the chemo, and after. The article is to be in the magazine after Christmas, probably February. I rang Breast Cancer Care to tell them about the article, and I asked if the magazine could print the helpline number.

Also been busy getting my china painting orders finished, and looking forward to Christmas.

I am still going to the hydro-pool once a week for physiotherapy, and I am so much more confident in the pool now. Dr Vaux is still keeping an eye on me about not doing too many hours at work.

Christmas Eve, and all the presents had been delivered as usual. We walked to the church; it was a lovely cold frosty evening, and we enjoyed the carols and service. Back home we had mulled wine in front of a cosy fire. We had decided to go out for lunch on Christmas Day, returning home for a relaxing afternoon. On Boxing Day, all the family came for tea. We are looking forward to the New Year, with Roger now working, Julie having the baby, and me feeling fit, so we hope it is a healthy New Year.

25

1995

January the 1st, and it snowed. We sometimes go on the village walk, but decided to go on our own. It was very cold as we walked past the church and along the footpath that goes across the field. We looked back to a wondrous scene: the ploughed field with the snow sparkling like crystals on the hedgerow, the church with the holly trees, dark green against the blue sky, and not a soul in sight. It was as if we were completely on our own. The footpath ended in the Hamlet of Otham, and we walked past Dr Vaux's lovely old house. Down the lane, over the hedge, we could see a beautiful chestnut horse rolling in the snow, and further on a small meadow with four cows blowing hot steam through their nostrils; it reminded me of when I was a girl, and the cows walked back to the farm for milking. It was nice to get home in the warm.

We were not to know, but this year was to be exciting in many ways.

I had been accepted as a volunteer for Breast Cancer Care, and went to visit my first client. I was a bit worried as it was my first time, but all went well.

We celebrated our thirty-sixth wedding anniversary; I feel as if Roger and I have been together always, but then I was only thirteen when he became my boyfriend. The word that would describe Roger is solid.

I went with Julie and Joe for her to have her scan. It was so exciting to see the baby moving about, and Joe thought it was great; I think it is a boy, but we will have to wait and see.

I received a nice letter from Professor Ellis which reminded me I had not had my injection. I saw Dr Vaux who said I must keep an eye on my weight, and now I have a problem with my waterworks so I have to take a sample.

My sister Nellie was to have gone in to hospital; she is to have a heart by-pass operation but it was cancelled, then three days later it went ahead. We were all very worried about her, but after two days she was out of intensive care which was good news. We were ready to go and visit her when Valerie-Joan rang to say she did not want any visitors, and five days later she was back home doing really well, except for a problem with her leg which was eventually sorted out, and she went on to make a full recovery.

I booked to start a basic English education course as I thought it would help with my writing; I enjoyed my first day.

I went to see Dr Keen at oncology for my check-up; he said all seemed well but would like me to have another mammogram before I see him next time.

Michelle came for a chat and told me one of David's friends, Jackie's brother, had died. The young boy had developed cancer in his leg and had part of it amputated, but he had been so brave when he had chemo. David had been at school with him, and he would visit us with his sister Jackie. David was very upset. It made me feel really down; it is not fair that a teenager should have to go through all that.

At the end of the month, we were all excited when the article was published in *Woman* magazine; it was a really nice write-up. When I went to writing classes the following week, Miriam, who is also attending the class, said she had seen it.

I now feel more confident with my volunteer work. Some of my clients know each other from the hospital and support group, so I was worried when Gwen phoned to say Stella, another of my clients, was back in hospital. Stella, a vibrant continental lady, always beautifully made up and dressed, was finding it hard to cope with her cancer, and I kept thinking about her. I went up to the hospital to visit her, only to find she had been sent home a few minutes before I arrived. On my way back to the car I saw her so we arranged for me to visit her at home. From the hospital I went to the hydro-pool, but Sadie was not there. Mal, who goes dancing with her, said she had been in hospital so I rang her when I arrived home. She said she would be at the support group tomorrow. On Saturday, I picked up Jill and Gwen to take them to the support group, and Sadie said she was feeling better. The speaker gave an interesting talk on aromatherapy, and demonstrated a massage on two of the ladies with her fragrant oils; they said they felt very relaxed.

The middle of February, and I had another fraught visit to have a mammogram. I went in and the radiologist went through the procedure of taking the X-rays. Then he told me to get dressed and wait while they checked them. After a while, she came back and said I needed to have some more taken, so undressed and dressed again, and then she came back to say I may need to return for an ultra-scan, saying, 'But I expect it will be all right.' Another week and a half waiting for the results, and I could not stop thinking about the scan, but then I received a letter from Dr. Keen to say they were clear. He said he had written so that I did not have to worry until I next saw him. It was very sweet of him, and it was a great relief.

Went to a volunteers' meeting and heard that the hospital is opening a room to give information to patients, so volunteers were wanted. I will do a day a week there. Also went to a talk about radiotherapy, and we were shown around the department; it was very interesting. It will help when I speak to clients about their treatment.

We are now in the middle of March; the weather is cold and we have had some snow. In the Roman year, also the English ecclesiastical calendar used until 1752, March was the first month. Scotland changed the first month to January in 1599. It received the name 'Hlyd Monath' meaning loud or stormy month from the Anglo Saxons and Martius by the Romans. On our walks, the birds are starting nest-building, and the flocks of starlings in the field by the river are making lots of noise. I love starting work early in the mornings; the Castle looks especially beautiful on frosty days. The daffodils are starting to push through the hard ground, and the ducks and swans look as if they are frozen in the moat until the bird man feeds them and they gather on the banks.

I find I get very tired, especially when I have been to work. The weeks fly by; I still do one day at the information centre at the hospital, and I am really enjoying the volunteer work for Breast Cancer Care, whilst fitting in china painting and looking after the grandchildren which of course I adore. I have always enjoyed doing all the things in the home; I like to have things in order, so housework, washing, ironing, and cooking are never a chore.

At the end of March, Trisha rang to say she was a grandmother; Lisa had had a little boy, James.

April, and the weather was warm and sunny which made us want to get in the garden. Easter Sunday, and all the family came; it was a hectic day. Easter Monday was more relaxing when Roger and I went to a country fair with wood turner, saddler, farrier, and all the activities associated with the countryside, birds of prey, horses, and dogs. The weather was kind; it was bright and sunny.

The end of April, and my dear friend Heather was retiring from the Castle. We arranged a tea party, and I was sad to see her leave; Heather was a special lady.

I went with Julie to have another scan, and we could clearly see the baby who now weighs five and half pounds. I am trying to get some knitting finished; we are all very excited.

I always look forward to the first of May, perhaps because it is my birthday month, but I love the bluebells. They remind me of when I was a girl, and Valerie-Joan and I would go off into the woods and pick armfuls (of course today this would not be allowed due to the preservation of wild flowers). It was once believed that bluebells rang out to summon fairies, and that any human who heard the sound would die. When the fields were full of poppies and big white daisies, the house would be full of vases of these. How lucky we are living in the countryside; driving to work is such a pleasure. Sometimes I take the long route, just to drive down the lanes; I love to see the rabbits, birds and, if I am lucky, deer.

26

SPAIN

We started our holiday on my birthday. Julie came to take us to the pick-up point; I am so excited, as always, when we go travelling, particularly when going by coach. As we were getting on the coach, Julie gave me a mini birthday cake to have when we stopped for tea, which was a nice thought.

The coach took us to Dover where we caught the late afternoon ferry to Calais and, after disembarking in Calais, we travelled overnight to Spain. We passed Rheims, Dijon, and Lyon, then slept all night, although the coach has comfort stops for people to stretch their legs, and for the smokers to have a cigarette. We awoke to bright sunshine, stopping to wash and brush-up, and have breakfast, and drove through some lovely countryside, then along the coast stopping at Fanals, Lloret, Canyelles, and at last arrived at Tossa De Mar, a lovely small fishing town.

We are staying at the Hotel Continental; it is one of the smaller hotels, and we have a nice room with a balcony that overlooks the swimming pool and, as we are on the edge of the town, lovely mountain views.

After a shower, we had a look around the hotel and walked down to the beach. Everywhere is so clean, and we were later to find out that the beach is cleaned every day, and everyone washes down outside their houses or shops. There are flowers everywhere; we have fallen in love with the town. From the beach, there is a lovely view of the castle and lots old buildings painted in soft pastel colours; there are no high-rise hotels. Most days we sunbathed in one of the little bays, and bought wine, bread, cheese, meats, and fruit for a picnic lunch. Some days, we walked up to the lovely old castle, and on the way back had lunch in one of the fish restaurants. At our favourite, we had sardines in garlic and coriander. The pace of life is so different, and lunch is never hurried; just sitting in the sun watching the people go by.

The highlight of our holiday was a trip to Barcelona, beautifully situated on its own Mediterranean bay. The best known streets are the Ramblas, a succession of wide streets with a central tree-covered portion reserved for pedestrians. One section is for the flower-sellers, another for birds - canaries and brightly coloured finches all singing in beautiful cages. There is a wonderful covered market with displays of bread, meat, fish, vegetables, chocolates, lace, leather goods and so much more; everything beautifully displayed. The highlight of the day was our visit to the Cathedral de la Sagrada Familia, the work of the wonderful artist Gaudi, still unfinished after his death in 1926, but work is still going on. I think it is the most magical building. The whole of the city is full of Gaudi's work; the fascias of shops and houses have this wonderful fairy-tale appearance, so typical of the Art Nouveau period which I love; it is my favourite period in art with the Pre-Raphaelites. There are also his sculptures in the gardens and parks. We had lunch in what is known as the Spanish village. I would have liked to have stayed in the city all day, but we were to visit the Monastery of Montserrat high up in the mountains; stunning scenery, a very peaceful place said to have inspired Wagner's Parsifal. It was then back to the hotel for dinner. Some days we bought hot bread and cheese, and went walking in the surrounding hills, sometimes not meeting another person all day, but finding ruined buildings and fields of sunflowers. Another day, we caught the local bus into Lloret De Lar Mar, a busy town famous for its nightlife, but it has a long sandy beach lined by a palm tree promenade, where we had ice-cream in one of the beachside cafés. Back in Tossa, we visited the local market and loved looking around the excavated Roman villa. All too soon we were back on the coach for our return home; we hope we can come back.

David picked us up from the coach station. On the way home he said he had something to tell us; we had had a flood from the tank in the roof. During the first week of our holiday, Julie had called to check everything was all right and found water coming through the kitchen ceiling. Upon investigation, she found water coming through the bedroom ceiling, and all the carpets in the bedroom, bathroom, and down the stairs were wet. Julie phoned Richard; he had arrived and called out John the plumber. Thank goodness they managed to sort it out. After we arrived home, we eventually had to have a new ceiling in the bedroom and kitchen, and new floorboards and carpets in the bedroom, bathroom, and on the stairs. So, not a very good homecoming.

The next day, I had to go into hospital for the day for my routine gastroscope. I saw Dr. Bird and he told Roger, when he came to collect me, that it had all gone well; he had taken a biopsy as usual, and Dr. Vaux would get the results. For the next two days, I was zonked out; just wanted to keep sleeping.

At the beginning of the next week, I am back at the hospital for a bone scan which involved going in for an injection of a substance that emits gamma-rays. The substance is taken up by the bone in the body. It means drinking for about two hours to flush it through the body, and then lying flat under the machine; it slowly comes over you, then back again. It is not painful; it just takes a long time.

The next day, I arrived home from my morning at the information centre to find a message from Mark, a colleague at work, to say a researcher from Sky TV was trying to get in touch with me about filming a documentary. At first I thought Mark was joking, but he convinced me it was true and gave me the researcher's number. Piu told me the film company was Cicada Films, and she found me from the article that appeared in *Woman* magazine. Piu explained there were to be thirteen programmes in which couples reveal the secrets of successful long-term and loving relationships; couples who had to cope with traumas in their lives. She arranged to come and see us the following Sunday.

Piu arrived and had tea with us. I liked her, and we were able to talk freely with her. At the end of the interview, she said she felt we were what they were looking for, but we would have to be interviewed by the producers. It sounded very exciting; the programmes are thirteen separate half-hours on each couple. Another week passed, when we had a call from Piu to say she was coming the next evening with one of the directors. I had to work during the day, so I rushed home. Roger managed to get home early too. Piu arrived with Maureen, one of the producers and directors; all went well, and the filming will go ahead. We now have to wait for a date to film.

The next morning, at eight o'clock, Julie rang to say they were dropping off Joe on the way to the hospital; she had started labour pains. After Julie and Marcus had left, I decided not to take Joe to school; as the pains were quite frequent, I thought it would not be too long before we had some news from the hospital.

Sure enough, just after ten o'clock, I had a call from Marcus to say we could go up to the hospital as Roger and I were grandparents again. Joe and I arrived to find Barbara, Marcus's mother, there with a blue balloon, so I knew we had a grandson. Alexander, a lovely seven pounds three ounce boy had been born at ten o'clock. I immediately rang Roger and all the family; everyone was so pleased, mainly that Julie and baby were both well.

That afternoon, I went to see Mr Jones about the results of my bone scan; there was some slight deterioration, so he would like me to have another check in three months. I was pleased nothing sinister showed. Also, he was still not worried about the glands under my arm; good news.

June had started off very warm, with each day getting hotter. There are not enough hours in a day. Julie was home from hospital, and I was going to her every day, taking and collecting Joe from school. I'm still going to the hydrotherapy pool once a week which I look forward to. Visiting Diane, who has now left the Castle, as I know she gets lonely, doing the volunteer work and the information centre, painting and attending my classes, plus there is the housework, washing and cooking. It is great that I am now feeling fit to do all of these things.

At the start of July, Andrew, my manager, told me Roger and I had an invitation to be presented to Princess Alexandra, patron of the Leeds Castle Foundation, who was visiting at the end of the month. What an exciting month.

July the eleventh, we were up early as the film crew was due to arrive at eight o'clock. We were feeling nervous and excited at the same time. We had nothing to worry about, as everyone put us at ease. There was Piu, and Frances, who was the other producer and director; then there was the film crew, Damon the sound man, Richard cameraman, and Jan, a handsome young man who I thought could be a model. It was to be a long hot day, in fact one of the hottest days of the year.

I was to be filmed on my own inside the house, and Roger in the garden. Then we were to do some shots inside together. I had prepared lunch, so we could save time rather than go out. In the afternoon, I was filmed china painting, then Roger and I going through our old letters, and me working on the word processor writing this book. The day before, I had taken our bikes down to the Castle as they were going to film us riding our bikes, and Roger fishing. We all drove to the Castle, changed our clothes, and with the camera on the back of a van, we had to cycle along behind. We changed again to walk through the gardens and beside the moat and, last of all, Roger fishing with the light fading. Frances said it had been a great day, and she was satisfied all had gone well. In typical filming language, she said, 'We will wrap it up now'. With hugs and kisses, they all left. We returned home to a house that looked as if a bomb had hit it, as all the furniture had been moved around, and plants knocked over. I hope it will not show in the film.

The next day I felt completely drained; it was as if we had exposed our whole life. I could not remember what we had said, and started to worry that the film will be too intimate.

David and Nina had bought a larger house; the one-bedroom house they were living in was now too small with Luke and Lucia, so it was moving day. We were to have the children, so they stayed the night and Roger took them to their new home the next morning as I had to be at work early. I was looking after Lord and Lady Thomson for lunch. Lord Thomson is chairman of the Castle Trustees. After lunch, I rushed home to change as it was the evening we were to be presented to Princess Alexandra. There was a reception in the terrace room, and the staff being presented was placed around the room. I had met the Princess before. She usually made a visit once a year, but I had not been officially presented before, and this was the first time Roger had been invited. The group moved around the room; the Princess's husband, Sir Angus Ogilvy, who is also one of the trustees, accompanied her and other local dignitaries. Our managing director, Mr Jackson, was introducing the staff to the Princess, and we had been told to curtsy. Mr Jackson had asked me if he could tell the Princess about my illness, and I said that would be fine; I know she is patron of cancer organisations.

Before we had time to think, they were standing beside us. Mr Jackson introduced me, and I told her my position, how long I had worked at the castle, and about my illness. He then moved back for her to speak to us. I introduced Roger, and she asked what operations I had had, and treatment. She thought it amazing that I looked so well, and she spoke to Roger about the effect that cancer and the treatments had had on the family. She said she had experienced it with her mother, and she made us feel very at ease. Her husband also spoke to us. I felt very honoured, and Roger said he felt privileged. I always say he is a bit of a roundhead, and I am the royalist, but I think he has changed his mind; he felt she was very genuine and caring.

It has been a very hot summer, and the grass is desperate for water. We had a storm last night, and I thought it would clear the air, but it is still very humid. David and Nina have settled in their new home, and Nina has been busy in the garden. I have been very worried about David. He is still having trouble with eating; he's in a lot of pain and looking thin, and it worried me so much I mentioned it to Dr. Vaux when I went for my injection. I felt he should see another doctor and, with our family history, he agreed and said he would write to a consultant and ask if she would see David. He had an appointment, and she arranged for him to have some tests.

I was feeling down after reading Alma and Ray Moore's book, *Tomorrow Who Knows?* Ray had his own programme on BBC radio; he had a deep mellifluous beautiful voice, and when I heard he had cancer in the mouth and was to lose that wonderful voice it made me wonder: 'Is there a God? Why Ray's voice?' Although the book made me feel so sad, it had a humbling effect. After he was diagnosed, he worked for six months and raised £100,000 for the BBC Children in Need. He showed such courage, especially during the last weeks when this awful cancer ate away his face.

August, and it is still so hot; the trees and grass are desperate for water. I had a phone call from a journalist, Ann Kent, the health editor with a magazine called *Take a Break,* who is writing a book, *Life after Cancer*, and would like to include my experiences; I am excited about this.

At work I had been busy looking after the conference people, DPS, who had helped Roger with some good advice, when he was out of work. I supervised a nice lunch for Lord Thomson, Mr Jackson, and Mr Cleggett, the historian; we had a chat about the archaeological dig that Roger and I, and the family, did at the Abbey, and I promised to let them read our notes and see the photographs we took.

I went to a Breast Support meeting, and took Carol and Jean. We had an interesting talk about aromatherapy, with a demonstration of massage with fragrant oils to relieve tension.

September, and it was Alexander's christening; the morning started very wet. The service was at Leeds church, then we went to the Culpeper rooms at the Castle, and had drinks in the garden followed by a lovely lunch. The sun came out and we all went for a walk round the gardens; the trees in the grounds were starting to turn orange and brown, the children collected lovely shiny conkers, and we also got lost in the maze, much to the delight of the children. It had been such a nice day.

I had a message on the answer phone to call Piu from the film company.

When I rang her, she said she would like us to do some press releases, so that should be interesting.

October is Breast Cancer Care awareness month. Sadie and I went into one of the big departmental stores in town, and we had a good day chatting to people, offering leaflets and getting donations for our pink ribbons. We also went into Body Shop, who are great supporters of Breast Cancer Care, and had a stand for two weeks which was very successful. It is great having the chance to chat to people, and we had quite a few men asking us questions about breast cancer in men, and also to chat about members of their families who had been diagnosed. Sadie and I also went up to London to a conference with some interesting speakers. One, Alison McCartney, a consultant pathologist married with three children, had secondary cancer. Alison had felt very lonely when diagnosed, and she longed to talk to someone who had 'been there'. She eventually came across a reference to the work of David Spiegel, a doctor and psychiatrist who worked in Stanford, California. The research that most interested her was on the increased quality of life that women with advanced breast cancer had felt after they had attended support groups specifically designed for them. The groups met up once a week for one and half hours. Sadly Alison was to die, but there are now groups all over the country.

Two weeks later, and I was going to the launch of the UK NATIONAL BREAST CANCER COALITION. It was a very exciting day. I went up to London, arriving at eight o'clock, so stopped and had a bacon roll and coffee, then walked to the Westminster Hall which is opposite Westminster Abbey. I was the first person to arrive, and met Nancy Roberts, chair of the UK. Quite soon we were joined by around three hundred ladies, who were welcomed by Alice Mahon MP and Liz Lynne, joint chairs of the all-party Parliamentary group on breast cancer. We proceeded to the House of Commons for a photo call - three hundred women of all ages and backgrounds including celebrities - symbolizing the three hundred women who die each week in the UK from breast cancer. We all wore bibs, pinned across our tops with 1/300 printed on them, and held hands around the railings of the House of Commons. The celebrities included Sheila Hancock, Diana Moran, Lorraine Kelly, and Glenda Jackson. We all walked back to the hall in a long line, handing out leaflets. I was privileged to meet some lovely people at lunch. Some of us went into the House of Commons for questions; it was all very interesting, and had been a successful day.

November, and had a message to ring *Options* magazine. They are sending their Contributing Editor, Margaret Rook, to interview me. Three days later, Margaret arrived and we got on well. She said she will also want to speak to Roger at sometime.

Back home, I had a phone call from Ann Kent from *Take a Break* magazine; she wants to do a write-up in the magazine. She will ring sometime to talk. It was lovely to hear from her, and I look forward to doing the article.

I have been trying to get my china finished for the craft day we are having at work. November is always busy at work, with companies holding Christmas parties, plus our usual conferences, lunches, and dinners. I'm still going to the hydro pool and have much better movement with my arm.

The craft day at work was organised so the staff could put their hobbies on show. Arriving at the car park, one of the guides from the Castle came over and asked me if I knew that Judy Woodman had died. I was stunned; Judy and I wrote regularly after both of us were diagnosed with breast cancer almost at the same time. Judy was a lovely lady, and she had had an awful time, going back for surgery a number of times, and having chemo and radiotherapy. She wrote some great letters of encouragement. It had not been long ago when I had popped into the Gate House office for a chat with her, as she was working part-time.

The day went really well, with lots of lovely crafts on show; a lot of talented people work at the castle. I could not stop thinking about Judy and, after we had finished, I sat in the car and cried. She was such a nice person, who had endured operations and treatment without complaining, and I remember her saying to me, 'we are not going to let this bloody thing get us.'

I have always loved the winter. This year, it has been very mild so far; the leaves have fallen in the garden, but there are still masses of berries which the birds fight over.

This month's support meeting was interesting. Dr. Keen gave a talk about Tamoxifen, and I also met one of my clients, Lynda. It is so nice to meet a client I have supported, during diagnosis and treatment, on the telephone. Lynda is a lovely lady who is looking well, and her latest results are good.

It was Judy's funeral today; the crematorium was packed with people, some having to stand. Mr Money who was the previous curator at the

Castle, and who Judy had worked for, gave a lovely address. When we left, Mike, Judy's husband, gave us all a red rose which was a nice thought.

A few days later, it was Diane's birthday so I invited Ros C, Jan, and Joan for tea with her. We had a pleasant afternoon, and Julie called in with Alex so the ladies could see him; he is a lovely little boy.

I spent a day at the hospital having a bone scan. When I got back home, the *Options* magazine rang and asked me to send some photos to go with the article that Margaret Rook is writing. She also rang to speak to Roger, and they had a long chat.

We are now in December. Awoke to a snowy landscape; it is very cold and the birds are still fighting over the remaining berries left in the garden. My Dad used to say that, if there is an abundance of berries, it is the sign of a hard winter; it is nature's way of feeding the wildlife.

I had a lovely letter from Judy's husband, Mike, who hopes we can meet up sometime; he is just coping one day at a time at the moment.

No work today, so I made my Christmas cakes and puddings. It really feels like Christmas is almost here now. I went for the results of my scan, and saw Mr Wilson, registrar to Mr Jones, and it was good news; the scans were fine, except it showed some osteoporosis of the bones in the neck, so to keep a check on it.

David came to tell me he had also had good results from his scan; it did not show anything sinister, and his consultant thinks it is due to the stress of running his business. While he was here, he put up the satellite dish so we will be able to watch the documentary. It has been a very busy month; I do not seem to have a moment to spare, and I am feeling really well.

Awoke to whirling snowflakes and a cold frosty day. We have been gathering holly, with lots of lovely berries on it this year, and the tree and decoration look good; the presents are wrapped, and the mince pies are made. Christmas Eve, we went to the midnight service at the church. It was bright moonlight, and the trees and hedgerows looked magical with the frost. The church was full as usual. Christmas morning, Michelle and Trevor came for a drink. After they had gone, we opened our presents and had lunch; it was a nice relaxing day. Boxing Day was a bit hectic, with all the family, but we enjoyed the day. Next morning, we had a lie-in and cuddle, and Roger said how lucky we were that it had been a good year.

27

AN EXCITING YEAR

I started the year by going up to London to the Chelsea and Westminster hospital. I had written and asked if it was possible for me to go to the hospital to photocopy my medical records as I needed them for writing this book. The hospital was very helpful and obtained permission from Dr. Phillips. When I arrived, they had the notes ready, and one of the secretaries helped me sort and photocopy them. For some reason, the next day I lost all I had written on the word processor. Thank goodness I had printed it all out. I felt miserable about having messed it up, but soon started concentrating and writing again.

Ann Kent rang about the article in *Take a Break* magazine, and said that Angela, a photographer, would contact me; not long after, I had a call from Angela to say she was coming at the end of the week.

I had another trip to London to do a workshop at Channel 4 for Breast Cancer Care; it was an interesting and informative day.

The snow that arrived at Christmas was still lying, but it was a wet and windy day when Angela the photographer arrived. She took lots of photos all over the house with me reading, sewing, and painting. I find it very hard posing for photos, so I hope they will be all right.

After Angela had gone, I had a call from one of my Breast Cancer Care clients, Katie, who was one of my first clients. She was very poorly, and in a lot of pain, and she was very upset. I suggested she rang her doctor and said I would ring her back later to see how she was. When I rang back, the doctor had been and given her some medication for the pain, and she was feeling much better. Katie had been quite poorly when I had first contacted her, and I had built-up a good relationship with her and her family.

TLC, the film company, rang to ask if we would speak to the press.

They said they would arrange it and we would be hearing from them.

A few days later, it snowed very heavily overnight, and my car would not start in the morning, so I walked to work through the back entrance of the Castle. It was the most beautiful sight, and I was the first person to walk through the park since it had snowed. In the wood garden the trees had icicles hanging from them, and it was like fairy land. The whole scene in front of me was magical: the Castle surrounded by a frozen moat, everywhere so still, and just the crunch of my boots on the snow, and the birds protesting that they could not get into the water. At the end of the day, Roger came to pick me up. He drove home carefully as the roads were very icy.

Next evening, Peter Edwards from the *Star* newspaper rang and said he would like to come with Peter the photographer to take some photos, and he was going to write an article promoting the film. On February the first, I bought an *Options* magazine to read the article that Margaret Rook had written promoting the film. It made me feel very emotional, and lots of friends and family rang to say they had seen it and thought it was lovely. One day, when I was working in the Fairfax Hall at the Castle, a visitor came up to me and said, 'you are the lady in the magazine; I shall watch your film.' It had been a busy time, and the problem was I had been rushing around so much trying to fit everything in, that I was having trouble with my eating. I lose the weight so quickly, and then it is difficult to put it back on. Peter came to interview Roger and me for the *Star* newspaper, then photographer Peter arrived and took some photos. Next morning, my niece Heather phoned to say there was a photo of us in the cable magazine advertising the programme, which is to be called *True Romance* (we were not too sure about the title!)

That week, our feet did not touch the ground. I had a phone call from Tony at the writing group to say he had received the *Star* newspaper and there was a nice article about Roger and me. That evening our copy came; Peter had written a lovely piece with our photo on the front page, and he had also written some nice comments in his column. We had a phone call from our local radio station, Radio Kent, to say they would like to send a James Grice to interview us, to go out on the radio the morning the film is to be shown on Sky TV.

On Sunday morning, James arrived. He was a pleasant young man who put us at ease, and got us to talk about our lives and what effect having the cancer had on our family, and about making the film. After we

An Exciting Year

had finished, he asked if I would go on the Barbara Sturgeon programme to talk about having cancer and writing my book. I said that would be great, and he said they would phone me. The next day, the phone did not stop ringing. First the film company rang and asked if we would go on a daytime talk show called *Kilroy;* the title of the programme was *Love Conquers All*. They would also advertise the film which is to be shown the next day, Valentine's Day. The *Kilroy* programme would ring later in the day to arrange transport to the studio.

We were up early, and it was a cold wet windy morning when the taxi arrived to pick up Roger and me. At seven thirty, we arrived in good time at the studio at Teddington, which is a nice setting beside the river. Everyone made us very welcome, and the PR girls who had been speaking to me on the phone came and told us what we would have to do. Some of the items we would be discussing were: Can love conquer all difficulties? Are there any circumstances where love is not enough? Can love last (long term)? After we had had coffee, we went into the studio where there was another couple that was to be featured on one of the *True Romance* programmes. The programme is well-organised; we joined in the discussion and very quickly the programme was ending. Back in the lounge, we were given coffee and nibbles, and the PR girls thanked us. Then Robert Kilroy came in and thanked us. I asked if we could have our photograph taken with him, and he was very nice and said he would love to.

The taxi took us back home, and there was a message waiting on the answer phone from Radio Kent, asking if I would go on the programme the next week. During the evening, Roger set up the television ready to record the *True Romance* programme the following day, and also the tape for the Radio Kent interview which is on the radio early in the morning before the TV programme. On February the fourteenth, Valentine's Day, the interview with James went really well, and when it finished, they said we had made a documentary but did not say what time it would be on. Nina, Luke, Julie, and Alex arrived, and they were very excited. There was a bit of a panic when I tried to get the video working because, as Roger had gone to work, obviously he wanted us to video it. Well, after worrying what the film would be like, we thought it was great. We both seemed relaxed and, as soon as the programme had finished, we had lots of phone calls to say how good they thought it was. The writers' group sent a letter of congratulations; people rang to say they saw us on *Kilroy*, and how they had enjoyed the programme.

The next day I felt exhausted. We had had so much excitement, it had caught up with me. I looked after Alex for the day, went into work to collect my rota for next week as I had been on holiday this week, and the ladies thought Alex was a gorgeous little boy, especially Ann who fell in love with him. The ladies who had seen the programme of me thought it was lovely. Whoever I talked to about it, they said they found it very emotional and had made some of them cry, even some of the men. Jan phoned and said she had it on video and was having some of her friends for lunch to show them. I wrote some notes for Radio Kent next week. On Sunday, we went to Frances, one of the producers, for a party. We drove up to London to her house, and it was so nice to meet the other couples. We were given videos of the film, and had a lovely evening.

One morning, that week, the post had a surprise letter from Sylvia, one of the girls I had worked with when I was sixteen, and had not seen since she came to visit our first home when Julie was about six months old, over thirty years ago. She had been listening to Radio Kent, and heard a couple speaking, and recognised Roger's voice. Then she heard the reporter say it was Roger and Margaret, and we were to be featured in a film, and I was writing a book. Sylvia rang the radio station and asked when the film was being shown, and how she could buy the book. They did not know, but gave her the number of Cicada films who had made the film. But by this time, the film had been shown, and Sylvia was very determined so she rang René, another of the ladies we used to work with, who I had kept in touch with. René wrote to me and we arranged for them to come to our house for the day; also Pauline who I had not seen for years.

Michelle from Radio Kent rang to confirm I would be at the studio for the Barbara Sturgeon show the next day.

Overnight it snowed, so I thought I would catch the bus rather than drive. Then Julie, Joe, and Alex arrived and said they were going to take me. We found the studio, and everyone made us feel at ease. I was taken into the recording room where Barbara welcomed me and asked who was with me. I told her it was my daughter and her children, so she asked them in as well. Because of the weather, the programme did not run as planned; in between interviewing me, she had to give weather updates. We chatted about having cancer, writing my book, and about being a volunteer for Breast Cancer Care. She said how well I looked, and what an inspiration I was to anyone diagnosed with cancer, and I told her that is why I am writing my book. I said that we read about the

An Exciting Year

sad cases of people who die, but there are an awful lot like me who live life to the full. Barbara is a lovely lady, and made me feel very relaxed. She also spoke to Joe and asked him how he felt when I was ill. We finished with her saying that when the book is finished, and hopefully published, she would like a copy, and for me to go back to talk about it. When we arrived back home, Sadie rang to say that a lady listening, who had been diagnosed with breast cancer, had rung her to speak to a volunteer, so the programme had been worth it. Again, the response to the programme was great; I had lots of calls and letters to say how much they had enjoyed the radio programme.

We are now into March; it's very cold, but the snowdrops and crocus are out, and our window box is very pretty with a mixture of colourful miniature bulbs.

March the thirteenth, and what an awful day. A man walked into a school in Dunblane, in Scotland, and shot sixteen children and a teacher; three children are critical. I was painting, and had my portable television on when there was a news flash. It was so distressing; it showed parents, grandparents, and friends running towards the school, and the agony on their faces not knowing if their children were alive. I shall never forget it. It was so emotional, I sat and cried.

Katie, my client who is very poorly, rang to say she did not want to have her chemo (I knew the feeling). She was frightened, so we had a chat and she said she felt better for talking and would go ahead with her chemo. Later in the day, she rang and said she felt so much better she had bought the magazine *Take a Break,* and in it was an article about her Margaret, as she calls me. She said it had really cheered her up. I told her I had not seen the magazine, but would go to our local newsagent to get a copy. It was on the health page, and Ann had written a nice piece, with a photo alongside. I rang Ann and told her I had seen it and was pleased.

Easter Monday, and for once I did not have to work, so Roger and I went to a country fair. It was held at Boughton Monchelsea Place, the lovely old house with deer in the surrounding park, and next to the church where David and Nina were married. It was a cold crisp day, and the fair was busy with lots of activities: clay-shooting, many of the old crafts being demonstrated, dog trials, and the falconer with his wonderful birds, plus the usual country ware stalls. It was a nice relaxing day.

Another day at the hospital. I went for my injection for a bone scan as usual; a dye is injected into a vein, and I have to wait for it to get into my system, but, as long as I drink lots, I don't have to stay at the hospital, so I went shopping before returning.

I was up early to do baking, and had a lovely day with René, Sylvia, and Pauline who came for lunch. I had not seen Sylvia for over thirty years, and Pauline I had not seen for thirty-five years when we had all worked together. We had lots to talk about, and after lunch we watched our film. They thought it was very good.

It was injection time again. Dr. Vaux was away so I saw a new doctor at the surgery. He asked me to tell him about my history because he said I looked so well, it was amazing that I had had stomach cancer and the breast cancer, plus so much chemo. He made me feel good. Next day, I saw Dr. Keen for my check-up and the results of my bone scan. It was good news; no cancer in the bones, just the same as my last scan, a slight deterioration, so continue to have check-ups. He was pleased with me and said, looking at me you would never know I had had my problems, which was great.

One of the ladies at work, Pat, is a great fan of author Catherine Cookson, as I am too. Pat's daughter, as a surprise for her birthday, had written to Catherine and asked for a signed letter for her Mum. When Pat received it, she was so pleased she asked me to paint a mug as a thank you present for Catherine. It was fine bone china on which I painted wild flowers and butterflies. I am very proud to have a copy of a letter that Catherine sent Pat to thank her, and also me for painting the mug so beautifully.

It was a lovely warm, sunny spring day; one more day and we are going on holiday. Ever since I was a young girl, and with my love of history and archaeology, I have always wanted to go to Egypt. I am so excited as that is where we are going.

28

EGYPT

We were up very early, at three o'clock, and waited for the taxi to take us to the airport. After twenty minutes, Roger rang and found it was waiting at the wrong address. I was worried we would not get to the airport on time, but we arrived at Gatwick with time to spare. The weather could not have been better, wonderfully clear flying over the mountains of Greece. We had breakfast on the plane and arrived mid-afternoon in Paphos, Cyprus. After a coach ride for one and quarter hours through barren countryside, we saw a Roman arena and drove on to the coast road past the Moullia Rocks, supposed place of Aphrodite's birth from the foam. At last, we arrived in Limassol and could not believe it when it started to rain - the first they had had for weeks. We boarded the cruise liner and were shown to our cabin. After safety instructions, we had time to settle in and have a shower before dinner and a cabaret; a long day.

    We got up very early the next day because we wanted to go up on deck to watch us sailing into Haifa; it was five o'clock and a lovely morning with a warm breeze. After breakfast, we went by coach to Bethlehem, which was not a bit like the story book idea I had. We drove past Rachel's tomb, the shepherd's fields, and went into the church of the nativity and touched the marble slab where Jesus had lain. Then we had a panoramic drive through Jerusalem. We had really looked forward to this day, but little did we know that Muslim militants had shot dead eighteen Greek tourists outside a Cairo hotel, with fifteen more tourists injured. An Egyptian Muslim militant group had admitted that it carried out the attack with the aim of killing Israelis to avenge raids on Lebanon. Because this had happened, there was security everywhere in old Jerusalem and, as we walked through the bazaar, we were told we could not stop, and had to keep walking. We arrived at the Wailing Wall, a small section of the western buttress-wall that surrounded the Temple compound built by King Herod in the 1st century B.C. It is the holy place most venerated by the Jews who have expressed their grief over the destruction of the Temple and the long exile, and their hope for their eventual return to the Holy Land. It is because the wall was the scene of so much lamentation and weeping, that it became known by non-Jews as the Wailing Wall. We were then going to the golden-topped Dome of the Rock, a spectacular structure at the centre of the Temple of the Mount, which is the oldest completely preserved relic of early Moslem period in the world. It was built in 691 by Umayyad caliph, Abd el-Malik, to protect the rock which is at the summit of the Temple Mount, believed in Jewish tradition to be the rock of foundation, a belief which was adopted by the Moslems. It is also thought to be the rock on which Abraham was to sacrifice Isaac.

Unfortunately, someone near the Wailing Wall had left a bag which the police thought could be a bomb so we were rushed back to the coach; I was very disappointed. We drove on to the diamond centre where I am sure our guides hoped we would buy diamonds. On the way into the shop stood a man, poorly dressed, selling beads. Later, we were sitting on the coach waiting for everyone to get on, when the same man walked across the road, stood by a car, and took off his old garments to reveal trendy shirt and trousers. He put the tray of beads in the boot of the smart Audi car and drove off, much to the amusement of us watching. Driving through West Jerusalem, we saw the Knesset (parliament), the Museum of Israel, and the shrine of the Dead Sea Scrolls, before returning to the ship very tired and ready to shower and dress for dinner. After another early start, we were now in Port Said and, after much messing about with the passports, we left the ship; it was a nightmare trying to avoid the people selling their wares. At last we were on the coach; all the coaches were to go in convoy with armed soldiers and police. It was very hot, and I was amazed at what poverty there was; on the side of the roads lived families under pieces of canvas. Some had a goat tied up, but they seemed to have no possessions, and there were old men and women on donkeys riding up the wrong way on the road.

As we got nearer to the city of Cairo, things changed and it became a more affluent society. There was a lot of security when we arrived at the Cairo Museum, and once again we had been looking forward to this day. Several years ago, there was an exhibition in London with some of the treasures of Tutankhamen which we had taken the children to see, so we hoped now to see more, but this was not to be, and we were not allowed anywhere in the Museum on our own; we had to stay with the guide. In the Tutankhamen rooms, there was of course much more than we had seen in London, but we were disappointed as we had so little time there. In the afternoon, we went to the Pyramids at Giza, and again, as soon as we were off the coach, we were surrounded by people trying to sell us items of jewellery, and rides on camels, but the guide said we did not have time for that; in fact we did not even get to look in the Pyramids. The next stop was the Sphinx, and this time we were surrounded by poor children begging; it was hard not to give them anything but we were told not to by the guide. The Sphinx is spectacular, much larger than I imagined. On the way back to the ship, once again the coaches were escorted by soldiers and police. At one stage, a car tried to overtake the coaches, so all the coaches were stopped while an argument went on with the soldiers and police. Eventually we drove into a lay-by while another argument went on; most of the soldiers were only young boys waving guns about in a very undisciplined way, which was quite frightening. Back at Port Said, we had then to get by the vendors with their fake designer goods, but as we tried to pass they would stand in front of us, and in the scurry I lost Roger and had to wait for him back on ship. At last, back in our cabin, we had a shower and prepared for dinner.

    Having sailed through the night, we awoke back in Limassol at midday, and were taken to our hotel where we would spend the rest of the holiday. After settling in, we had a stroll around the town and down to the beach with Stella and Peter whom we had met on the cruise. Next day, we decided to go on one of the excursions and visited the castle where Richard the Lionheart was married; we also saw the ancient city of Curium with its wonderful mosaics and amphitheatre. We stopped for coffee, and then at a sponge factory which was interesting, and I bought some sponges for using with my china painting. In the afternoon, we lay by the pool; it was nice just to relax.

    Next morning after breakfast, we sat on the balcony waiting for Stravos from Etko which Roger's company buys a lot of its wine from. When they knew Roger was going to be staying in Limassol, we had been invited to go to the winery. We had a fascinating morning; wine-making is rather like cooking. If the basic rules are followed, the final results should be good wine, but as each cook will have an individual touch so will every wine-maker. The temperature of fermentation, the length of time it is allowed, the choice of wooden barrels or stainless steel tanks, the age and size of the casks, and the period before bottling; the wine-maker has complete control over all these factors which will influence the character of the finished wine. So after our tour, we were invited to taste the wines, then given a box of the wines we liked and driven back to our hotel, with an invitation to go out to dinner with Stravos and his wife the next evening.

After lunch, we walked around the old town, buying our presents to take home, and then met up with Stella and Peter to have dinner.

Stravos and his wife collected us from the hotel, the following evening, and we drove up into the mountains to a typical Greek Cypriot restaurant; it was full of local people, with only two waiters who were rushing around carrying plates all up their arms. We had a meze; this is small dishes to start, but they get bigger with each course until we each had a whole fish, followed by a dessert of little pastries filled with nuts and honey. It was very difficult for me not having a stomach, so I nibbled a little from each course. I don't know why I find it so difficult to tell people the first time I meet them that I have had my stomach removed, and have a problem with eating; it would be so much easier if I did. We had a very nice evening. It was fascinating just watching everyone; some tables singing, others getting up and dancing. Back at the hotel, within half an hour I was in the bathroom as usual; my body did not like what I had eaten.

On our last day, we met up with Stella and Peter to have our usual coffee and pancakes together before leaving for the airport. Phaphos airport is situated near the beach, so as there was a delay with our flight we sat on the beach until we were ready to leave. On arriving at Gatwick, we said our goodbyes to Stella and Peter, exchanging addresses to keep in touch.

We arrived home on the Wednesday. I had tried not to think too much about doing an abseil on Sunday for Beat Breast Cancer Imperial Cancer Research. As I do not like heights, I was beginning to wonder what made me say I would do it, but when people knew I was, and what it was for, they were eager to sponsor me, so this gave me encouragement. I went to the Breast Cancer support meeting, and Pam the breast care nurse told the ladies, who donated £24 which was great.

Sunday April 28th. It is the abseil today; a very warm and still day, thank goodness. I did not sleep too well, and could not eat anything because I felt sick.

At last it was time to go. We arrived at the library tower at Springfield in Maidstone, and I was told then that this was the highest building in the town - and it looked it! Lots of family and friends came to support me, and Roger looked rather worried. I went to sign in, and the girl there said I could go up for a trial run if I wanted. I said no way, once would be enough. The instructors were from the army, and at last they said I could go up. Arriving at the top, I realised just how high it was when the soldiers said to wave to my family and friends, and when I looked over they were so small I could not see who was who. Then they were putting on me the harness, helmet, and gloves. Around the top of the tower were railings, so the first task was to get over them. Unfortunately, as I am only five foot one, I could not get over, so a chair was brought for me to climb on. I was holding on for dear life, then I was over and the solider said I would have to let go of the railings and hold the rope. It took all my courage to let go; I seemed suspended in the air so they told me to put my feet onto the wall and sort of walk down. It felt as if I was going down forever. I could then hear cheering, and I thought I had done it, and glanced down only to see what looked like matchbox toy cars. I still had a long way to go, but at last I heard the soldiers saying I had done it. I touched the ground in a bit of a trance, but everyone was clapping and cheering, Roger was kissing me, and people were taking photos. Back home we watched the video that David had taken, and I felt sick again. I could not believe I had actually done it.

Julie's mother-in-law, Barbara, told a businessman friend that I had done the abseil so he sent me £1,000 pounds donation; in all I had raised £1,700.95. The great thing was that the businessman then sent £1,000 for the next two years, so doing the abseil had raised £3,700.95 which I was so pleased about. After the abseil, my body was not too pleased; for the next few days I felt I had pulled all my insides and my back. I think it was because I had been so tense when doing the abseil.

May had a letter from the journalist Margaret Rook to say there was a nice letter in *Options* magazine from a lady who had read the article about us.

My fifty-sixth birthday was a good day to begin with. Roger and I went out for a meal, but when we came home there was a message to say one of his colleagues, who had been diagnosed with breast cancer, had died. A week later, Nina's Mum's partner had been diagnosed with bowel cancer. I really wanted to hear some good news; I just think how lucky I have been.

I went for my regular endoscope. Now Dr. Stevens has retired, I see his successor, a pleasant young man. He told Roger that all looked well, and unless I have any problems he would see me in a year. So, that was good news. As usual, I could not stay awake on the way home, and next morning had a sore throat; it took two days to feel my self again.

June went to the support meeting; it was great to see so many ladies who are looking fit and well and living life to the full.

The weather was good, and very hot. It was Alex's first birthday and, after his party, we all went down to see the hot air balloons at the castle. As usual, I had to work, starting at five o'clock in the morning; this is because they fly in the morning and evening, weather permitting. It is a wonderful sight - balloons of all descriptions floating over the castle, and their reflections in the moat, some landing in the moat, and as they fly off they are chased by vintage cars to where they land, so the cars can bring the passengers back to the Castle. At the end, the cars all drive around the croquet lawn in front of the Castle. After I finished work, I went to join the birthday party. The children had a wonderful time watching all the activities; it was a lovely end to Alex's first birthday.

Journalist Margaret Rook rang to ask if she could write an article about us for the *Mail on Sunday* magazine; it sounded quite exciting, and she would ring again to discuss it.

My lovely client, Katie, rang to say she was having lots of problems. She was coming near to us to visit relatives and asked if she could call round to see me. I said I would love to meet her, but unfortunately they got lost and could not find us. Another client rang who said she is having a bad time; she has a large family, some still young, and is naturally worried about them.

Ann Kent sent me a signed copy of her book *Life After Cancer*. She had dedicated it to all of us who had shared our experiences with her, which I thought was a lovely thing to do.

During the first week in July, we went with Michelle and Trevor to the open-air concert at the Castle. The concerts are held on two weekends; we have to work one, and are given tickets for the next. We arrive early to get a good picnic area, then set up our tables and chairs, and have nibbles and champagne. Trevor usually makes the main course, and I do dessert. Everything else we share, salad, bread, cheese, and of course wine. I drive so the others can have a drink.

The atmosphere is wonderful. As soon as the gates open, everyone rushes through the castle grounds to where the stage for the orchestra is situated with the castle in the background. Picnic hampers, and chairs and tables with cloths and candelabras are set up. During the afternoon, the orchestra practices, and it is time to sit and watch the people; it can be quite entertaining. The celebrated conductor, Carl Davis, conducts with famous orchestras like the Royal Liverpool Philharmonic, together with notable soloists. Lots of people dress up in fancy dress, or dinner suits and evening dresses, and a variety of hats. As the evening draws in, all the tables light their candles; it is a wonderful sight with the Castle floodlit. The concert ends with my favourite hymn, *Jerusalem*, and *Rule Britannia*, and the *1812 Overture* being performed with fireworks and cannon of the Royal Artillery, and a sea of waving flags - a sight not to forget.

At the end of July, we decided to have a week's holiday so we took our little caravan to a site up on the downs. It is so picturesque, surrounded by woods and fields and views of the downs, and in the early evening the rabbits run and jump around the caravans. The first night we had the most terrible storm, but we seemed safe and snug. The next morning was clear and very hot; we had two days just relaxing, reading, and walking. We went into the local village to buy hot bread, pastries, and cakes, and to look in the antique shops. Some evenings, we walked along the lanes and had a drink in the little country pub. We did not want to go home; it had been a lovely relaxing week with good weather.

The first thing I did, when we arrived home, was to ring my client, Katie. I spoke to her husband first, and he said she may only have weeks to live; I was so upset. I rang the next day and spoke to Katie; she asked if I would go and visit her. I said I would in two days, on my days off from work. The next day, I supervised a wedding and did not finish work until twenty past two in the morning, then had to be up to start at seven o'clock the next morning. I felt worn out.

My day visiting Katie was rather hectic. I was going by train, but as I was leaving, Julie arrived and said she would drive me as it was going to take about an hour by train. We drove onto the motorway, and I do not know where we went wrong, but we ended up going to Dover instead of London. We came off the motorway, and Julie took me to the railway station. I arrived at Katie's to find her very poorly, but she was very pleased to see me, as was her husband whom I had spoken to quite a lot on the phone. Katie said she hurt so much, and asked if I would sit on the bed and hold her. When it was time for me to leave, Katie asked if I would visit again; I said I would. I arrived home at six-thirty, feeling very emotional. Roger suggested we went out for a meal as it was late for me to start cooking, which I was thankful for.

Next day, I was at work again by seven o'clock in the morning, and did not get home until seven thirty. I rang Katie and spoke to one of her daughters; she said Katie had been taken into hospital after I left. Next day, I had to work a double; went in at eleven o'clock and finished at three the next morning. How I got up the next day, I do not know, but after rushing around preparing dinner and cleaning, I went into work to supervise a wedding. I had a nice day, but it was another late night, and then had two days off.

I had an exciting day when journalist Margaret Rook came to do the interview for the *Mail on Sunday;* she said six million people read the paper (thought, that's a bit frightening). We had a nice day, and I felt the interview went well; in the afternoon I drove Margaret back to the station.

I rang Katie again but she is still in hospital.

August seemed to have been so busy, working long hours and doing doubles; that is a function during the day, then staying on to do another in the evening. I like to have order at home, as well as having the grandchildren which I love, and have also been picking Joe up from school and taking him to scouts. Roger usually picks him up when he has finished, and takes him home. Sometimes he stays with us and I drop him at school next morning. I am also trying to do my writing and painting which I find so relaxing, plus fitting in the volunteer work. Went for my B12 injection, and Dr. Vaux asked me how much work I had been doing. I said quite a lot, and he said how much, and when I told him he said I must cut down.

At the end of August, I had a day off. Before Roger went to work, he brought me a cup of tea and the newspaper in bed. I opened it to see *Life After Cancer* by Ann Kent, then I saw a photo of me; it was an article promoting Ann's book in which I had shared my experiences. It was a nice piece, with some of the other people who were in the book. Later I had a phone call from Margaret, the journalist, whom I had done the interview with for the *Mail On Sunday* supplement, saying that, now I had been in the *Daily Mail*, they would not do the other article. She was very cross, saying I should have told her I was doing that article with Ann. I tried to explain I did not know it was going in the *Mail*. I said Ann had asked if I would mind promoting the book, and I had said yes, not expecting it was going in a daily newspaper. I was really upset as I was looking forward to Margaret's article because it was not so much medical as how I felt having cancer and how it changed my life. I felt it would be an inspiration to others who had been diagnosed with cancer. The next day I was still worrying about Margaret's reaction, and decided I would have to write to her. I really wanted her to know how I felt, so I wrote and explained that I really did not know about the article. I had no idea about the world of journalism and I hoped we would stay friends. Margaret answered my letter, and understood I had been naive.

I went to the Breast Cancer Support group meeting. Although I have had friends and a client die of cancer, we always hear about the people who die but there are an awful lot of us who do survive, and going to the support group makes you realise this. The trouble is, in newspapers and on television, it seems to make more news when someone dies, particularly a personality, than if they survive. This was one of the reasons I wanted to do Margaret's article.

Sadie and I went to Breast Cancer Care head office in London for a days training in telephone skills; a long day but gained a lot from it.

At the end of that week, H.R.H The Duke of Kent was visiting the castle and I was asked to serve tea. It was held in one of the cottages. Michelle and I served sandwiches, cakes, and tea; our curator said we would need the silver teapot from the Castle, and this was brought over. He proceeded to explain how to make and serve the tea; we both smiled at each other (I think we knew what we were doing.) The Duke did not eat or drink anything, but when he left he thanked Michelle and me for a lovely tea!

I arrived home from work to find a message on the answer phone asking if I would ring Paul, Katie's husband. Katie had died. It was such a blow; we had become very close. I spoke to her daughter, and she asked if I would go to the funeral. She would let me know when it would take place.

I travelled by train to Katie's funeral, and, after the service, two ladies asked me if I was the Breast Cancer Care volunteer Katie had told them about. They were from the local support group, and kindly gave me a lift back to the station. I arrived back in time to go to work although I really did not feel like going in. Katie had been one of my first clients, and I was finding it hard to cope with her dying.

Three weeks later, I attended a Breast Cancer Care Loss and Bereavement course which helped me learn skills, knowledge, and understanding, with an exploration of my thoughts and feelings about death.

The weather had turned very cold, and the mornings remind me of hop-picking days.

It has been four years since my last operation. Today I am lucky to be so fit and well, especially as eating is so difficult and trying to keep on weight.

During the summer, we had decided to have some bantams I have always loved chickens; they are such contented birds, scratching and clucking, and the bantams rewarded us with eggs, and also chicks. The grandchildren loved them.

In October, Sadie and I went for a training course on relationships at Harrogate. Richard and Sandy drove us to the station. We went to London, then to York, and finally arrived in Harrogate. We were worn out, so after meeting the other ladies on the course at dinner, we all decided to go to bed. We awoke to a sunny day; it was quite an intensive morning, followed by a quick lunch, so we decided to walk into the town. We were in a hotel on the edge of a park. I love Harrogate; it is full of flowers in pots and hanging baskets, lovely shops, and the famous Betty's tea rooms. One of my china suppliers is in the town; as I normally have to order from their catalogue without actually seeing the china, it was a treat to go to the shop. Then it was back to the hotel for more training in the afternoon. We worked until three thirty the next day, and then had the long journey home, arriving at eleven thirty.

Sadie rang to say that TVS, our local television station, wanted to interview us. They were doing an item on how much stress is caused to breast cancer patients waiting for results. A machine had been invented that gives instance diagnosis. We were to say what a difference it would have made to us if we had not had to wait; I feel once you know, you can cope with the diagnosis, it is the not knowing which is hard. The studio rang me to say they would film us at Sadie's house in two day's time. Arriving at Sadie's to do the filming, I felt a bit nervous but it seemed to go well. I went home to watch, as it was to go out on the six o'clock local news health slot, but it didn't, and was shown the following week.

Back home after the filming, I found my little white bantam had died. I think it had got wet. They do not like the wet weather, and it had rained most of the week.

I went for my check-up at Mr Jones's clinic, and saw one of the registrars. He obviously had not checked my notes, because after examining my breasts and under my arms, he suddenly poked me where my scar is for my stomach operation, and said, 'what is all this then?' I felt like saying, 'well, if you had read my notes, you would know.' After explaining about the stomach cancer, he said I was very lucky to have come through it and the other operations, and look so well. He asked who was checking me for it, and I said, since the breast cancer, usually at this clinic when I came for my breast check. I also said that I had regular endoscopes, and my G.P. when I went for my B12 injection. He next said he thought I should come off the Tamoxifen; I explained that I was also on HRT, which I had already told him, and that Dr. Phillips and Mr Jones had decided I should stay on both. He said we had better stay with what they had advised and go back in six months. I had hoped it would be a year as it is now four years since the breast operation.

It is now December, and the days just fly by. We are very busy at work so I have been working long hours. I went for my B12 injection; Dr. Vaux said he hoped I hadn't been overworking. Also went for my check-up with my oncology consultant, Dr. Keen, and he was very pleased with me and told me to go back in six months. I cannot believe another year has nearly gone.

The weekend before Christmas, I had the Sunday off so Roger and I wrapped the last of the presents. It is cold, windy, and we have had snow, so perhaps it will be a white Christmas.

Christmas Eve, and it was very cold when we walked to the floodlit church for the midnight service. Christmas Day was quite hectic with the family. Boxing Day we had on our own. New Year's Eve, and it snowed all morning. Roger was worried about me going to work and, because we live on a hill, it is always difficult to get up onto the main road, but I managed it. The roads were dreadful, with cars stuck in the snow drifts, and part of the way I had to drive on the wrong side of the road. At last I arrived at the Castle and it was still snowing. We had a meeting because we thought we may have to cancel the evening, but guests started to ring in to say they were still going to try to get to the Castle. The staff was told we could stay the night, as there was spare bedrooms, so I rang Roger. He thought it was a very good idea, as he was worried at the thought of me driving home at four o'clock in the morning. The evening went really well, and when I got up the next morning it had stopped snowing. I drove through the grounds to go home, and as usual it was a wonderful sight, with the Castle surrounded by the frozen moat, and the ducks and swans skidding on the ice. What a lovely start to the New Year.

29

A FULL YEAR

I arrived home at about ten thirty after staying the night. It had been a long night going in at two o'clock the previous afternoon and working until four o'clock the next morning. The roads were treacherous with snow and ice, and I had to crawl home. I was so exhausted that I slept the rest of the day; Roger cooked dinner and said I would make myself ill if I kept working like this.

January the tenth was our thirty eighth wedding anniversary, and we still have the snow. It was the staff party and, as usual, we went with Michelle and Trevor. It was a good evening; we arrived home around two o'clock. The next morning I had a phone call asking if I could go into work; the supervisor who should have been on duty was ill.

I went for a mammogram as Roger said he could feel a tiny pea-size lump in my breast. I couldn't feel it, but it was safer to have it checked. My first thought was, 'hell, not again.' The mammogram was clear, thank goodness.

Whilst china painting one day, with my little TV on, they announced they were going to be showing a series of programmes titled *True Romance*; this was the title of our programme. I rang Maureen, one of the producers from Cicada films, and she explained that the BBC was going to show selected episodes although she had not known about it until her daughter had phoned her at the office and yelled down the phone, 'Mum, one of your programmes is on telly now.' Maureen said she would send us a list showing when our programme would be aired.

It was time for my injection. Dr. Vaux was on holiday so I saw a new doctor at the surgery who, after reading my notes, said it was amazing how I had come through everything, and after taking my blood pressure, said it was like a teenager's. I felt quite chuffed by this.

February, and today our film was shown on BBC. It was ten minutes shorter than the original, which was good; they had cut out the only bits we did not like. It was very emotional. Once again it looked as if the book was finished, and the BBC had people ringing in to ask where they could buy it. I had a call from Cicada films to say the BBC had had calls from ladies wanting to talk to me so I said I would. One was an American lady who was visiting a relative with cancer, and another lady from California, visiting her sister who had cancer, said she was so touched by the film and wanted to buy the book. I had to explain to everyone I spoke to that the book was not finished. The California lady gave me her telephone number to ring her when it was finished. Once again, lots of family and friends rang. One was Nat who had been one of my managers at the Castle, and had now moved to Oxford. I missed her at work; she was great fun, and she thought the programme was great. The next morning, I had more calls from people; one a doctor who said I was an inspiration to people who had cancer. After the last call, I stood in the kitchen and had a cry; I was so pleased we did the film as it had had such a good effect. Four days later, I had a phone call from Sandy, the lady from California, to say she was leaving for home and wanted to just have a chat before she left, which was lovely. I also had a call from Mr Herbert who had been my form teacher when I was at school; he had seen the programme. Heather, my niece, thought Roger should be the next Parkinson because he had come over so well on the film.

March, and a message to say my brother Ted had had an accident on his bike; he was knocked over but could not remember anything about the accident. I didn't think he looked too good, and he may have broken a bone in his neck. By the end of the month, he was home and improving.

I do get tired, but I am now working full-time. In May, I went for my endoscope; I had lost some weight and had been having quite a lot of pain. Dr. Bird said I had a sore place, but medication should heal it. He said if the problem persists, he will see me again. The endoscope must have rubbed my throat; because it was so sore, eating was difficult. Four days later and I was still having trouble speaking.

At the beginning of June, I went for my check-up with Mr Jones. He was pleased with me; he could still feel the glands but was not worried and told me to go back in six months. As I was dressing, I overheard a conversation Mr Jones was having with a colleague; he referred to a Diana Spencer, and was discussing her case, which it did not sound too good. As

A Full Year

I knew a Diana Spencer at work, I was rather worried. I did not see her often; she worked only the occasional evening as she had two little boys. When I went into work that evening, I made some discreet enquiries; no-one had seen her but that was not unusual. So I hoped it was not her. A few days later at work, I was told Diana had been diagnosed with breast cancer. Of course I did not tell anyone what I had heard at the hospital. The next day she phoned me. I had been thinking so much about her because her Mum had been diagnosed with cancer and died last year. Diana had phoned me when her Mum was really poorly and said she wanted someone to talk to as she was finding it so hard - the thought of losing her Mum. Diana was so attractive, tall slim with long blonde hair, but when she phoned me about her own cancer, I had to tell her we were going on holiday in two days, so would ring her as soon as we arrived back home.

It had been such a rush, as I had worked the last six days. One of the other supervisors had gone sick so I had to work extra time, on top of trying to do the housework, washing, getting my painting orders finished etc. I was so pleased we were going on holiday. I took my canary, Sunny Delight, over to my other friend Diane to look after; she loves birds. Then I took the bantams to Julie. Woody, one of the bantams, had laid her fiftieth egg, and we also had some chicks. Bantam eggs make wonderful cakes; they are saffron yellow, and so light, plus I find I can digest them well. My body doesn't like chicken eggs very much.

I had been to Dr. Vaux for my injection, and he said the weight loss, sickness, and tiredness was due to the hours I was working, so he did advise me to cut down. Roger said he agreed, so I asked if I could work two or three days or nights. Andrew, my manager, said it was fine to do that, but if anyone was sick I would have to step in, so hopefully after our holiday this will happen.

30

BACK TO SPAIN

At last we were on the coach going to Dover. I had not arrived home until two o'clock in the morning from work, and then had to pack and fit in a hairdressing appointment this morning, so as soon as I was on the coach I slept until we arrived at Dover. On the ferry, we went for a meal in the restaurant, and at last I felt we were able to relax. Off the ferry in France, we drove through the night, and when we awoke, we were in Spain. We stopped to wash and have breakfast, arriving at our hotel at lunch time. We are staying in Tossa De Mar, the lovely fishing town where we stayed in 1995. This time we are in a different hotel, large rooms with a balcony overlooking the local nursery school. The children walk past the hotel in a long line, attached at the wrist by rope so no-one gets lost. They are so sweet, so small, and some only just walking; they wave to us as they pass. We shower and unpack before going to walk around the town, hoping it has not become commercialised. We find it is just the same; beautiful golden, clean beaches, and flowers everywhere. It was festival time in Tossa, and the local people celebrate the blessing of the boats. That evening we meet Beryl and Arthur, the couple we are to share a table with. It is a second marriage for them both; Beryl's first husband had a heart attack when he was forty, and died. They are a nice couple.

    Some days, we walked up to the old castle, and would have a lazy lunch sitting outside our favourite restaurant while we drank wine and ate sardines. We went on some lovely walks up into the hills, where we would suddenly turn a corner and find a field of sunflowers. We stopped for our picnic lunch while admiring the wonderful views. A day in Barcelona was the highlight for me. After our first visit, I fell totally in love with the city and the architecture, and the work of the great artist Gaudi is wonderful. I always say, if ever I become rich I will have a holiday there and stay in one of the beautiful hotels. We went to the cathedral where the Spanish Princess is getting married, and everywhere there were preparations for the wedding.

Back in Tossa, the local people entertained us with traditional dancing in the town square. We also followed the procession of fishermen and clergy carrying religious objects down to the beach to bless the boats. I went into the local church to light a candle for Diana. Another evening we went to an open air concert held in the excavated Roman Villa; held in candlelight and truly magical.

One evening, we watched Brazilian dancers at the hotel, and another night, the wonderful Flamenco dancers and guitar players. After dinner, we usually went for a walk to the town square where there was music, dancing, and artists drawing portraits, so I had mine done. Roger thought it was a good likeness. All too soon we were on the way home, but we had had a super holiday.

We had only been home for five minutes when I had a phone call from Michelle at work to say I had to be in work at seven o'clock the next morning. I finished at four o'clock, so as soon as I was home I rang Diana, my young friend who had been diagnosed with the breast cancer, to see how she was; she is finding it hard and so is her husband. I also rang my other clients; one is Lin, who had a mastectomy, who has been trying to decide if she should have a reconstruction, but she has not made up her mind; she needs more time to think about it. All my clients are doing well at the moment.

Sadie and I went to London to attend the C4Ward Forum which was launched following a Channel 4 programme and workshop, to explore how the needs of women with secondary breast cancer, and their partners and families, could best be served. Following the workshop, an on-going forum was established, consisting of women living with primary or secondary breast cancer, health professionals, and representatives from leading cancer charities such as CancerLink and CancerBACUP, and others who wish to influence and support the agenda. It was an informative and interesting day.

I spent another day in London at Breast Cancer Care, for training this time. It was about fund-raising and talking to the media, and was a good day.

Julie's father-in-law, Ken, had asked me if I would give a talk at one of his dinners. Well, having never done anything like that, I was a bit stressed.

He said it would be for about half an hour, so I prepared my talk. The trouble was that, to read my notes, I would have to hold it up in front of me to see it, so I had to learn it off by heart. Roger and I had been invited to have dinner with the group first. The chairman said they were running a bit late so could I shorten my talk. I did not know how I could, but thought: I just hope I do not overrun. I was quite terrified when I stood up to speak, but fortunately, once I started, I was fine. The chairman said he wanted me to call the talk, 'My Wonderful Life'. I was not too sure about that at first, but after thinking about it, I have had a wonderful life, and the talk went well. Roger said he felt quite emotional.

In August, I picked up Julie, Joe, and Alex, and we drove to Rochester to meet Nina, Luke, and Lucia. We were going to see David and a business friend, Mark, depart for Romania. The local press and TV were there also. They were taking a van with donations of clothes, shoes, and toys to children in an orphanage in the town of Deva, located in the Transylvanian mountains. The journey to Romania was through Belgium, Germany, Austria, and Hungary, and when they arrived back home they said they had to trade two hundred cigarettes and a bottle of Scotch for the papers they needed in Hungary and Romania. There were sixty-five orphans aged between three and fourteen. Mark and David found it heartrending and tragic to see the children who have nothing. Mark had made a similar trip some time ago after seeing the plight of the children on TV; they only had one toilet and shower, but with the help of another organisation, Task Force Romania, and Mark, they now had six toilets and showers. With winter coming, it was essential to get them warm clothes and shoes and toys for Christmas. After they left, we had a worrying two weeks when Nina phoned to say she had seen on the news that two aid workers had been killed near where David and Mark were. Eventually the killers were caught, but we were still worried until they arrived home safely.

Time again for my check-up at oncology with Dr. Keen. He was very pleased with me, and said, as I am still under Mr Jones, I need not see him again, so that was good news. Sometimes I feel as if the hospital appointments never end.

It has been very hot so the family decided to have one of our family days out. We all packed picnics and went to our local park where there is a miniature railway which the children can ride on, and we watched the boats on the lake and had a game of rounders. It was a lovely relaxing day.

Julie told me Marcus had a surprise for me; we were going to Paris on the Eurostar through the Channel Tunnel. When Richard knew, he asked if Sandy could go with us for her birthday, but it was to be a surprise. We also asked Nina but she couldn't go. I was up at five o'clock to be ready, and Richard took us to Ashford, the Eurostar station. Sandy did not know where we were going until we were at the station and they announced the next train was for Paris. We were served a lovely breakfast on the train, and in no time at all we were in Paris. Thank goodness Sandy can speak French, but we did get a bit lost to start with; having decided to walk from the station, we found ourselves in a cosmopolitan area with shops and market stalls. Then at last we could see Sacre Coeur, which is perched atop Montmartre Hill, so we found our way to the bottom of the two hundred and thirty-four spiralling steps, and slowly made our way to the top. The wonderful Basilica of the Sacred Heart was built from contributions pledged by Parisian Catholics as an act of contrition after the humiliating Franco-Prussian war of 1870-71. It was consecrated in 1919. Arriving at the top of the steps, we had the most wonderful panoramic view of the city. The inside of the church was as stunning as the outside, and as always I like to light a candle, as did Julie and Sandy. We walked down to Montmartre which is full of cafés, restaurants, and artists painting portraits and Parisian views. I could have stayed here all day. We took a taxi as the girls wanted to shop. Then we felt it was time to eat, and found a restaurant in a tree-lined avenue. After lunch, more walking, and we passed a park with men playing boules, the game not unlike lawn bowls but played with heavy metal balls on a sandy pitch. All too soon we were back in a taxi heading for the station. On the Eurostar, we were served a super dinner, and too much wine!

We had had a great day. It was a day I would never forget, as the day we had been to Paris, Princess Diana had died in a car accident. Roger has an alarm clock with a radio that comes on to wake us. After our day in Paris, I was worn out so I had slept really well, and was woken by a voice saying that Princess Diana had been killed in an accident in Paris. She was with her friend, Dodi Fayed, who also died; he was the son of Mr Al Fayed who owns Harrods. The only person to survive was Lady Diana's bodyguard, Trevor Rees-Jones. When I realised I was awake and not dreaming, I ran downstairs to put on the television and it was true. All day they were giving reports of what had happened. It was as if the whole world was in shock. Every day brought more news and pictures; it was so sad to see Prince William and Harry going to look at the oceans of flowers

Back to Spain

that people from all walks of life had laid outside Buckingham and Kensington Palaces.

The day of the funeral was one of the saddest I have experienced; more than a million people assembled to watch the cortege carrying the Princess's coffin through the streets to Westminster Abbey. Roger and I watched the scenes on the television; the music was wonderful, Mendelssohn, Bach, and Dvorak. Elgar's Nimrod brought even more tears. One of the most heart-rending moments was when I saw on the casket a posy of white rosebuds from Prince Harry with the word 'Mummy' written in a childish hand, a bouquet of white tulips, and another of white lilies, her favourite flower, from Prince William and her brother Charles. After readings from Princess Diana's sisters, Elton John, accompanying himself on the piano, sang *Candle in the Wind*. He struggled with his emotions but managed to get through it. Earl Spencer, her brother, gave a powerful but beautiful address and, when he had finished, the crowds outside and in the parks where enormous TV screens had been erected, began to applaud. As we watched we could hear this, and as it drifted into the Abbey, the congregation joined in. The Princess was buried on an island in the centre of an ornamental lake in the grounds of Althorp House, the Spencer family home. After leaving the Abbey, the hearse was showered with flowers, and at one stage they had to stop to clear the windscreen. Just five days after Diana's death, a lady whom she said had inspired her and was her friend, also died; Mother Teresa. At a requiem Mass for Diana, Cardinal Hume said, 'Two of the best known and loved women in the world have died within one week; they had much in common, they were friends and they were concerned with helping the poor.'

Three days later, Julie rang and said, 'Shall we go up to London to see the flowers?' Joe and Alex enjoyed the train ride. We walked from Westminster Abbey to Buckingham Palace to Kensington Palace; it was an amazing sight and it made you wonder if there were any flowers left. We arrived back tired, but glad we had made the journey - something we and the boys would not forget.

The next weekend, Nina rang and asked if we would like to watch Lucia doing her dancing exam. She does ballroom and modern, and we love watching the boys and girls; they are all so talented. We enjoyed the afternoon. Lucia already had many certificates and trophies as she had been dancing since she was three and half.

September the sixteenth, and it is five years since my last operation.

Once again I have recovered really well from the operation, and the chemo and radiotherapy. My hair has grown back, but not curly this time. The last time, although I had straight hair before I lost it, when it grew, it was very curly; it is just great to have hair again, curly or not. I still have my problems with eating, and spend a lot of time in the bathroom especially if we have been out. Sometimes the pains are really intense and I feel a bit frightened, and think, 'has the cancer returned?' It is natural that I would have some concerns, but I think it is something I have to live with due to not having the stomach.

November, and we are as usual very busy at work, with lots of late nights. Roger asked what had happened to cutting down! I have been doing all the usual Christmas preparations and baking. I have had new clients from Breast Cancer Care, whom I enjoy talking to and visiting, and I speak frequently to Diana, sometimes taking her to the doctors. She is very poorly, and finding the treatment hard going, but does not complain.

Christmas Eve, and I went to work supervising our friend Trevor's company's Christmas lunch which the staff enjoys doing. The guests left after lunch, so not too late finishing. Later, Trevor and Michelle came for supper, and Roger and I went to midnight service. We had had snow at the beginning of December, but it was now cold with a hard frost. I always put the turkey in to cook when we come back from church, and leave it in all night. On Christmas morning I got up to check it was okay and, there in the lounge, was a writing desk that I had admired. Roger had bought it for me, and Rose next door had kept it in her house so Roger could surprise me. We had a lovely day on our own. Boxing Day was more hectic, with all the family.

I had a nice surprise when Kate and Sam, my friends who had been living in Hong Kong, came to visit us with their boys; they are a lovely family.

New Year's Eve, and thank goodness the weather is better than last year when we had so much snow I had stayed overnight at the Castle. I went in as usual at two o'clock as we always have a lot of preparation. A lot of the guests enjoy it so much they come back each year. The evening went really well, with the piper piping in the New Year, and the chef, Gerry, carrying the haggis around the room, and Andrew, our Scottish manager attired in his kilt, making a speech. As the guests left, they said it had been a super evening. I arrived home just before three o'clock in the morning.

31

A HORRIBLE YEAR

The year started very wet. One week into January and it had been raining almost continuously since Christmas.

Diana rang; she was starting her radiotherapy.

I had some good news; Valerie-Joan and Sid had become grandparents again. Their daughter-in-law, Hayley, had had a little girl.

Once again, it is our wedding anniversary; thirty-nine years. Sometimes I feel as if Roger is part of me; we seem to know what the other one is feeling and thinking.

Andrew, my manager, said he was pleased how the New Year's function had gone; there had been lots of compliments, and I was to supervise a function for Princess Anne, so I am looking forward to that.

I rang Diana, and spoke to her mother-in-law; Diana had been taken into hospital, but her mother-in-law said she will ring me to let me know what is happening. A horrible start to the next day when Phil phoned; Diana's cancer is now terminal, and he would like to come for a chat, so we arranged a day next week.

Roger has been having problems with his hands; the doctor has arranged for him to see a consultant. David had the same problem, and had an operation which was successful.

It is nearly the end of the month already. I had two new clients to speak to this week; sometimes one phone call is enough to answer any worries or information the ladies need.

I was feeling a bit stressed as Phil, Diana's husband, was coming for a chat. I find it easy to talk to lady clients, but this would be the first man so I was a bit apprehensive. I didn't know Phil until Diana became ill. I had seen him at the staff parties at the Castle, and thought of him as very sporty and macho. When he arrived, we got on well and arranged to talk again. Sometimes it is easier for the families and friends of people who have been diagnosed, to talk to someone outside the family.

It was my lovely friend Joan's birthday, so I made her a cake and took it round on my way to work. I had to go in for a briefing for Princess Anne's visit. It was an interesting afternoon; with royal visits there is so much security and planning. Joan said she would want to know all about the function next time I saw her.

At the monthly support meeting, a young lady came and spoke to me. She said she was Trudie, and did I remember her? She had lived in a house at the bottom of our garden when we lived in Leeds, and gone to school with David and Julie. She told me she had been diagnosed with breast cancer at thirty; now, two years on, she is doing well and is married with two young children. We are having a fashion show at the support group, and some of us are going to model; that should be fun.

We had a really nice evening when Hywel and Pat Herbert came for dinner; we had lots to talk about as our interests are the same. He had been my form and art teacher at school, and we have kept in touch over the years. I had gone to his china painting classes when I had finished my chemo. They live in the village of Detling where I was born.

At the end of February, I had a phone call from Diana asking if I would take her to the doctors; the poor girl is very overweight with the treatment, and is having trouble walking. It was also an opportunity to have a chat about her trip to Lourdes. When I was having the chemo for my stomach cancer, we parked a little way from the Westminster hospital and had to walk past a tourist office advertising trips to Lourdes. I so wanted to go; I had read about Bernadette Soubirous, a fourteen-year-old peasant girl who saw the Virgin Mary in a series of visions in a grotto near the town. Bernadette had become a nun and was canonized as St. Bernadette in 1933. These events set Lourdes on the path to becoming one of the world's most important pilgrimage sites; many sick people go there seeking cures. For people of the Catholic faith, it is sacred; a place as Mecca is for Muslims, the Ganges for Hindus, and the Wailing Wall in Jerusalem for Jews. Each time we passed the offices, I looked at the posters advertising the trips, but at the time, with Roger having so much time off work taking me to hospital, and the cost of petrol, I could only look as I knew we could not afford to go. Roger and I have talked about it since I have been well, and if we had made the trip, would I have thought I was well due to going there? I think I probably would.

A Horrible Year

Diana felt it had helped her. It was not quite what she had expected; it was quite gaudy with many tacky shops, and so many people. Apparently, miraculous cures are rare; the last medically certifiable case took place in 1987, and was recognised by the church as a miracle. Diana had brought me back some holy water; we had a nice afternoon.

I went into work early to supervise the dinner for Princess Anne. As President of Save the Children fund, she was the guest of honour at the Institute of Directors - Kent Grand Charity Dinner. It was attended by the chairman, and his wife, of the Leeds Castle foundation, the Rt Hon Lord and Lady Thomson of Monifieth, and many local dignitaries including the High Sheriff of Kent, Mr Edwin Boorman, and chairman of the Institute of Directors, Mr Graham Webb. The last time the Princess had visited the Castle, I had been privileged to serve her tea, and she was not all as the press present her. This time I was even more impressed with her; we were told it was her fifth engagement that day. On conclusion of dinner, slides were shown of HRH on tour for Save the Children fund, and she spoke about the work done by them. It was a great evening and we were pleased it had gone well.

I seem to be back working long hours again. I went for my B12 injection, and Dr. Vaux said he hoped I was not working too much! I never have any spare time; with all the usual things us ladies have to do, I am up early to clean and feed the bantams, also to collect their eggs as, any excuse, and the hens go broody.

Trying to get my writing and china painting done, and looking after the grandchildren is all full-time without going to work. Then there is the volunteer work; I can talk to clients while I am painting but the paperwork has to be kept up. There are never enough hours in a day, but I get fitter all the time so life is great.

I had a busy day and evening looking after Rosamond, one of the other supervisor's daughter's wedding in the Fairfax hall; a lovely day.

At the end of the month, I had to go into work for a meeting. We finished early so I thought I would call on my other friend, Diane, who lives near the Castle. Since she left work, I usually pop into see her every two weeks. It was rather lonely where she lived, so I tapped on the door and called out who it was. She answered that I should go in and, on opening the door, I found her on the floor. She had fallen and could not get up; she said her arm hurt. I went next door to her neighbour, Betty, and after a while we persuaded her to let me take her to the doctor, who after examining her said I would have to take her to the hospital as she thought Diane had broken her wrist. It was about four o'clock when I had arrived at Diane's house, and eleven o'clock when we arrived back from the hospital; she had broken it and it was in plaster. After helping her to bed, I arrived home at nearly midnight. I was worried that Diane would not manage on her own, so was about to ring her sister when Diane rang to say her sister was there, and she was going to stay with her, so I went over to see her before they left. It was a good thing she stayed with her sister, as quite a few times she passed out. Eventually she was taken into hospital and found to be diabetic, so she had to move out of her lovely little cottage and into a warden-assisted flat. However, she still kept having falls, so she went into a nursing home. Diane was rather stubborn, and would never go to the doctor. I had been concerned some weeks before when I had taken her to Rye for the day, when walking back to the car she had asked me to hold on to her; I thought she was just tired. She wanted to go to the garden centre on the way home, and we were looking in one of the greenhouses when she suddenly fell on top of four boxes of little cuttings and crushed them. The man who owns the garden centre is quite grumpy, so I got Diane on her feet and said we had better escape before he saw the damage we had done. I felt a bit guilty, but was too frightened to tell him.

It was the day of the support group fashion show. It went very well and we had a lot of fun doing it. One of the ladies, Carol, has been raising money for equipment for Mr Jones. Her husband videoed it, and the local newspaper came to take photos; it was a great success.

While Diane was staying with her sister, I rang and asked if she would like to come to tea. I also rang Joan and invited her as well. A week after they had been to tea, I had a phone call from Joan's niece to tell me Joan had died while staying with her sister. Joan had told me how much she was looking forward to staying with her. Roger and I were so upset; Roger often did jobs for Joan, and I enjoyed my visits to her, and her letters. As usual, after she had been for tea, I had a nice letter from her saying how much she had enjoyed the afternoon. I was so glad I had asked them.

I did have some good news when I had a letter to say that Margaret Rook, the journalist who did the articles for our film, had had a little girl.

I felt a bit down the next week at the sad news of the death of Paul McCartney's wife, Linda. It seemed to shake the whole country, especially the many women living with breast cancer, and their families and friends.

A Horrible Year

For some time after her death, the Breast Cancer Care helpline was flooded with calls from anxious women stunned at the news. The clients I was given, were wanting reassurance, or was the same thing going to happen to them, especially the younger women. The volunteers taking calls said a large number were about what they could do to protect themselves and daughters whose mothers had breast cancer. What were the risks for them? Also had calls about Tamoxifen after press coverage of the US trials. There was the positive side to Linda's death in that it raised the awareness of breast cancer.

This month has been full of sadness. It was Joan's funeral, but it was nice to meet her sisters and their families of whom she was so proud. I was asked back to the house, but I declined as I feel that is private for the family.

May, and I picked up Diana as we were going to see Amanda, who used to work with us at the castle, for lunch. Amanda is another person who wrote such nice letters to me when I was ill. I feel so sad when I see Diana and think about her husband Phil and her two young boys. She is so ill, but we had a nice day with Amanda.

On my fifty-eighth birthday, I awoke to Luke and Lucia singing happy birthday on the phone. Julie came on her own as Alex had not been well the last few days; he has chickenpox. I had a lovely day. Roger and I went to Brighton where we had a nice lunch, and he bought me a beautiful amber pendant. Brighton is very cosmopolitan; the oldest quarter is the Lanes, narrow twisting, brick-paved passages lined by 17th century fishermen's cottages that are now mainly antique shops. In the centre is Brighton Square, surrounded by pavement cafés and entertainers. There is a large marina and, on the sea front, a variety of hotels and terraced boarding houses. One of the town's churches, St Nicholas's, dates from the 14th century, and among those buried in the churchyard is Martha Gunn, 'queen' of the dippers, the attendants who looked after women bathers in the 18th century. On the outskirts of the town is Sussex University, but the most outstanding landmark is the Royal Pavilion, built for the Prince of Wales by Henry Holland in 1787, and later frequented by William IV and Queen Victoria. Holland reconstructed the original seaside villa as a classical building with a rotunda and dome. In 1815, by the time the Prince of Wales had become Regent, John Nash, architect of Regents Park in London, rebuilt it with a larger onion-shaped dome, tent-like roofs, pinnacles, and minarets in the style of an Indian Mogul's palace. It is full of beautiful furnishings and treasures. I had had another lovely birthday.

I had a nice surprise when Nat, who had been one of my managers, rang to say she would be visiting the Castle the next day and hoped to see me, so I said I would go in early. I had supervised some very nice functions with Nat; one was a dinner for the Maidstone local board of directors on the 185th anniversary of the founding of the Kent Institution. On the seventh of December 1987, the *Caterer and Hotel Keeper* selected the menu to be considered for Menu of the Month award. We did not win, but the magazine printed our menu, including our names: Peter, our sous chef, Nat, the food and beverage manager, and myself as supervisor. We were all quite pleased about that.

Roger had his appointment to go into hospital to have his operation on his hand. I left him there in the morning, and collected him in the evening. He said it was quite comfortable and not too painful. He had Carpal Tunnel syndrome; the nerve is trapped and caused him a lot of pain, especially at night and driving. The surgeon frees the pinched nerve by cutting through the tough membrane this gives immediate relief. Sixteen days later Roger had his stitches out. The operation had been successful. He is to have the other hand operated on at a later date.

At the end of the month, I went for my check-up at Mr Jones's clinic. It is now six years since I was diagnosed with the breast cancer, and twenty-one years since the first operation for the stomach cancer. I saw the registrar who, after examining me and looking at my mammogram, decided it would be safe to go back in one year unless I had any problems. It was such good news, and I was so pleased. I knew Roger would be relieved; he worries so when it is my check-up.

Diana had asked me if I would arrange for some of the girls from work to visit her on her birthday. She does not look the Diana the girls knew before her treatment. It has made her put on a lot of weight, and she has lost all her beautiful blonde hair; her legs are very swollen so she has trouble moving. I thought I should warn the girls, so they would not be too shocked when they saw her. We decided we would take the food and wine, so sorted out who was taking what. We had a lovely evening. Diana was so pleased to see everyone, and I think the evening was also good for her husband, Phil. After we left, some of the girls were overcome, as seeing Diana had been very emotional for all of us.

July, and I'm still busy at work. I had a very hectic but nice day when I supervised Alistair, one of our previous manager's wedding; we did not finish until two o'clock in the morning.

A Horrible Year

I had been looking forward to going to a china painting seminar, but was a bit apprehensive about driving there as I had not been to the area before; thankfully I found it. I had a super day. We had coffee on arrival, then demonstrations all day by famous china painting artists, an exhibition of painted pieces, and stands selling china, brushes, and paints - everything for the painter. We had a lovely lunch, and I met some nice friendly ladies. After tea, I was on my way home.

I rang Phil but he sounded down; he said Diana was poorly and in bed.

I had a day off. When I awoke it was raining, which was disappointing as I was having Joe and Alex for the day. When Julie brought them, it had stopped so I decided to take them to the beach for the day. By the time I had sorted out our picnic, the sun was shining. Minster-in-Sheppey is about twenty minutes' drive, and we quite often go there on our family days out. Sheppey is Saxon for 'sheep island', and much of the island is sheep farming. We were heading for Minster, which has a wide beach backed by a grassy slope and low cliffs - perfect for walks and picnics. An Abbey was founded here in the 7th century by Queen Sexburga who became the first Abbess of the nunnery there. It was eventually knocked down in the Reformation of the 16th century, and only the gatehouse survives. The parish church of St Mary and St Sexburga contains fabric of the original nunnery church. Elmley Marshes, along the Swale, is perfect for the many wildfowl and waders, and redshanks, lapwings, teal, white-fronted geese, and widgeon are just a few that can be seen. With the sun shining, we had our picnic on the grassy slope and then walked along the beach inspecting the pools for crabs and small fish. Alex had a paddle, and had the tide been out we would have searched for winkles. Joe said Granddad loves eating winkles after cooking them and getting them out of their shells with a pin. When I was young, we always had the winkle man call on a Sunday, and we would have shrimps and winkles with bread and butter for tea. After ice-creams, we arrived back at the car just as it started to rain. We had to wait before we started back as it rained so hard and became very dark, but at last it cleared and two tired boys slept all the way home.

At the end of July, it was my sister Barb and brother-in-law Ted's fiftieth wedding anniversary so I popped in on my way to work. During the evening, I rang Roger and he said there was a message on the answer phone for me. He said he had not listened to it, which I thought was odd, as he knew it was for me. It was late as usual when I arrived home, and

Roger said he had listened to the message but had not wanted to tell me on the phone. It was from Phil to say Diana had died. Roger held me, and I could not stop myself from crying; I had become very close to Diana these last few weeks. I could not believe it had happened; it was only a month ago when we were with her for her birthday. I was so pleased we had all gone that evening; she had so enjoyed it. The next morning, I phoned Phil. He asked if I could go round; we had a long chat about Diana, and he asked if I would ring the girls and tell them.

It was so hard having to tell people like Shirley, Viv, Gail, and the two Ros's who had known Diana for a long time and been to her birthday. Some of the girls very kindly said they would ring other girls for me. I found it very hard going into work that night as we were all so upset.

I was off work the next day, but felt mentally exhausted, and I was meeting the ladies from the hydro group for tea. I didn't feel like going, but one of the ladies, Eileen, was moving so I wanted to see her before she left.

Arriving home, Phil phoned and said he would like to go back to the Gatehouse rooms at the Castle after Diana's funeral, and could I arrange it.

Next morning, I was just getting myself organised for the day when Michelle rang and asked if I could go into work to look after a small lunch. After I had finished, I spoke to my manager, Andrew, about the arrangements for Diana's funeral; he said to tell Phil he would sort it out for him. I rang Phil that evening, and he was pleased with the arrangements.

I had a bad night; kept waking up and having to go to the bathroom. Today was Diana's funeral; it was a lovely service, but very emotional. Afterwards, Phil and the family were going to a service at the crematorium. He asked me if I would like to go with them, but I said I felt it was for the family so I would go to the Castle with the girls, and we would wait for him there. It must have been one of the hottest days of the year, which did not help. On the way home, some of us went to look at the flowers; it had been so hot, they were looking very sad.

The next day, Gail rang to see how I was which I thought was nice and thoughtful of her. When I went into work, Ros was very upset; I said we must try and think about the lovely tall blonde Diana we knew, and think about Phil and the boys who were her pride and joy.

After all the sadness, we had some exciting news. Julie thinks she may be pregnant, so is to have a scan.

It has been lovely weather; very hot really. It's nice to come home from work and have a glass of wine and dinner in the garden. My niece

A Horrible Year

Heather's daughter, Chloe, is getting married. We were looking forward to seeing all the family. On the day of the wedding, it was lovely. The reception was held at the hop farm which has now been converted to hold weddings and various functions; there is also a museum of hop growing and local crafts. It is also home to shire horses, and twenty-five white cowls of Victorian oasthouses gleam in the sun. In one of these, the reception was held; we all had a lovely day.

Roger was supposed to have another operation on his other hand, but when we rang there was not a bed available, so it has now been booked for the beginning of next year.

It was time once again for my endoscope. Roger took me to the day ward at the hospital, and the staff said they would ring him when I was ready to go home. All went well, and there did not seem to be any problems. Dr. Bird told Roger that, so long as I did not have any trouble, I could come back in a year.

Roger and I had a nice evening with Julie's mother and father-in-law, Barbara and Ken. Julie and Marcus had bought us tickets for an open-air concert with Shirley Bassey. We took champagne and a picnic, and it was a lovely warm evening.

Roger had been taking his Mum to the hospital to visit Harry, her partner, who had been ill for some time. On the first of September we had a phone call to say Harry had died. The next two weeks were quite hectic for Roger as he had to sort out the funeral arrangements. Maura, the flower lady from work, arranged the flowers for us; they were, as always, beautiful. I looked after Alex while the family went to the funeral.

We had good news when Julie had her scan and it was confirmed she is having a baby, so we are all very excited.

It was Richard's thirty-eighth birthday - makes me feel quite old.

I have always said I would like to ride a horse. Alex had been having riding lessons for a while, when Julie asked if I would like to go with them for his lesson. When we arrived and booked in, they said, 'two of you today'. I thought they had made a mistake, when Julie said I was having a lesson too. I was very nervous; the horse seemed enormous. Sitting on a horse was so different to what I thought it would be; I just felt as if I would topple off. The riding instructor said I was to relax, as the horse would sense I was nervous, but I could not. We were walking through the woods when she asked if I would like the horse to trot. I said no way, I would definitely fall off. Back home, my bum hurt so much I had a job to sit down. When Roger came home I was sitting on a cushion so he asked what was the matter, what had I done? He of course thought it a big joke, especially when I said I thought I would fall off, and then he laughed and asked if I would like to have lessons! Now when I watch a gymkhana, I admire their courage to jump the high fences. Riding is something I do not think I will try again; to be honest, I was terrified.

I had been looking forward to supervising a lunch for our chief executive and his wife, Mr and Mrs Sabin. Their guests were the artist, Graham Clarke, and his wife. I was an admirer of his work when I first became ill in 1997, and helping at Sutton Valance School. There had been a collection for me. Graham was not well known, but I had seen some of his work and longed to own one of his paintings, so decided to use the collection to buy one. Graham Clarke is quite a distinctive looking gentleman, large with lots of hair and a huge beard, a much admired artist all over the world now, so it was a good investment. His latest work was an etching of the Castle which he had been commissioned to do. Appropriate to the Castle, he gave it the title, 'Wilt thou marry me', depicting Henry the IV, so when they came on sale in the Castle shop, I became the proud owner of another Graham Clarke. I have met so many interesting people at the Castle.

I went to see Phil. He is coping well with the boys, and trying to sort out how to look after them when he goes back to work. It is hard to imagine what it is like if you are in his situation when one parent dies.

It is now October, and we are getting excited about our holiday. It is a special one because, in January, we will have been married forty years, our Ruby anniversary. We had been trying to think what to do to celebrate, so decided on a cruise, going to some of the places Roger had been to when at sea, and always wanted me to see them. We are due to start our holiday in one week, so have been getting organised. As usual, I have been working long hours, and have had a lot of orders for my china paintings, and more new clients, and the ones I already have with Breast Cancer Care that I am regularly in touch with. I try to visit my other friend Diane once a week as she is in the nursing home; she is still lonely. I have also been knitting and sewing for the new baby. Having the grandchildren Luke, Lucia, Joe, and Alex, I love living in the country. There is always something to do, and they love walking in the woods, feeding the ducks down on the pond, and fishing with Roger.

Going on a cruise is a good excuse to buy new clothes, so I have had to fit in shopping.

32

BARCELONA TO MIAMI – THE CRUISE

David picked us up at five o'clock and took us to Heathrow airport for our flight to one of my favourite cities, Barcelona. Arriving there, we went by coach through this wonderful, exceptionally beautiful city. Everywhere there are the modernist architect Gaudi's buildings, and we passed the Guell Park and Picasso museum. The modern Barcelona is laid out in tree-lined avenues, and there is of course the Las Ramblas which runs inland from the two hundred foot Columbus monument close to the harbour. We were sailing on the SS Norway, said to be the most beautiful cruise liner afloat. It was once the legendary transatlantic liner SS France, which was then purchased and re-named by the Norwegian Cruise Line. She has been restored to her former glory, with art deco murals, marble statuary, a two-storey Broadway theatre, and a magnificent art deco ballroom. There is a fitness centre and a beauty salon. The Champs Elysee and 5th Avenue are chic 'streets' of boutiques, and of course, there are the Casino, and a disco, with dancing to the Arti Shaw orchestra, or listening to the piano in the Windjammer lounge.

The cruises have a theme, and ours was Romance of Music. Once on board, we were taken to our cabin which is very nice. We had to assemble at certain points for a safety check, and were shown how to put on a life jacket. Luke had been very worried about us going to sea, and said he hoped the ship would not sink like the Titanic. Nina had assured him it would not. Lunch time, so we made our way to the dining room. I can see it is going to be difficult for me, and I will have to miss out some of the five courses. There are so many places to choose to eat, apart from the two main dining rooms and outdoor buffets, or Le Bistro, and of course, there are the midnight buffets with the chocoholics delight, and each afternoon, ice-cream.

After lunch, we had a look around part of the ship; it's too big to see everything in one go. We had afternoon tea on deck, and then just relaxed until it was time for dinner back in the dining room, which looked wonderful at night. The next day, we sunbathed on deck, with music from the calypso band, and I went and had my hair done as it was the Captain's welcome party; we had champagne and nibbles, and our photo taken with the Captain. We were up early as we had arrived in Malaga, Spain. We went ashore to the Alcazaba, a fortress begun in the 8th century when Malaga was the principal port of the Moorish Kingdom. Ferdinand and Isabella lived here for a while after their conquest of Malaga in 1487. There is a wonderful Roman amphitheatre sitting in the middle of modern buildings. From the walls of the fortress, there was a magnificent sweeping view of the bay of Malaga, and there were orange trees and bougainvillaea everywhere. We also saw a religious ceremony walking through the streets with an effigy of the Virgin Mary surrounded by flowers. Back on board, and after dinner at midnight, was the chocoholic buffet with wonderful ice sculptures. I so wanted to eat some of the chocolate delights, but had eaten too much for dinner. That night, we were cruising through the straits of Gibraltar.

For some while, I had had an embarrassing problem that, like lots of ladies, I did not like to talk about, stress incontinence. When getting a cold, I usually get a cough which made my problem worse. I did not realise it would happen, and it almost ruined the cruise. I awoke feeling ill; I was obviously running a temperature, had a sore throat and a dry cough. I just felt like staying in bed. Roger gave me some paracetamol, but I did not feel like breakfast so Roger went on his own. We sunbathed, and I slept most of the day, but the cough was getting worse as the day wore on. Each time I coughed, I could not stop wetting myself which I found so distressing. I still had a temperature, so we thought I should see the doctor as, by the end of the day, I was feeling worse. By the time we went to the medical room, it was closed, so we bought some cough mixture and looked to see if they sold pads, because the more I coughed the more I wet myself. But they did not sell them, so I had to pad myself with toilet paper; it was awful. Dinner was a nightmare, as I coughed and coughed. After dinner, we went to our cabin where I dosed myself up as much as I could in the hope that I would feel better when we arrived in Madeira. We had both been looking forward to visiting there as it was one of his ports of call when Roger was at sea.

Barcelona to Miami - the Cruise

After a restless night, the cough was worse, but we were ready to watch the ship dock. Roger was amazed; he said it did not look like the same place - so many more buildings. We had docked at Funchal, and had decided to go on the tour to the Botanical gardens and wine-tasting. Funchal nestles in a beautiful bay protected by mountain peaks, and as soon as you step ashore, everywhere is a panorama of colours - bougainvillaea, jasmine, hibiscus, and orchids, plus masses of semi-tropical species. The climate is very warm but comfortable. The coach took us on a sightseeing tour of this lovely island; the roads are narrow and steep especially when arriving at the Botanical gardens where we had stunning views from the terraced slopes, not only wonderful flowers but huge beautiful butterflies. Madeira is also famous of course for wickerwork and embroidered goods; apparently the embroidery work is said to have been started by an Englishwoman, a Mrs Phels. She opened a school to teach needlework to help the women of Funchal whose families were suffering hardship because of a blight that killed a year's harvest of grapes. It is also possible that Flemish settlers brought it to the island, centuries before. But most famous of all is the wine, so our next call was the wine tasting. Roger was looking forward to that. This dark brown wine was Madeira's most important export during the 17th century. The wine is fortified with brandy, and ranges from dry to sweet. It derives its distinctive rich character from the volcanic soil of the island's vineyards, which are some of the most steeply terraced in the world, and from the unique process of aging it in baking rooms for several months after fermentation. This process was adopted after the discovery that wines benefited from the prolonged heat of storage that it underwent during tropical voyages. It is also aged in oak casks.

The day was spoilt with me coughing and wetting myself; it was very upsetting. It was quite emotional when we were leaving; we were standing on deck, and lots of people came down to the docks to wave us off.

It was Julie's thirty-seventh birthday, so we rang her from the ship to say happy birthday. Each day I went to the craft hour to see the demonstrations, and participate in the various crafts. I started chatting to a lady who said she was on the cruise as a treat because she had just finished her treatment for breast cancer. I told her I was a volunteer for Breast Cancer Care, which she was interested to know all about.

When we decided on a cruise, as I have said, Roger wanted to go to some of the places he had visited when in the Merchant Navy, but did not want a cruise where we would keep stopping at lots of ports. He wanted mainly cruising, so this was one of the reasons for going on the SS Norway; it would be more relaxing.

After cruising the Atlantic Ocean for twelve lazy days and glittering nights, we arrived in Charlotte Amalie St Thomas in the Caribbean. The island's real attraction is its natural beauty. Columbus discovered what are called the Virgin Islands on his second voyage to the New World in 1493. Legend has it that he named them in honour of the 11,000 virgin followers of St Ursula who were martyred in the early days of the Christian church. The people of the islands are colourful, with stories and folklore originated by their ancestors. In the harbour were some wonderful ships. We had to go by tender, and it was a sight not to forget, with turquoise water, rows of red-roofed white buildings, fabulous flowers, bougainvillaea, huge hibiscus, and yellow trumpets set against a backdrop of green mountain forests. Ashore, its streets are lined with every kind of shop imaginable, and outside each one a tall dark man with the biggest of smiles, showing brilliant white teeth, telling everyone passing to have a nice day. It is a shoppers' paradise, with the bustling market square, and of course it is duty free. Arriving in the town, we went in one of the open-topped buses for a tour of some of the island. The scenery was stunning overlooking Megens bay, which is one of the world's top ten most beautiful beaches. As we drove higher, it was a tropical paradise with exotic flowers and birds, and also very hot and humid.

Back in town, and as it was our ruby anniversary, Roger wanted to buy me a ring; some of the finest quality jewels are sold in the Caribbean. We chose a ruby and diamond ring, and then once again we were back on the tender back to the SS Norway.

I seemed to be coughing all the time, and had no control over my bladder. I tried not to drink very much which is not what you want to do when you keep coughing; it was a nightmare. The rest of the holiday was spent cruising the Caribbean, and the weather was wonderful. We had hoped to see whales, but we were not lucky, although on one occasion some of the passengers were lucky and saw one. We saw lots of flying fish, but very few birds while at sea. There was so much to do; the shows were great, lots of different music, the art shows, fashion, and beauty demonstrations. We had an interesting tour of the bridge and, on our last night before arriving in Miami, had champagne with the Captain. We were up early on our last day on board, arriving in Miami at six am. We wanted to be on deck to see our arrival. Miami is the 'Magic City', full of distinctive and eclectic neighbourhoods. Coconut Grove is known for its cosmopolitan culture; its colourful bars and boutiques attract a mixture of artists, artisans, and writers. After breakfast, we said our farewells and were transferred to our hotel. I felt like a movie star; the hotel suite was wonderful with huge windows overlooking the city. We would have liked to stay longer, but all too soon the holiday had come to an end and we were on the long flight home.

Richard and Sandy were at the airport to meet us. It had been a great holiday with memories of some beautiful places and a wonderful cruise.

As much as we enjoyed the holiday, it was good to be home. My cough was no better, or the waterworks; I seemed to be wet all the time (I hate it, it is so embarrassing), but at least I could get some proper pads. I made an appointment with Dr. Vaux; he said I had a prolapse of the bladder and thought I would need an operation. He would make me an appointment with a consultant, and in the meantime would fit a rubber ring inside me (yuck!) Not the most pleasant of things, and I was to have a week off work to hopefully get rid of my cough which was making the problem worse.

The next few days, I was feeling a bit down. The ring was making the bottom half of me ache, and not helping much, and the cough was still bothering me.

I had a call from Stanley, my dear friend Heather's husband, to say she was in hospital, so not a good day. Arriving at the hospital the next day, I was shocked to see Heather looking so thin and poorly, but as always very active in her mind. She's a very knowledgeable lady, and it's so sad to see her so unwell.

I rang Phil to see how he was; he said he was coping quite well, but has his bad days which are to be expected. Now back at work, I'm trying to fit everything in as usual. Julie went for her scan, and all is well with her and the baby. Rang Stanley Heather; not sounding very good, so next day went to the hospital to see her and was shocked to see how she had deteriorated in such a short time. I am very worried about her.

Had an interesting evening when Roger and I went to the village of Headcorn to a talk by the author Nigel Nicolson on writing an autobiography. Nigel Nicolson is the younger son of Vita Sackville-West and was brought up at Knole and Long Barn, and after 1930 at Sissinghurst Castle, where he still lives. He has written several books on architecture and social history, as well as edited the three-volume edition of his father's diaries, Sir Harold Nicolson. Roger bought me his book *Portrait of a Marriage* which he signed for me.

Two days later, I had a message to say Heather had died. How sad I feel; she had been a good friend, a lovely lady.

I had been asked if I would help with some research into lymphoedema; this can be one of the side-effects after having breast cancer and its treatments. It is not known why some patients develop this condition, and others do not. The research team at St George's hospital in London had asked me to have some tests done, as I have not had the condition which affects people in different ways; swelling of the arm including the hand and fingers is the most common symptom. Roger said he would drive me to the hospital. We were there three hours, one hour of which was spent trying to find a good vein to take a sample. Roger said he didn't know how I sat there having needles stuck in me for so long. In the end a paediatrician came in and managed to get a vein, but the doctor said next time they will do different tests. On the way home we stopped and had a meal; it was not a good idea because as soon as we arrived home I had to rush to the bathroom. I do sometimes feel frustrated about going out to eat, and, although I am careful what I eat, my body nine times out of ten rejects it.

I still have my cough, and the waterworks are even worse, so I hope I get an appointment soon.

It was Heather's funeral, but although I was supposed to work, I was allowed to attend. I took Ros C., Lily, and Anne from work; it was in the lovely village church of Leeds. I will miss Heather. She was a little bit unconventional; sometimes while serving teas at work, we would miss her, and she had gone for a walk around the gardens. She had a great love of music and art, and was involved in village life and the church, and loved travelling, especially to America to see two of her daughters who live there with their families. Heather and Stanley had had six children. Dickon, the youngest, had died as a teenager with cancer. Heather once told me God must have wanted him, and she accepted that; they also had grandchildren and great grandchildren.

Next day, I had a phone call from my friend Trisha to say they were grandparents again; their daughter Lisa had had a little boy, Thomas, a brother for James, and both were well.

It is now the end of November, and the last local Breast Cancer support meeting of the year, so I picked up Jean. There was no speaker this month as we had a quiz, and our group won so we were pleased about that. Time for my B12 injection again, so had an appointment with Dr. Vaux. While waiting in the surgery, I was reading the newsletter and it said Dr. Vaux was going to retire. I felt very upset. I really feel if it were not for him (and of course Dr. Stevens and Professor Ellis and his team) I would not be here today. I have always felt so confident with him. He asked how I was getting on with my waterworks problem, and I said it was a nightmare, I am having to wear awful thick pads. He said he would write to the consultant and get things moving. I still have my cough which is not helping.

Our boss, Andrew, takes the managers and supervisors out once a year as a thank you. We went to the local bowling hall, then had a meal in a wine bar; a pleasant evening. One of the nicest things about working at the Castle is the camaraderie of the staff.

We are now into December, so Roger took a day's holiday. First he had an appointment at the hospital with his consultant as a follow-up to check the operation he had on his hand. That went well so we went off to do some Christmas shopping. Next day, I did something stupid. I was up early, drove my car to the park-and-ride car park, and went into town on the bus. I wanted to try and finish the Christmas shopping, so had some very big boxes and bags. On my way to catch the bus home, I saw Di T from work. She said, 'come on, I'm going home so I'll help you with the bags and take you home. Arriving home, she helped me take everything into the house; I was so grateful. After Di had gone, I had to drive to West Malling to collect Roger's Christmas present. I went out of the house, locked the door, and turned round to get into the car - no car - I thought someone had stolen it, then like a fool I remembered I had driven to the park-and-ride car park that morning. I had been so grateful for the help and lift with Di, that I had totally forgotten when we were driving home. I had to walk to the car park to get the car, but it started to rain and, by the time I got to the car, I was soaked. I felt such an idiot.

Arriving back home, I felt wet and exhausted. We had dinner, and then I spent the rest of the evening in the bathroom having diarrhoea, and retching. My body was telling me once again I had done too much. Sometimes, looking back, I wonder how I managed to fit so much in while working. The next day I felt a bit of a grot, but was up early, did the usual housework etc., made a bread pudding for our neighbour, Charlie, did some ironing, managed some painting, and wrote Christmas cards before going to work. I had a very hectic evening and did not finish until two thirty in the morning. Thank goodness I had the next day off, as my body really ached.

I had been feeling very worried since Julie told me she had a problem with her breast. I said I really felt she should see her doctor, so I had Alex while she went for her appointment. He is referring her to the breast clinic. While Julie was gone, I took Alex to see Father Christmas at the local garden centre, and then we went to Detling to my Mum and Dad's graves to put on a wreath. I like to do that at Christmas, as Boxing Day was my Mum's birthday. We collected Joe from school, and when we arrived home Julie was back. I had a call from Phil asking if I could take him into town. He doesn't drive and he seems to be having a bit of a bad spell at the moment, but he said the boys are coping well. It is such a lot for a man to cope with, especially at Christmas.

Back home, I put marzipan on my Christmas cake and went to see Diane; I had a chat and cup of tea with her. She is settling in better at the nursing home now. Richard and Sandy called with their Christmas presents; they are going to Sandy's parents for the holiday. Roger and I then did our usual delivering of presents to my sisters, Nellie and Barb, and nieces, Valerie-Joan and Heather.

It is two days before Christmas, and Julie still has not had her appointment so I thought I would ring Pam the breast care nurse. She said I should ring my consultant Mr Jones's secretary, which I did and she said they had not received a referral from Julie's doctor, so could not do anything until after Christmas. I was not too pleased. Christmas Eve, after work, I went to Julie's, as a friend was dressing up as Father Christmas. It was very hectic but the children loved it. We then called on David and Nina and the children before going to church for the midnight service which I love; it feels like Christmas, especially when it is a crisp frosty night as we walk back home. All too soon, Christmas is over. I rang the breast clinic for Julie, and she has an appointment next week. Back at work for New Year's Eve dinner, and at midnight once again, we have the piper piping in the New Year, and Gerry the chef carrying the haggis around the room. The guests said they had had a wonderful evening. When they had all gone, and we were locking up, I walked out onto the terrace. It was three o'clock in the morning, and what a wonderful sight: the Castle floodlit against the purple sky, and the reflections in the moat. As I drove home, I wondered what the New Year would bring.

33

OUR RUBY WEDDING YEAR

The first day of the New Year, and I saw a woodpecker on a tree opposite our house - such a treat. We do not get that many varieties of birds, but he was chased away by a magpie.

Not a good start to the New Year, with Julie having her hospital appointment at the breast clinic. I have not been able to stop thinking about it; in fact I was nearly out of my mind worrying about it. She waited two hours, and then saw a lady consultant who said there was nothing to worry about; it was fatty tissue and not sinister. I hope she will not worry now. I felt sort of okay about Julie, but must admit not 100%, and then she said she wasn't happy. She had checked the name that the consultant said it was, and it means something totally different, so she is going back to her doctor.

We went to the Castle staff party with Michelle and Trevor, held as usual at one of our local hotels, but we did not enjoy it so much this year. The food was not up to standard, and the music was so loud we could not have a conversation. Next morning, we drove down to one of our favourite places, Rye, one of the ancient towns attached to the Cinque Ports. At one time, Rye was almost encircled by sea. It was heavily fortified against the medieval French, but its influence declined when the harbour silted up in the 16th century; today the sea has receded. On a small hill with cobbled streets and lovely old buildings, there is the church with its 16th century clock and 18ft free-swinging pendulum, whilst weather-boarded and tile-hung houses, some with timber frames, are all over the town.

We were staying at the Mermaid Inn, opened in 1420 and one of the oldest in the country. Arriving at lunch time, we were shown to a lovely room with a four-poster bed overlooking the cobbled street, and after settling in, we walked around the old town which is full of antique and art shops. We had lunch in a quaint restaurant with a huge inglenook fireplace with a log fire. Back at the hotel, we bathed and changed for dinner which was served in the lovely old dining room; a superb meal and wine, and coffee was served in a cosy lounge which again had a huge inglenook fireplace and a lovely log fire. I had been careful not to eat too much as I did not want to spoil the day by being in the bathroom for the rest of the evening.

Next morning, it was so nice to have a lazy breakfast and read the newspapers before leaving; we wished we could have stayed longer. It is the tenth of January, our fortieth wedding anniversary, and we are meeting the family for lunch at an old country pub which has a great restaurant. They had reserved a table for us, and Julie had arrived with balloons; as always, when the family are together, it was a happy noisy lunch. Back home we had lots of cards, presents, and flowers, but then I had a disaster. I had worn the ruby and diamond ring Roger had bought when we went on the cruise. I had delayed wearing it until our anniversary. I went to the cupboard under the stairs and, as I came out, banged my hand hard on the door. When I looked I had lost one of the rubies. I was in such a panic. We looked and looked but could not find it; I was so upset. The next morning I took everything out of the cupboard but still could not find it. Roger said not to worry, we could have it replaced. When I did take it to the jeweller who has done work for me before, he said it may take a while to find another ruby of the size and colour to match, but he did thank goodness.

It was time to go up to St George's Hospital to continue with the research into Lymphoedema. This time it was to carry out investigations on the blood vessels and blood flow in the arm. Roger came with me and was there about two hours; the doctor did not think he would need me again so that is good. They say it is still early days, and the results of their work cannot yet translate into better treatment or prevention into Lymphoedema, but research is continuing.

Once more it was time for my B12 injection. Dr. Vaux asked how I was getting on with my waterworks problem; he thought it a good idea to keep the ring in, and he would try to hurry my appointment with the consultant.

A few days later, I went for a mammogram. The nurse was most impressed with my previous history; she said I was a walking miracle. I just hope the scans are okay. Three days later, I had a bit of a scare when the post came; there was a letter from the hospital. I nervously opened it and it was from Pam Wright the breast care nurse with information about the support group. I was so relieved; when I saw the envelope I thought it was bad news from my scan.

February, and the bulbs are just peeping up in the garden; the snowdrops are out and spring is on its way. Breast Cancer Care rang to ask if I would collect a cheque from a shopping centre near us. I said I would love to. Julie is coming with me next week.

It was injection time again, and I was feeling sad as it would be the last time I would see Dr. Vaux as my doctor, as he was retiring the next week. I feel that without his care I would not be here. If he had not sent me for an endoscope when I started to have the stomach problems, the cancer would not have been diagnosed so soon. He was so caring, especially when I was having the chemo, by offering to administer the chemo three weeks out of the four so that I did not have to travel up to London every week. Then of course, when I was diagnosed with the breast cancer, and the hospital doctor had said to leave it six months. Dr. Vaux said he was not happy with that and referred me to Mr Jones who said, six months and I would not have been here. I have always felt so confident with Dr. Vaux, so his replacement will have a lot to live up to.

Had a nice weekend with Luke and Lucia. We took them shopping, and to the local leisure centre; they were worn out so slept until late the next morning.

It was the day I was going to collect the cheque, so Julie and I set off with instructions from Roger as to how to get to the shopping centre. I don't know quite what we did, but we got lost and eventually arrived back where we had started. I was worried as I did not think we would arrive on time, so we asked a postman for directions. I rushed in while Julie parked the car. The shop, Superdrug, had been updated so it was also a ceremony to reopen it, and as I arrived the Mayor was just about to cut the ribbon (which I was supposed to be doing). I was then presented with the cheque. We had photos and interviews for the local press, and were given a goody bag as a thank you, so all went well in the end. Superdrug has raised a lot of money for Breast Cancer Care, and without people like them, they would not be able to continue helping people with breast cancer.

Had a phone call from the BBC about a documentary they are making, and when I told them we had made one, they said they could not use us as it was too soon after the previous one.

Sad news when we had a message to say Roger's friend, Colin, who owned the trout farm where Roger fishes, had died. He had been in hospital and had an operation, and all seemed well. Roger had taken his wife in to visit the night before, so it was quite a shock.

March started wet and windy, but has settled down now and we have had some nice sunny days. The daffodils are out, and the catkins, and we saw primroses and dog violets on one of our walks. We think blue tits are building a home in our nest box so we will keep watch on them.

I had my appointment to see Mr Kefford, the consultant gynaecologist, about my waterworks. He said I need an operation, and he hopes to do it as soon as possible. I do not want another operation, but I cannot go on wearing pads; it is horrible so I need something done.

The crematorium chapel was full for Colin's funeral. Colin was well-known; not only did he run the trout farm, but he was involved in country sports, especially shooting. After the service, we went back to the farm, and Colin's wife, Brenda, gave Roger one of his shooting sticks. Roger was very touched.

I had been looking forward to supervising another wedding. It was a great day; Morland and Victor, the couple getting married, were from the USA. They had a film crew with them, and were staying in London, so they were filmed out and about and at the hotel, together with all the preparations at the Castle. They were having the ceremony and reception in the Gate Tower. It was a long day; I worked from nine thirty in the morning until eleven thirty that evening. The two waitresses with me were Marguerite and Maureen, and it was a lovely day - all such nice people - and they sent us a copy of the film to watch. And as with lots of functions, we received such nice letters to thank us.

At the end of the month, I was attending a Supporting the Supporters Workshop with Breast Cancer Care. I travelled by train to London; it was being held at a retreat, the Kairos Centre, which is a lovely old house set in beautiful gardens. I had a room overlooking the garden. Early morning and evening, foxes came and played on the lawns. I think we all arrived with a little trepidation, and began to wonder what we had let ourselves in for, but we were put at ease and warmly welcomed by Dorothy, our counsellor for the weekend. We had tea and met the other volunteers, then an early dinner and went to bed at eight thirty; I cannot remember the last time I went to bed that early. The weekend seemed to fly by as we learned to loosen our bodies with gentle exercise and relaxation (so much so I went to sleep during one of the exercises, although I was not on my own; Betty Westgate, the lady who founded what is now Breast Cancer Care, did also.)

We also had meditation and visualization. On Sunday we had a break, and four of us walked to Richmond Park. It was a warm sunny day with lots of families walking and riding bikes, and of course the deer - the males looked very majestic with their huge antlers. On the way back, we all had ice creams. It was a very therapeutic workshop, and I met some nice ladies.

I felt a bit apprehensive; it was injection time, and the first meeting with my new GP, Dr. Godsmark, a young doctor who I like and feel confident with.

At the weekend, Nina said Lucia was in the dance team which was giving a demonstration, and would we like to go? We enjoyed the evening; when Lucia was three, she started ballroom and modern dancing lessons and has done well in her exams, being chosen to be in a team of dancers going to Blackpool to represent the dance school.

Twenty-third of April, and at nine o'clock in the evening, we had a call from Marcus to say Julie was in labour; they would be dropping Joe and Alex off to us shortly. We went to bed at twelve o'clock - no news from the hospital. Marcus arrived at seven o'clock in the morning to say Julie had had the baby, and we could go to visit. As it was a Saturday, Roger was at home so we could not wait to get to the hospital. Julie was in a room on her own, and lying in the cot was a lovely little girl with black hair, Claudia Margaret.

In May, I celebrated my fifty-ninth birthday, and two days later I was back at the hospital to have the tests for my waterworks problem that has been getting worse all the time. The tests were not very pleasant, and they gave me stomach ache; I just hope it is not too long before I get the results.

I had a nice week. HRH Princess Alexandra, as patron of the Leeds Castle Foundation, was opening the New Lady Baillie garden. Lady Baillie was of course the last owner of the Castle. The staff had been invited to a reception in the Castle for the Princess. I picked up Di and Gail on my way. It was a lovely warm evening, and there were drinks and nibbles. The Princess came and spoke to us, also her husband Sir Angus Ogilvy. The Rt Hon Lord and Lady Thomson also had a chat with us; we know them quite well. Lord Thomson is chairman of the foundation, so he and his wife are frequent visitors to the Castle. During the evening, Paul the head chef asked the three of us if we would like to go to the kitchen and see the preparation going on for dinner, then into the dining room. Stephane Boudin designed this room in 1928; displayed around the room are pieces from Lady Baillie's collection of 18th century Chinese porcelain. The

William IV mahogany dining table, with its white painted Louis XIV style chairs, looked wonderful laid with the silver and crystal, and as usual beautiful flower arrangements by Maura, the castle florist. There are also five beautiful Louis XVI Aubusson pastoral tapestries hanging around the room. We then decided to walk around the new garden which had been designed by landscape architect, Christopher Carter, on the site of the old Lady Baillie's aviaries, and enjoyed the new terraces with panoramic views across the Great Water. The folded terrace wall encloses sun traps for Mediterranean and sub-tropical plants, and when the garden is fully established, it will provide flowers all year round.

The next day was the official opening of the gardens, and after the opening ceremony I had been asked to look after Princess Alexandra and Sir Angus Ogilvy while they had a private meeting with Lady Baillie's daughter, Mrs Remington-Hobbs, who was ill at the time. I felt it a privilege to have been asked to look after them, and the next morning I went into work to supervise breakfast for Lord and Lady Thomson.

June started off warm and sunny; our garden is looking nice and colourful with the bedding plants. I had an appointment at the hospital for a check-up. The young registrar, who saw me, did not read my notes properly as he said I shouldn't still be on Tamoxifen. I explained why I was on them and said I was sure it was in my notes, so after checking he said he understood it was because I was on HRT, and keeping me on them was due to my previous history and not having a stomach. He said I should have a bone scan and would make an appointment for me. I had to ask for the results of my last mammogram; he found them at last and said there were no problems, thank goodness.

David's thirty-fifth birthday. I wonder where the years have gone; eight days later and it was Roger's sixtieth birthday. I had made arrangements for Roger and I to go to the small seaside town of Whitstable. I had been trying to find out what I could do that was different for his birthday, and he had mentioned that he had never had oysters. Then I read an article about Whitstable; it was becoming very popular for artists, and the Hotel Continental had been refurbished in Art-Deco style, and of course the restaurant is famous for its oysters. At the hotel, which is situated right on the beach, we had a room overlooking the sea with great views. After settling in, we walked into the small quaint town; lots of art shops, a book shop I could stay in all day, and an old-fashioned sweet shop. The harbour has its fishing boats and tall net huts, and has been famous for oysters since Roman times. The old fishermen's huts have now been converted to holiday stays, and are owned by the hotel. Back at the hotel for dinner, we tried the oysters for the first time. I wasn't keen on trying them; I had been told they were slimy and just slid down your throat. Roger said I must try them so, after a lot of persuasion, I did. They were not at all as I had been told; I found them absolutely delicious. We had enjoyed our stay so much; it was great sleeping with the sound of the sea outside our window, and we had fallen in love with the town. When it was time for us to leave, we decided we would be back before too long. Back home the next day we had a BBQ for all the family.

The following day, I had another surprise. I had booked for Roger to go fishing at Lakedown Burwash at a fishery owned by Roger Daltry, the famous rock star from the group the Who. At the fishery, which is set in beautiful grounds, we went to the fishermen's hut and were greeted by a man not much taller than me, with short blonde curly hair, who looked vaguely familiar. I later realised it was Roger Daltry; he no longer had the bushy wild hair he had when the group was very popular. Roger enjoyed his day fishing and said he had had a great birthday.

An outing to Ascot had been arranged at work so Roger and I picked up Michelle and Trevor and drove to the Castle as we were joining the coach there. The weather was kind, warm and sunny. We had a picnic lunch when we arrived at the racecourse, and sat and admired the fashions and hats; some were quite outrageous. We had a bet of course and watched the races, but did not win. It was an enjoyable day although we would not be fussy about going again.

My waterworks problem is not improving. I do hope I get a hospital appointment soon.

Had Alex and Claudia for the day; she is almost two months old, and a dear little girl. It was a lovely day so we went for a walk to feed the ducks on the pond.

The next day, I went to work in the afternoon as I was supervising an evening function. When I arrived home, Roger asked if I had realised something was missing from the garden. I had grown a bay tree from a small cutting twenty years ago; it was now 5 ft tall and I had shaped it like a ball. It stood in a very heavy pot outside our front door and was much admired; it was my pride and joy and it had been stolen. It was so heavy it would have needed two people to have lifted it; it must have been stolen during the night. I rang the local neighbourhood-watch policeman who said it had probably been sold at a boot fair; I was devastated.

I had an appointment for my scan. The usual procedure: a small amount of radioactive dye is injected into the arm, and the dye needs to concentrate in the bones for about three hours before the scan can be performed. I have to drink as much as possible but need not keep the bladder full, thank goodness; with my waterworks problem I would not have been able to hold on to it. I decided to wait at the hospital; it was a chance to see some of the staff I knew. I no longer helped at the information centre as there had been changes, and it had been difficult getting to the hospital after returning to work. The three hours was soon up, and the scan took about an hour.

The first Sunday in July, and Claudia's christening day. We were having lunch in the Gate Tower at the Castle, and I had taken the cake, menus, and place names down in the morning. I had painted sweet pea fairies on these, and also on a christening plate; Claudia's birth month flower is the sweet pea. The christening service was at Leeds church, and she wore the family christening gown that had been made out of my wedding dress, first used for Richard. At the Gate Tower, the dining room looked lovely; crisp white table cloths, sparkling glasses, pink and white posies on each table - as usual, Maura's floral arrangements were beautiful. After lunch we went for a walk around the grounds, then back to the Gate Tower for tea and cake. The waitresses all looked after us really well. A lovely day.

I had won two tickets for a trip on the Sea-Cat ferry to France. We awoke to a really hot day, and left early for Dover. We had coffee and croissants on the way over, and docked at Ostend. We had decided to go by train to Bruges. It was beautiful; lovely old buildings, shops with wonderful chocolates, and lots of lace shops. We decided to take a boat trip, and it reminded me of the canals in Venice; there were flowers everywhere. We had lunch outside a restaurant, watching the world go by. We would have liked to have stayed longer, but had to catch the train back to Ostend; we did not want to miss the last Sea Cat home.

The next day was back to normal at work; by six thirty I was supervising breakfast. We always look forward to the Japanese flower ladies, a group of ladies from Japan who stay the week. They would have flower arranging some days, when a florist would come to demonstrate, and other days were spent visiting gardens. At the end of their visit, they would give me and the ladies who looked after them, the arrangements they had done. They were always so polite; we loved having them.

The next event at the Castle was when Elton John gave an open-air concert. He had cancelled the previous concert when he had been taken ill. As usual with these sorts of events, lots of organisation is needed; the concert stage and seating were on the Cedar Lawn which has a wonderful view of the Castle. There were two performances on the first night. I was supervising a surprise party. A lovely young man, Mike, had arranged it for a friend, Damien. Another surprise was that the guests had tickets for the concert. They arrived at the Gate Tower for dinner, and after the main course they went to the concert. Then they came back for the rest of the meal. It was one of the nicest functions I supervised, and I had a lovely card from Mike and Damien thanking me. On occasions like that it was worth working the long hours.

Time for my endoscope again, and Roger came to collect me; as usual I was so sleepy I could not remember what the doctor had said, but he told Roger all looked well. He had taken a biopsy, and my GP would get the results. As always, my insides did not like me having the endoscope; it took about two days for my body to get back to normal.

We were nearing the end of July, and it was the Oyster Festival at Whitstable where all sorts of activities were going on during the week. We went at the weekend when there was a parade through the town, and the blessing of the boats, and the local Morris dancers were performing. There were a lot of art exhibitions, and in one we bought a small watercolour because it reminded me of my Dad's garden. We had oysters and lobster for lunch, then walked to the gardens above the beach and watched bowls being played by a group of ladies. It reminded me of a Beryl Cook painting; all shapes and sizes taking the game very seriously, and the men getting told off for interfering in the ladies' game. We moved on to listen to a group of young people playing in a brass band. On the way home, we stopped at a tea shop at the tiny village of Ode Street which is so small it is more like a hamlet; there is a pub, and a small craft centre with the tea shop. Back home I had my usual spell in the bathroom when my body says I have eaten too much.

Over the past weeks, I have had new clients from Breast Cancer Care to speak to, and of course I'm still in touch with my other clients.

The last day of July was a happy and sad day, Janet, my friend who moved to Newbury, was back here for one of her son's wedding at Thurnham church, overlooking the pilgrim's way. It has the grave of the famous Kent cricketer, Alfred Mynn (Mighty Mynn), who died in 1861, although his better known memorial is in the adjoining parish of Bearsted where the sign on the village green depicts the top-hatted batsman defending his wicket. Also nearby are the remains of the Norman castle. The wedding went well, and Janet looked great in her wedding outfit, with a stunning hat.

It had been a year since Diana, my lovely young friend, died, so after the wedding, Roger and I went to put flowers on her grave at Bearsted churchyard. How sad I feel; she was so young, but Phil and the boys are doing well.

August is very hot. Luke and Lucia came to stay. They awoke early as they wanted to see the eclipse; and were excited that it was going to get dark so soon after breakfast. We were prepared for it to start, when Lucia went back to sleep and missed it. It did get dark, but not completely; we watched it on television and some parts of the country were in complete darkness. Luke couldn't stop talking about it.

It was the middle of the month, and such a nice warm Sunday that Roger and I decided to walk to Gidds Hill where I had lived as a young girl. The house then was surrounded by woods and fields, but now a housing estate had been built almost up to the house. We parked the car at what was once the old hamlet of Grove Green, and walked through the housing estate past the old farmhouse that is still there. Up until 1996, when it was burnt down, was Grove Green church; I know at least one of my sister Barb's children was christened there. It was very small with a corrugated roof, and had been built around 1903. The lanes I played along are almost unrecognisable with new houses. We walked up the road where the banks were a mass of wild strawberries when Valerie-Joan and I were young, and the woods that are on each side of the road were full of chestnuts in the autumn. The house we lived in has now been modernised, but not spoilt; the facade is still the same. Then past what was the cricket field, now full of houses, and past the old allotments, where my Dad spent many hours, which are still there although not used any more. My Dad would not believe it is the same place if he came alive today. We walked along the side of the field where Roger and I would walk hand in hand and kiss before we were married, and some nights we would walk there hoping to see the badgers and watch the rabbits; there was no clubbing for us. We picked blackberries on the way back to the car. The next day it poured with rain, and in Sussex they had a mini hurricane.

I had a nice day at work; went in at eight o'clock in the morning and did not finish until seven o'clock. I was working with Ros C. The clients had lunch in the Gate Tower, and then we walked them to the vineyards where Trevor Fermor, who is the Castle's official viticulturist, was doing a tour and wine tasting. The vineyard may be situated on the same site as the one recorded in the Domesday Book in 1086. The wine, that is sold in the Castle shops and restaurant under its own label, is from a blend of Muller Thurgau and Seyval Blanc grapes. Riechensteiner and Schonburger vines have been planted recently to widen the range of wine produced in the future. The clients really enjoyed the afternoon, and went back to the Gate Tower for tea.

It was time for our holiday, so on our first day we went into town to see if we could get a last minute booking. We were in luck; we could go the next day to Greece. It was a rush to get sorted out; we took Sunny Delight, my canary, to Nina to look after, and I have never packed at such short notice. David took us to the airport, and in no time at all we were landing in Greece, and had to catch the ferry to Thassos where we were staying. On the ferry was the dancer Wayne Sleep, a pleasant young man who made conversation with the other travellers. On arrival, we had transport arranged to take us to the hotel with three other couples who were staying there. It was the first time we had been self-catering abroad, and I was a bit apprehensive, but I need not have been. We had a super apartment with a front balcony overlooking the pool and garden bar. I loved our back balcony; the forest came right down to the building, and between the trees was hanging sparkling white bed linen and towels. I had taken my water-colour paints and knew this was a scene I had to paint.

I thought Thassos was a beautiful island; it is known as the 'Green Island' because of its thickly forested mountain ranges and tracts of olive and fruit trees, which in the past have suffered from fires. That evening we went into town for dinner, and it was so warm we were able to sit out on the quayside. It was great to have breakfast sitting on the balcony, the tall trees full of birds. We thought we would investigate the beaches as we only had to cross the road and there were white sandy beaches as far as we could see around the coast line. We had them to ourselves; as it was September, most of the visitors had gone home.

One day we had a boat trip around the island; we saw little Greek villages, cream and terracotta houses all jumbled together. Another day we wandered around the classical ruins. We walked up a path through old houses with lemon trees, and chickens scratching in dry ground, up to the amphitheatre where the archaeologists are excavating. It nestled in the forest above the town, and one evening we joined a tour for dinner, then walked up to the amphitheatre to see the sun set over the mountains. It was a very relaxing holiday; some days we just picnicked, read, and did painting under olive trees on the edge of the beach. At the end of the holiday, we left the apartment early to catch the ferry back to the mainland, and at the airport we saw Wayne Sleep again. I asked him for his autograph for Lucia. I told him about her dancing, and he said if one of his workshops came to our area, to bring her along. It had been a lovely holiday; the only problem was my waterworks; I was wearing awful large pads, and I seem to be waiting ages for my hospital appointment. My eating was quite good, not too many times spent in the bathroom; the Greek food agrees with me. David met us at the airport, and soon we were back home after collecting my Sunny Delight. He was happy to be home singing his heart out.

October, and it is Breast Cancer Care awareness month. Sadie had a stall in the town shopping centre for Breast Cancer Care and the Hospital Scanner Appeal. I helped to man the stall; it was a success, with a lot of support and people making donations. Most knew about Awareness month and wanted to share experiences of themselves, families and friends. A lot of interest was shown in the work of Breast Cancer Care, especially that we, the volunteers, had had breast cancer. The interest shown by teenagers was good too. It was a great week.

At the end of the month, we had a nice day. Roger and I had been invited to the official opening of the new bridge over the river Medway in Maidstone. Roger had an invitation because he was a member of the Len Valley Action Group, local people who had been clearing footpaths and repairing stiles along the Len Valley. It was to open up the footpath that goes from Rochester through Maidstone, Yalding, and Tonbridge. Of particular interest to the group, was all the information gathered; apparently, twenty-nine mills were recorded on the Len and its adjacent feeder stream. The original mills were corn mills which were converted to be used as fulling or paper-making mills. Not far from where we live, there is Thurnham Mill, in Otham Lane, which stands at the junction of the parishes of Otham, Leeds, and Thurnham. It was built in the 1820s by the Cage family of Milgate, and leased to a Robert Blinkhorn in 1829. The mill was working until the 1930s.

We arrived at the new bridge, where local dignitaries had assembled, which is part of the new river walk. The official opening was by the Duke of Kent, and after the ceremony he walked across the bridge, speaking to people on the way. He asked Roger if he had anything to do with the new river walk, and Roger explained how the group had been clearing the paths as part of the river walk. After the ceremony, we were invited to watch a film about the walk, and were given a copy; an interesting day.

It was time for our support group meeting. I miss Pam who was the breast care nurse and who started the group; she has now retired. Lin, one of my clients, was there looking very well. It was good to see her and to chat to the other ladies.

November, and I developed dreadful pains in my lower half. I had had them for a week, so thought I should see the doctor. He was not sure what it was, but thought I may have an infection, maybe to do with the trouble with my waterworks. It is now so bad I am wearing awful thick pads, and having to take extra clothes to work to change into. I am to take antibiotics and to have an X-ray and blood tests. I just hope I get an appointment soon to sort it all out. The tests were all clear, so I am now to have a scan.

We are nearing the end of the month, so I have started Christmas shopping. I took Diane to meet Jan for tea at Biddenden; it was a cold crisp day, but nice and cosy in the picturesque timbered tea room - a chance to catch up on our news. The next day it was time again for the support group meeting; the last one before Christmas, so we had a quiz and raffle which Sadie organised. I helped by selling the raffle tickets for her. The group is always well-attended, and some are the same ladies who have come since it started, but we always have some who are coming for the first time. It is good for them to see those of us who are a few years down the line, and looking so well.

I went for my B12 injection, and Dr. Godsmark had my results from the scan and X-ray. All seemed well and he felt sure my problem was to do with the waterworks, so he would write again to the hospital to try and get an appointment as I had waited so long. Roger had to go to the hospital for a hearing test; he is finding it difficult to hear in one ear, plus he suffers from Tinnitus, which is most unpleasant – a constant hissing in the ear. He has to have more tests.

I love this time of the year when the children have their nativity plays. Julie picked me up, and we went to see Alex as an angel; he was very good, and remembered his part. Next day, Nina rang to ask if I would like to see Lucia as a fairy; seeing them in their plays is one of my favourite parts of Christmas. At the weekend, Roger and I took Luke, Lucia, Alex, and Claudia to see Father Christmas at the local garden centre; they all had their photo taken with Father Christmas, and then we went to see the rabbits and birds before returning home for tea.

We were busy as usual at work with bookings for Christmas lunches and dinners. Some of our clients come every year, such as the Chamber of Commerce lunch which I supervised that week. I also looked after our chairman and his wife, Lord and Lady Thomson, for lunch. We always enjoy looking after them; such a pleasant couple, and they always find time to chat to me and the waitresses.

It was nice to supervise a winter wedding when Sandra, our new Sales and Marketing Director, had her wedding reception at the Gate Tower. The dining room, beautiful with candles and floral decorations, and the Christmas tree in the reception room all gave a wonderful ambience to the rooms; as with all weddings it was hard work, but the staff enjoyed the day.

The week up to Christmas was hectic. I have new clients from Breast Cancer Care, and I like to ring them to wish them a happy Christmas and healthy New Year. I have been getting my china orders done, wrapping presents, and delivering them.

Julie rang to say that Joe, Alex, Claudia, and she were feeling so ill she did not know what to do, so I rang her doctor and asked him to make a house call. He was concerned when he called that they were so poorly, and called again later in the day. He said it was flu; there was a widespread occurrence of a particularly nasty strain in many parts of the country, and it is very infectious. I wanted to go round, but Julie said no, she did not want me getting it. Christmas Eve, we took the presents but did not go in. I brought her washing and ironing home with us to help. As usual we walked up to the church for midnight service; it was pouring with rain and we got soaked on the way home.

I awoke Christmas morning feeling so ill. I had not felt so grotty since I had been on chemo. I did not realise flu could make you so ill, and knew what Julie and the children had felt like. Boxing Day, David and Nina and the children were supposed to come to lunch, but I felt worse, and anyway I did not want to pass it on to them. I went to the doctors two days before New Year's Eve, and he said not to go to work. This is how it gets passed around, and it was not a good idea going to work where there is food, as I also have a cough. I felt too grotty to stay up to see the New Year in, so went to bed. New Year's day, Julie called in; her first time out since before Christmas. She and the children still look poorly, and she has lost weight.

I wonder what the New Year will bring.

34

YEAR 2000, ANOTHER STAY IN HOSPITAL

The first week of the New Year, I had a call from Breast Cancer Care to ask if I would give information on Teletext. They wanted to know if breast cancer screening was worthwhile. I definitely think it is; if I had not had a mammogram, I would not have known I had breast cancer, and I feel it saved my life. This was shown on Teletext a few days later.

The end of the first week in January was my first day out since before Christmas. The flu really pulled me down, and I still have a dreadful cough although I am beginning to feel better. We decided to go to Tunbridge Wells, an elegant Regency town famous for its medicinal waters discovered by Lord North in 1606, and you can still take the waters today. There is also the lovely Calverley Park and a raised promenade fringed by Lime trees at one end of the town, and the unusual rock formations from eroded sandstone on Rusthall Common; one is Toad rock, and other unusual rocks are at nearby High Rocks. We wandered around the book and antique shops, had tea in the 'Nutmeg' tea shop where the waitresses wear long black dresses and white caps and aprons, and serve delicious home-made cakes and pies - all very civilised.

That weekend was also our forty-first wedding anniversary; a quiet one after our Ruby last year.

Julie had still been worried about the problem with her breast, so had decided to see my consultant, Mr Jones, at his private clinic. He said he was 120% sure there was not a problem, but he would take a biopsy; he did not like the look of two moles she had, so she would receive an appointment to have them removed. Breast Cancer Care rang with a new client for me to speak to, and I also had a call from Phil, the husband of my friend Diana who died; we still keep in touch and have a chat.

I have been looking forward to a weekend at Whitstable. We wanted to go away the weekend of our anniversary, but this was the nearest we could get. As usual, we stayed at the Hotel Continental in the same room overlooking the beach. We had a wander around the old town, and had booked lunch at Wheelers, a tiny fish restaurant, and tiny it is; the room at the front serves all fresh sea food to eat at the counter or take away - the oysters are the favourites - and in the back is the smallest restaurant with three tables; it was once the parlour of the house, and the original fireplace is still there. Their crab cakes are out of this world. They do not sell wine but you can take your own, and they will supply the glasses and opener. After lunch, we walked back to the hotel, stopping at the fish market which has the most wonderful display of fresh fish and seafood. We had dinner that night in the hotel.

At the end of our stay, we decided to go to Port Lympne zoo for the day as it is on the way home. We like to take the grandchildren to either Port Lympne or Howletts - both are owned by John Aspinall. He bought Howletts in 1958, and built it up into one of the world's most important zoological collections, with breeding groups of gorillas, tigers, African elephants, and many others. We like Port Lympne because of its tigers and rare cats. At the beginning of the main drive are the snow leopards, wolves, and tigers, then you arrive at the top of a stone stairway with the most wonderful views over Romney Marsh, the sea, and, on a clear day, France. At the bottom of the stairway are enclosed gardens with fountains, and then into the beautiful house. It was once owned by Philip Sassoon in 1912 when he succeeded his father's baronetcy, parliamentary constituency, and vast fortune. He employed a number of leading artists to decorate the rooms with murals, the most famous being Rex Whistler's Tent Room with its imaginary Georgian scenes and tromp l'oeil map of the gardens and tent roof. In another room, are murals by Arthur Spencer Roberts, the well-known wildlife artist; it took three years to complete the mural depicting South East Asian animals and birds. The Martin Jorden room murals depict wild nature around the world, not only on the walls but on the ceiling where an ocelot looks down on you; I think it is a magical house. You can walk round the park or travel in a tractor Safari shuttle; we had a ride as far as the Barbary lion enclosure. The males are magnificent with their huge manes; further on are more tigers and the beautiful ocelot, small margay, lynx, fishing cats, and many more. There are always the gorillas that give endless entertainment. We had a lovely weekend.

February, and Roger went for his hearing test; he needs to have more done. Julie had her hospital appointment to have her moles removed. At last my cough is better, and Trisha came for a chat; she too had had a dreadful cold. I was up at five thirty, an early start at work, as I was looking after the pike fishermen. Once a year, the men working on the estate can fish in the grounds for pike which grow very large in the moat and have a liking for ducklings. We served the men and women, who were fishing, with breakfast and lunch.

I had Luke for the day. He wanted to go to the castle; he loves the Maze, and the Grotto which is the underworld with mythical beasts created out of shells, wood, and other materials. At the end of the tunnel, there is a shell phoenix, and finally the Green Man about to spring out of his cave. The aviaries have a lovely collection of birds, and a successful breeding programme. Lastly we went to the story-telling. Next day it was the support group, so I left Luke with Roger and, after the meeting, picked up Lucia. Then Julie came with Alex and Claudia, and we went to the local leisure centre to the Polar Experience; the children love it. We came back home for dinner, and once again I am sure I am more worn out than the children.

March, and I had been looking forward to going to Westfield House, Wakefield, for a china painting course. I am going to take my City and Guilds Certificate so I have to attend certain courses. I decided to travel by train but it was a disaster. It was so difficult trying to carry bags and negotiate the escalator. Roger had taken me to Maidstone station. Arriving at Victoria, I then had to catch the underground (which I hate), then the train to Wakefield. After struggling on to the train, I found myself in first class so had to move up the train. There was only one seat, and I had to leave my bags where I could not see them. At last I arrived at Wakefield station, took a taxi to Westfield House, and was welcomed by Celia Shute and her daughter, Jan. They were worried that I had not arrived. I was introduced to the ladies, one of whom I had met on my first course. Celia showed me to my room, which overlooked the garden, and I joined the others for dinner. Our days were spent painting. Celia is such a good tutor, very patient; I learned so much. After dinner, we would paint for a bit, then some of us would sit in the lounge and chat, often going to bed quite late. I had a better journey home, but arriving at the underground, the escalator was not working so I had to walk up what seemed like a mountain with my bags. I had to stop and rest at the top; my heart was beating so fast. At last, I arrived back in Maidstone and rang Roger who picked me up. Although I had a great time, it was good to be home.

I had Gail, Shirley, and Di over for lunch; we found plenty to talk about and had a nice day. At the weekend, Phil had invited me for a chat and coffee, and to see the work he has had done on the house. Before Diana died, they were going to make some changes, so Phil decided to have the work done. Diana's aunty was there; so nice to see her again.

My sisters, Nellie and Barb, and nieces, Valerie-Joan and Heather, came for lunch. We had a lot to talk about. I had recently gone up to Nellie, and she said she had something to tell me. It came as a bit of a shock, but apparently our Mum and Dad had not been married until my Mum was pregnant with me. The story was that my Mum had been married to a soldier who was supposedly the father of our eldest sister, Phyllis. He had gone away to war and had not come back, so after some years, Mum met Dad but she could not get married without knowing where her husband was. It was not until one of my sisters wanted her birth certificate that all was revealed. Our Mum had given them to Nellie before she died. When my sister asked for hers, to get a passport, they realised they all had different surnames. The strange thing was I had had to get a new birth certificate, because when I had gone to get a passport they would not accept it as it was a tiny piece of paper with very few details; it did not even say if I was a boy or girl so I had to go to the registrar of births and deaths to have a full one. I had always wondered if my Dad was my Dad, because he never showed me any affection and I have to admit I did not have any paternal feelings towards him. So were my Mum and Dad really married? Although there is a marriage certificate, it says she was a widow, but was she? My Dad did not like visitors or Mum having friends; he was very private. Was this because he did not want anyone to know about their circumstances? We will never know; our Mum and Dad took their secrets with them when they died.

I had been working hard on my written work for my City and Guilds, plus the painted china that I have to take with me in May.

I had been looking forward to going to Rusthall, near Tunbridge Wells, for a writers' surgery. Michael McMillan, whose publishing history covers scriptwriting for theatre, radio, and TV, was Rusthall's writer-in-residence until the summer. He was offering a writers' surgery once a month for writers, and would-be writers, so I had booked a session. He was very helpful, and gave me lots of good advice which inspired me to write on.

David had been with his friend Mark on another trip to the Number One Orphanage in Romania. They had taken seventy boxes of clothes,

Year 2000, Another Stay in Hospital

shoes, towels, blankets, and toys, and collected more on the way from their German friends. After a four-day delay at the border between Hungary and Romania, they arrived at the orphanage with their consignment of boxes. They were misinformed about the paperwork they needed, so they left the van at the border, and got a taxi to the orphanage to spend time with the children and help with some painting.

Back at the border, they collected the van and drove back to the orphanage. David said the look on the children's faces when they arrive, makes it all worthwhile.

On Claudia's first birthday, all the family went out for lunch. I had bought Claudia and Lucia matching dresses which they looked really sweet in.

Roger and I had a super day in London. We went to the Art Nouveau exhibition at the Victoria and Albert museum. There was Lalique and Tiffany glass, Lalique jewellery items by William Morris, sculptures of the beautiful Alphonse Muca women, and Charles Rennie Mackintosh furniture; I think it is a wonderful period in art, and it was a great exhibition.

Lucia had been chosen as part of the team of dancers going to Blackpool, representing the dance school. The week before they leave, families can go and watch them perform what they will dance there, plus they are presented with their exam awards. I went along with Nina and her Mum; the children danced really well and we enjoyed watching.

May, and I am going back to Westfield House in Wakefield for the second part of my City and Guilds china painting. I have all my painting and written work finished from the last course. This time we are both going up; Roger is going to do some fishing. When we arrived, Celia said Roger could stay as well instead of going into bed and breakfast, which was good of her. As always, a nice group of ladies; it is wonderful not to have anything else to do but paint all day and evening. We painted roses and strawberries. After lunch, we went for a walk with two of the ladies, Margaret and Lisa. Roger had a good day; he caught ten trout and brought them back for Celia, but Margaret, who helps with the cooking, was not too keen on touching them. At the end of the course, Roger took me to see where he had been fishing; it was in the beautiful grounds of a hotel. We walked across a bridge to have lunch in the restaurant overlooking the river; then the long drive home.

I was upset to receive a phone call from my lovely friend Ros C. Her husband Dennis, who had been one of Richard's teachers when he was at grammar school, had been diagnosed with a form of cancer. Dennis had been poorly since he retired; he is now waiting to start chemo.

On my sixtieth birthday, Julie came during the day with presents and a cake. It was a nice warm day, so we took Claudia to feed the ducks. Julie said I should get changed to go out when Roger came home, but would not say where he was taking me. We went to Souffle, the lovely restaurant on Bearsted Green. We had a super meal, and the food did not upset me which was a bonus, as it usually does when I go out. Next day, I had a nice lunch with Sadie, Pam, Gladys, and Jane. Jane has Parkinson's disease so we try to choose somewhere that is easy for her to get to. She is a lovely gentle person, and was a nurse who worked with my sister Nellie. Gladys is another lovely lady, whose young daughter died leaving two small girls. We all attended the support group and went to hydro together, so we meet up every so often. The ladies at work had asked if I was having a party for my birthday, and I said no. Then I had a super surprise when Michelle rang to say some of the girls from work were going for a drink, and she would pick me up and meet the others at the pub, first picking up Gail who had just moved into a new house near where Michelle and Trevor were moving to. Arriving at Gail's, Michelle said she wanted to go in and see the house. Gail came out and said she was not quite ready, so could we go in and wait. We walked into the lounge, and a shout went up, HAPPY BIRTHDAY. The ladies were all there, and they had arranged a surprise birthday party for me. I was quite overwhelmed; they had kept it a secret so well, I had no idea what they had planned, more so when I discovered they had bought me a bay tree to replace the one I had stolen. They also gave me vouchers and a beautiful bouquet of flowers, and they had bought Michelle a rose bush as she had recently had a birthday. We both had a cake, and there was food and drink that everyone had contributed. It was good of Gail to have it in her new house. I went home and had a few tears; the ladies have always been so good to me when I have been ill. They have always given me such encouragement; it was a great sixtieth birthday.

Ros C picked me up and we went to see Sue who used to work with us; she had an accident and is now in a wheelchair. Bill, Sue's husband, has been looking after her with the help of carers. He has had a heart operation but he copes really well. I keep in touch with Sue by letter, and Ros and I visit when we can. Ros is coping well with Dennis's illness. Although they have had a few setbacks, he has now started his treatment; I think about them often.

At last, I went to see Mr Kefford, the consultant, and he explained the

Year 2000, Another Stay in Hospital

options for the operation. I did not want to have an epidural anaesthesia, but he said that would not be necessary as he thought a new type of operation he was doing, would work well for me; I would get an appointment shortly. He was a bit funny; he noticed in my notes that I was going for my endoscope the next day. He said, 'Oh dear, that is brave having that done.' I replied that I was used to having them as I had had them for the past twenty-four years. He said he had one last year, but never again! I said I didn't think it was that bad; he laughed, and shook his head.

The next day, I was not feeling so brave when Julie took me to the hospital. I saw Dr. Bird; it was the same as usual. I was too sleepy to know what he said, but he had left before Roger came to pick me up. The nurse told him my GP would get the biopsy reports. I still worry each time I go, about the cancer coming back. I miss Nurse Kate Wrelton; she was in charge of the ward when I first had the endoscopes with Dr. Stevens. She has now retired, but we exchange Christmas cards; it is nice to keep in touch. I did not have the usual sore throat, although it did upset my insides; I just felt raw. Two days later, I went for my check-up at Mr Jones's clinic and saw one of his registrars. They are always different ones; he did not read my notes again, and wanted to know why I was still on Tamoxifen as it is eight years since I had breast cancer, and it is usual to stay on them for five years only. Once again I have to explain it is because I am still taking HRT, and Mr Jones and Dr. Philips agree that as I have had my stomach removed, and a hysterectomy, it is best for me to stay on them. He said I did not seem to have any other problems, which was good news.

It's June, and David's thirty-sixth birthday. I finished the written work for my City and Guilds, and also did the paperwork for Breast Cancer, which I do not like doing, but it has to be done. We all went to Alex's fifth birthday party at the local village hall. I did some face painting, so we had tigers, flowers, fishes, and spiders; the children enjoyed it. The day before Roger's sixty-first birthday, we went to an antique fair and bought two china Ladro geese and an Edwardian brooch. Then I took him for lunch at Souffle, the restaurant we had been to for my birthday. Next day, all the family came for a BBQ; another nice day.

Joe had his fifteenth birthday; I cannot believe he will leave school next year.

I was very upset to have a call from Sylvia, one of the girls I had worked with when I was a teenager. She had got in touch after hearing Roger and me on the radio. Sylvia had one daughter, Michaela, who had not been married long. They had just moved into a new home, and were having a BBQ. They had invited Michaela's in-laws, and Sylvia and her husband Colin, when Sylvia had a phone call to say go down quickly. Sylvia had only spoken to Michaela a short while before, but arriving at the house was told Michaela had gone to sit down, and had died; she was thirty-four. Poor Sylvia and Colin; Sylvia had longed for a child, and had been married for a number of years before she at last had the daughter she wanted. How devastating to lose her so young.

I have now had my appointment to go into hospital. The night before, Roger and I had been invited to a talk and wine-tasting at Biddenden Vineyard, which Roger's firm does business with. It was a very interesting talk and an excellent buffet, and of course a chance to taste the wine. I did not have time to think about going to hospital.

On the day before I went in for my operation, in preparation for my admission, I had to go to out-patients for a blood test. I collected my forms from the ward, and had the test. I was not looking forward to another operation, but I was fed up with having to take pads and a change of clothes to work, plus I did not want to go out on my days off from work. Roger and I had always walked a lot, but this was not easy when I was losing water all the time. When I had first gone to the hospital and had urodynamic tests - these measure the changes in pressure when the bladder is filled and emptied - the surgeon told me I had a severe problem caused probably by my medical history of having two major stomach operations for the cancer, and the total hysterectomy, plus I had three large babies, ten and nine pounds. I had also always been very tiny, and he thought the TVT operation would suit me. Next morning, I rang the admissions office to see if there was a bed, and was told they would ring back half an hour later. They rang to say there was, so I could go in.

Roger took me. When we arrived, it was a bit of a rush getting all the notes taken. I was taken to the operating theatre at twenty to two, and arrived back at four o'clock. The operation I had was a TVT, Tension-Free Vaginal Tape procedure. The operation is performed by making two small incisions in the vagina, just beneath the urethra, after which a special instrument is used to place a tape under the urethra; the tape will rest completely tension-free under the urethra, hence the name Tension-Free Vaginal Tape. The tape will rest like a hammock under the urethra, supporting it during straining so there is no leakage of urine. The whole operation normally takes only thirty minutes, but with my previous history the whole procedure took longer. Generally, no post-operative catheterising is necessary. Arriving back on the ward, I was told all had gone well and I did not have a catheter. Roger came in to see me, but I cannot remember much as I was so sleepy. By the early hours of the morning, I was in a lot of pain and could not pass water, so had a catheter fitted. It was taken out the next day, then had to be put in again. Julie came in with Claudia; they were going to Disney Land Paris, so hope I will be home when they are back.

I stayed in hospital for five days; the nurses said it is usually overnight, so I was a bit unlucky. The day before I was going home, the doctor said I would have to keep the catheter in for another week, so I had a little tap fitted and, when I wanted to spend a penny, I turned the tap on. Roger collected me from the hospital; it was lovely to be home. Next morning, I had a bit of an accident; I had my shower, and spent a penny thinking I had turned my little tap off. I dressed, and decided to ring my sister Nellie. When I came off the phone, I realised my dress was wet so went to the bathroom to investigate; I had not turned my tap off properly, so I had to have another shower and change. After that I was very careful to turn off my tap. I had lots of visitors and phone calls, and as always the family and ladies at work were very supportive.

I rang the hospital at the end of the week, and they said I could go in the next day, hopefully to have the catheter taken out. I was there until early afternoon; the catheter was taken out, and I had to keep drinking water to make sure I could spend a penny. I had no problem at all, so I was allowed home. Three days later, I went to my GP for my B12 injection, and he said I was not to go back to work until I had my check-up with Mr Kefford. Normally the time off work is two weeks, depending to some extent on the type of work you do. It is important to avoid heavy lifting, so that the wall of the abdomen is not strained, as this could cause the leakage problem to return. Also, I am not to drive. I was so pleased I had the operation as it worked 100%; it was brilliant not to have to wear the awful pads. Stress incontinence is one of those problems women do not like talking about, so when I spoke to my friend the journalist, Ann Kent, and told her I had had the operation, she asked if I would participate in an article in a magazine that she wrote articles for. It was the ideal opportunity to persuade other ladies to overcome their embarrassment, and to encourage them to get help from their GP.

In August, Julie, Marcus, and the children moved to a bigger house at the village of St Michaels, near Tenterden. The house is just five minutes from the school. I had been with Julie to see the school, and we were impressed. Tenterden is a delightful town with weather-boarded houses, antique shops, and a 15th century church tower made of the famous Bethersden marble. Its high situation makes it visible across the weald, and at one time the tower was used as a beacon to guide shipping. We looked after the children while they moved, and I felt very tired after they had gone home. Claudia is quite a little podge to carry, and I was still being careful not to lift. I do get tired, but the doctor said that is to be expected after having a general anaesthetic.

Ros C picked up Diane and me, and drove us for lunch with Jan who lives in old Romney. I love the flat marshlands, and it is difficult for anyone standing in the village today to believe that once an important waterway reached right up to the town quay; of course it was a long time ago. The church is interesting, standing as it does aloof from the village in a field with one solitary old yew tree. Dedicated to St Clements, it has a fine timber roof with rare King posts, and an 18th century Minstrel's Gallery. In 1960, part of an early 13th century painting of a rose design was uncovered. As always we had a super lunch, and admired Jan's lovely garden.

Ros said her husband had had a setback, and was going to the hospital the next day. I also had my appointment for my follow-up check. Mr Kefford, the consultant, was his usual jolly self, and was very pleased with how things are going. I told him it was great not to have my problem anymore. On my way out, I saw Ros and Dennis as they were going in.

Had an appointment with my GP, Dr. Godsmark, and he said I could go back to work in a week's time. I was looking forward to going back; I had an early seven-thirty start my first day, with Gail, Di, and Ros S. It was a long day; we did not leave until seven o'clock. The organiser gave us chocolates, a CD, and flowers, but I was worn out.

September twenty-eighth, and it was Richard's fortieth birthday. We had arranged, as a surprise, for him to have a flight in the Leeds Castle balloon, and Julie had also decided to send Marcus as well. We all arrived at the Castle and went to the Cedar lawn where the balloon would take off; the weather was good, and the whole month had been really warm. We did not know that Richard does not like heights until we were there, but, once up, they both thought it was a great trip. They flew over the Castle, across the surrounding countryside, and landed in a field where they had champagne.

I had passed my china painting City and Guilds, and the certificates were to be presented at the British Porcelain Artist Convention near Wakefield. We decided to have a holiday in Yorkshire. I could go to the convention which was on for two days. It was held in a building on the edge of a large park, so we booked a hotel on the edge of the park, arrived in the evening, and had a nice dinner and an early night. The first day of the convention, Roger came with me. There were demonstrations all day by well-known artists, and an exhibition of painted pieces. I saw some of the ladies who were on the last course I did, and we were presented with our certificates. That evening there was a special dinner which we enjoyed. Next day, Roger went fishing while I attended a workshop with the brilliant young artist, Mark Jones. I had much admired his work; he was an excellent tutor, sharing his knowledge with us. I thoroughly enjoyed my day, and Roger had a nice relaxing day, fishing.

We had decided to stay the rest of the week in the Yorkshire Dales. We booked in to the local inn at Malham, a traditional country inn. It stands in the centre of the village, and we were told it was at least 150 years old. Our room had a four-poster bed and overlooked the stream which comes from Malham Cove. After settling in, we had a walk around the village. Next morning, we were up early and set out for a twelve-mile walk; only one problem, it was raining, but not to be deterred we left the village. Even in the rain, the scenery is wonderful: Malham Tarn and the high white cliffs of Highfolds Scar, and the natural limestone pavement, the natural amphitheatre of Malham Cove. We felt as if we were in another world; not another person in sight. The breathtaking gorge of Gordale Scar, with its waterfalls and beck which runs into 'Janet's Foss' where there is a waterfall and pool which was used originally as a sheep dip in times past. If ever there was a place with fairies, this was it, I thought; it looked like a fairy dell.

Back at the inn, very wet and tired, we had a bath, and then dinner in the oak-panelled dining room with its open stone fireplace. Next day, we drove through the scenic Ribblesdale to Settle, a small market town with its narrow streets and Folly Hall. Also known as Preston's Folly, it is an unfinished 17th century house with an elaborate front that contrasts with a very plain back. Once again it started to rain, so we drove back to the inn. Despite the weather, we enjoyed some lovely walks. Today, the limestone scenery attracts the visitors; in the Middle Ages, it was the monastic settlement, then the sheep fairs, and later, lead and zinc mining. On our last day, the sun came out, so we went for a short walk and enjoyed a cream tea in the village. This seemed to upset me, and I spent a while in the bathroom; sometimes, not having a stomach can be a bit of a pain. It was great being able to walk once more, without worrying about my waterworks; the operation was brilliant. On the way home, we stopped at Haworth, but were disappointed; it had become rather commercialised and not the same as when we visited a few years before.

Back home, I had been looking forward to going to the singer, David Essex's concert. I always have to do a bit of persuading to get Roger to take me, as he prefers classical music, but as always he came away from the concert saying he enjoyed it. I certainly did.

The rest of the year went quickly.

Roger had said I should think about giving up work, as it takes over and we cannot make plans because we never know what days I will be working until the weekend before, and then it was too late to make arrangements. I still enjoyed supervising; I had looked after some super functions, and met such interesting people. One memorable wedding was a couple from the musical *Star Light Express*. They had some very theatrical guests, but were all very nice. Coming up to Christmas, I had worked some very long hours and, although I feel so much better since my operation, I do get tired, and there are a lot of things I want to do.

The weather had been awful, with storms and lots of rain, and this had caused major flooding, particularly in the villages near the river Medway. Some poor people lost everything; it was to take months for some people to go back to living in their homes.

There were the usual Christmas preparations. I had a nice evening when we went to the charity carol concert in the town centre and saw Anne and Jean from work. Worked up to Christmas Eve when I supervised a wedding; I love looking after winter weddings.

I had a nice surprise when Michelle invited Roger and me to join Trevor at the New Year's dinner in the Castle. It was a lovely evening, very civilised. At midnight, we were supposed to all go outside and watch the fireworks, but the weather was so awful, we watched from the Castle windows. It was a lovely end to the year.

35

TIME TO RETIRE

We started the year with our usual stay at Whitstable, for our forty-second wedding anniversary, but the rest of the year was to have changes for me.

The article written by Ann Kent about my TVT operation appeared in *Choice* magazine; it was an excellent informative piece.

Richard's wife, Sandy's mum, had been poorly and was in hospital. She has had some treatment and recovered well.

I went up to Wakefield for one of my china painting courses. I had decided to go by coach, and it was so much better. I enjoyed the journey; not at all stressful as when I went by train. It was a great course, learning how to do lustres; Celia and her son, Glen, were our tutors. Glen, like his mother, is an excellent artist and a great tutor; as always I enjoyed the stay. I had missed Roger, so was glad to be home.

Every year, some members of staff are invited to have lunch with the trustees, and this year Betty and I, who had worked at the Castle for many years, were invited. I met Betty and we went to the Castle together. I sat next to Lord Armstrong who was to be the new Chairman as Lord Thomson was retiring. Lady Thomson brought Sir Angus Ogilvy, Princess Alexandra's husband, over for a chat; he is a lovely man.

We had another scare with Julie who had been having problems. Her doctor sent her for a scan, and she was told she had a cyst on her ovary; we were so worried. Next she saw a gynaecologist who took a smear and blood test, and said she would get a hospital appointment in two weeks, and it seemed certain she would need a hysterectomy; it was a nightmare. We were going on holiday to Spain, and I didn't want to go, but Julie said we must. Julie and Claudia took us to meet the coach, and I felt sad waving as the coach drove off.

We had only got as far as France, when I started having toothache. By the time we arrived in Spain, it was driving me mad; I could not eat or sleep, and I had never had toothache like it. In the morning, we went to a chemist who gave me a spray to numb the tooth. It did work for a short while, but next day it was really aching again, so I asked the courier if I should see a dentist; she did not advise it. She suggested I should see a pharmacist at the chemist. I told her I did not have a stomach so there was certain medication I could not take. She said she would write a note, explaining in Spanish. The pharmacist read the note and just looked at me saying, 'no stomach, no stomach'. She seemed more interested that I had no stomach than about the problem with my tooth. The Spanish pharmacist can prescribe antibiotics, which she did, plus strong paracetamol. As soon as I started taking them, it was bearable, but it took three days before I could say it had gone, and I could start enjoying the holiday.

We took a boat trip along the rugged coast to Blanes. The couple with whom we shared a table at dinner were on the boat, and they were going on to the Mediterranean gardens as we were. On landing, we caught the little open bus to the gardens. It was a very hot day; the displays of flowers were stunning, and we saw the most beautiful large butterflies and dragonflies. Roger collects cacti, and they have a wonderful collection; some are huge with great bright flowers. There are some panoramic views across the coast as you walk around the gardens. We caught the little bus back into town and had lunch in a restaurant beside the beach. Then it was back on the boat, and back to the hotel for dinner after a very pleasant day. Pat and Charlie, with whom we had shared the day, were good company. The next day, we rang Julie to see how she had got on at the hospital. Not very good, she said; they were not at all organised, and did not have her scan results, although the blood results looked quite good. She had to go back in a week. It was such a worry. Julie was to have her fortieth birthday in October, and we wanted to buy her a large Ladro china figurine; we chose a lovely mother and baby. We then had a lazy day, and an ice cream in one of the beach cafés.

The weather had been so hot that we waited for a day which started a bit cooler to do a walk that went to the top of a mountain. It was quite a hard climb, and I was a bit worried as there were signs warning of wild boar. Thank goodness we did not see any. On the way back, we investigated the Roman villa remains. We were up early the next day for another boat trip, this time to San Feliu. We did not think much of the town, but the walk along the coast was stunning; there were the most beautiful villas and gardens. The local market was held not far from the hotel, and the displays of fruit and vegetables were fresh and colourful. We bought Spanish dresses for Lucia and Claudia to dress up in. On our last day, a taxi took us and two other people to Loret-de-Mar to wait for our coach. The other couple was not together, but staying in the same hotel. One of them, Juliet, we discovered, lived quite near us and mentioned she was going to visit the Castle with her daughter. I told her I worked there, and she said she would ask for me. Once again we had had a good holiday, apart from the worry about Julie.

Back home, I had an appointment to see my dentist. She thought we could leave the tooth now; it had settled down, and she felt it could have been that I had been tense and stressed worrying about Julie. We went to the hospital for Julie's appointment; they did not instil any confidence in us. They could not find her notes, and the consultant was saying she would still need a hysterectomy, and chemo was mentioned. Julie said she would like a second opinion and then, as we were leaving, a nurse brought in the notes. When we left, the consultant gave Julie her notes and asked her to put them on the table outside. There was no-one there, apart from other patients, so anyone could have picked them up - we felt they were very disorganised.

Claudia stayed with me, and Joe and Alex were at school, while Julie's friend, Christine, went with her for her appointment with the consultant I had seen, Mr Kefford. She was very relieved, as he did not think there was anything sinister, and said he would like another scan. After Julie arrived home, I remembered the nurse doing the last scan and measuring the cyst, saying it had grown. Mr Kefford said the scan he was shown had shrunk, so this was the reason for having another scan. After her next visit, it was very good news. Mr Kefford said the cyst had gone, just as he thought it would. It was due to the menstrual cycle; thank goodness she had not had a hysterectomy.

Not long after this came another blow to us all when Julie told us Marcus had decided family life was not for him, and was leaving. I hope one day she will find someone who is right for her; she is a great mother who enjoys every aspect of looking after her family.

I had made the big decision to leave work, but when I spoke to Andrew, my boss, he asked if I would work until the end of August. I agreed, but did not want to tell anyone until nearer the time. In June, I had to say I was leaving when the ladies working with me were talking about people leaving, and Shirley asked me if I was thinking of going. Well, I could not lie, so I said I was. There was a silence. I don't think the ladies believed I would leave.

The chairman of the Leeds Castle Foundation, Lord Thomson, was retiring and had invited the staff to a farewell evening on the lawn in front of the Castle. Lord and Lady Thomson were the perfect hosts as always, making sure they had a chat to every member of staff while the managers served drinks and nibbles. There was to be a dinner for Lord and Lady Thomson later that evening, and Lady Thomson took some of us to see the dining room set for the dinner. As always, the room looked beautiful - sparkling glasses and silver - but Maura, the florist, had created the most stunning display along the middle of the table, very tall slim vases with a blue and white theme of carefully chosen flowers. Lady Thomson was thrilled with them. It was a lovely evening.

I had not wanted to leave before August because I had promised to supervise the wedding of one of our managers. Anthony was marrying Maxine, who worked part-time at the Castle, and they had asked me to paint china gifts for the bridesmaids. The day arrived, and the reception was held in the Fairfax Hall, dating in part from 1680 and now restored, which was perfect for a wedding. On arrival, drinks had been served on the terrace overlooking the Castle. It is always hard work having a wedding in the hall, because during the day it is open as a restaurant to the day visitors so, when it is closed at five o'clock, everything must be ready to set up the room. It looked lovely with white linen and sparkling glasses, and Maxine had wanted Maura to arrange the flowers in the tall vases she had used for Lord and Lady Thomson's retirement dinner. They looked lovely, and Maxine looked a beautiful bride. It was a great wedding and, as it was to be my last at the Castle, also rather sad as I had enjoyed all the weddings I had looked after.

The week after, Gillian Gray, a local journalist, came to see me to give advice on my writing. She's a very pleasant lady, who also writes children's books. She was very encouraging, and gave me some good advice, and said I should try and get published.

August thirty-first was my last day at work, and I was up at five o'clock for an early start. I was working in the Castle with Linda, our manager, and Ros C. A leaving party for me had been arranged for after work that day. I felt quite ill; I was worried about making a speech, and whether anyone would turn up. Lynda let me leave early so I could go home and change. I kept feeling emotional, and driving home there were a few tears. When I arrived back at the castle, I had to sit in the car for a bit to get myself together. It was a great leaving party; so many people came. The ladies had also invited staff who had left, even Sue in her wheelchair with her husband, Bill. Such a nice thought, and a lovely surprise, the ladies had asked Roger. Andrew, my boss, made a very nice speech and then it was my turn; I managed to get through it, and Roger said he and the ladies found it touching. I had so many presents that Michelle had to bring some home in her car. So much thought had gone into choosing the presents, and a very special one was from Marguerite and John. She had been taking photos of everyone since she knew I was leaving, and I had a wonderful album of Castle life and staff. Paul, the head chef, had put on a lovely buffet.

I had not been feeling well all that day and, by the time I went home, I had an awful pain in my chest and down my arm. It woke me during the night, and I spent the rest of the night sitting up. The next morning, I had an appointment for a blood test, so I told the nurse. She said I could not leave it, and must see the doctor. Dr. Godsmark gave me a spray, and said I would have to have an ECG and X-rays. That night it was very painful, and I was worried because my Mum had had angina. The next day, I had been really looking forward to going to the wedding of Stewart, one of our chefs, and Claire, who worked at the Castle, but the pain was so bad I could hardly move, so we were unable to go.

It took about a month before the pains disappeared. In the meantime, I had all the tests but nothing could be found. Dr. Godsmark and I think it was because I had become very stressed, and there had been the problems with Julie's health, and Marcus leaving, plus it was a big decision to leave work after twenty-three years, but I wanted to finish the book and do things I could not do when working.

Bubbly Ros S. had organised a lunch for me at her house. Gail, Shirley, Anona, Di., and the other Ros were invited; the dining room was decorated with balloons, and there was even a cake. Ros and the others had gone to a lot of trouble to make it such a nice day, especially as Ros's mum was ill. She had been diagnosed with ovarian cancer, and was having a bad time with treatment and stays in hospital. Earlier in the year, I had been to see her when she was having one of her stays in hospital; not only was Ros coping with her Mum being ill, but her Dad also was having treatment for cancer.

Although I loved my work at the Castle, what I gained most was the great friendships I made. There was the lovely young Tina, who was the supervisor when I first started; she left to start a family, and now has two boys; her sister-in-law, Shirley, whom I have known for many years; her Dad, Ted Filmer, was the stone mason at the Castle until he retired, and brother Anthony works in the gardens; Shirley, attractive with dark hair and blue eyes, is a great gardener, and in the summer some of us ladies go for what we call Shirley's garden party, to admire her garden - it is full of hanging baskets, borders of flowers, and water features. Then there are the two Ros's - one is blonde and bubbly, adores her animals, especially birds, who at one time worked in the aviaries at the Castle. The other Ros is everyone's favourite; she never has a bad word to say about anyone. We often joke with her because she is always late, but she is a lovely caring person. Gail, who did a five-year art course which was a great achievement, looking after her family, going to work and to college. We both like the same art and books, so we always have plenty to talk about. Val and Anne are two friends who like to work together, and we would tease them because they like to talk a lot, but they are great fun to work with and always call me Madge, which some of the other ladies hate me being called. Marguerite always remembers everyone's birthday, and is great with her camera. Viv, who I always ask how her love life is going; Ann, whose daughter, Anita, worked with us at one time, now lives abroad, and Ann loves to visit her grandchildren. Yvonne who always found time to write the most entertaining letters when I was ill, which was much appreciated. Anona who always looks well-groomed; Sue Hook who is always rushing around and loves her garden. Di who has been very brave; one of her little daughters died of cancer - something none of us want to have to cope with. Michelle who has always found time to visit me when I have been ill, and Roger and I have enjoyed going to the open-air concerts and having dinner together with Trevor, her partner. Unfortunately, Michelle does not cook, but fortunately Trevor does and has cooked some great dinners, plus Roger and Trevor share a love of good wine. The lovely Linda, one of the managers, and young Rose. Mark and Anthony, supervisors, and Rosamond, Maureen, Gillian and Sue. Then Irene and Pat, and her daughter, Nicola. The ladies who have looked after the bar, the two Sue's and Pam. Maura the florist with her wonderful arrangements that have given so much pleasure to everyone. Judy Murray, in the offices, who kept me going with her entertaining letters when I was ill. Beverley and Lynda Duffield both have lovely personalities and are perfectionists in their work. Anne, who is kind and religious, has worked nearly as long as me at the castle; Margaret and all the office staff. Darleen and Sue who work in reception, and the ladies who work in the Fairfax Hall. The kitchen departments - Betty, Annie, Angela, Janet, Gerry, Peter, Steve, Adam, Damien, and Giles, Dan, Richard and Chris. Of course there are those who have left or retired; Pat and Ernie, our very good neighbours from Leeds who got me the job at the castle. Andrew Wilson, Humphrey Shepard, Phyllis, Pat, Pam, Mary, Roy, Sylvia, Daphne, Graham, Freddie, Alastair, Nigel, Ron, Angela, Victor, Jean, Lily, Gladys, and Dave Banks who was our first head chef, Richard and Kathy, Vera, Joan, Ethel, Iris, Julie, and Kay; Ron and his son Nathan; Mr Borrett who had been butler to Lady Baillie who I loved working with for his entertaining stories of life at the Castle and when he accompanied Lady Baillie to her home in the Bahamas. I have been so lucky working with everyone at the Castle. I cannot name everyone but they are all caring, conscientious and loyal, as are Trisha and Jan.

On the eleventh of September, Trisha came for the afternoon. When she rang Jim, her husband, to ask him to pick her up, he told us to put the TV on. We do not usually watch the television when she comes round because we have too much to chat about, but we put it on and the most horrendous thing was happening. We thought it was an accident that a plane had flown into one of the Twin Towers at the Trade Centre in New York, but as we watched another plane appeared and went into the other tower. We could not believe it was really happening, and as we watched it all became even more horrendous - the men flying the planes were suicide pilots. The aftermath was dreadful; the towers collapsing and so many people killed. Something we will never forget.

After my retirement, I had time to do some of the things I did not have time to do when working. I started water colour classes and had more time to visit friends. One morning, I picked up René; we were visiting Sylvia, who we used to work with, who lived at Queensbough, on the Isle of Sheppy, I love this area with its marshes and bird life. We got a bit lost, but eventually found Sylvia and Colin's house. It was the first time I had met Colin; I liked him very much, he was a gentleman. We chatted about old times when we were working in the sixties.

I went to the theatre to watch Lucia's dancing show. She is doing so well; she has passed more exams and has a large collection of trophies.

When I was working, it was missing occasions such as this that was upsetting.

Julie's fortieth birthday, and we all went out for lunch at Detling. Also there was my brother Ted and his family celebrating his eightieth birthday; he still looks young and handsome for his age.

On one of our trips to Whitstable, I had bought a large print of a young girl. I wanted to know more about it, so I took it to Canterbury, to an art shop, as there was to be an expert on prints and paintings to give advice. We were told it was the Willow Tree, probably by Gladys Dawson, a 1930's illustrator of children's books.

I had a phone call from Lady Thomson, inviting Roger and me to the House of Lords for tea, and she sent a letter so that the police would let us in. November, and a very cold day, we arrived in London at Westminster Abbey. We saw the Field of Remembrance, as the weekend before had been Remembrance Day, and also went into the gardens to see Rodin Sculptures. We checked with the policeman and he showed us where Lord and Lady Thomson were waiting to greet us, and they gave us a wonderful tour of the House of Lords. It was so interesting, and we were introduced to some of the other members. We also went to listen to question time, and then had tea which was delicious. Lady Thomson gave me House of Lords chocolates; she said they had invited us as I had always looked after them so well when they were at the Castle. A day not to forget.

At the end of the year, I thought I would have a Christmas lunch for some of the ladies I had worked with. Also, as a surprise, I invited Pauline who used to work with us and who we had not seen for a very long time. I was up early to prepare everything. The two Ros's, Gail, Shirley, and Michelle arrived, and everyone wanted to know who else was coming. Pauline arrived, and it was as much a surprise for her as the others; she thought she was coming for a cup of tea with me. We had a great day talking over old times.

Roger and I took the grandchildren Luke, Lucia, Alex, and Claudia (Joe now too grown up) for a trip on the Santa Train from Tenterden. Once the train started, Father Christmas came round with his elves and gave the children presents, drinks, and chocolates. Roger and I had sherry and mince pies. Back at the station, at the end of our ride, was an old-fashioned carousel, and I said to Roger, 'I have always wanted to have a ride on one of those.' He replied, 'well, here is your chance.' But I could not get up on the horse; they were too high, plus I had to hold

Claudia who was too small to go on her own, so Lucia, Claudia, and I went in a sleigh, and Luke and Alex went on the horses. We all enjoyed our Santa trip.

Once again it was time for writing cards, and receiving them to hear news of friends. I had a card from journalist Margaret Rook, who is now married; she sent a photo of her two lovely children. It is always good to hear from Margaret. Roger's cousin and her family sent news from America, and we had cards from Mrs Malby, the children's teacher from primary school, and Rita Pizzey who I went to school with. We haven't seen each other for years, but always exchange cards. Now is the time to decorate the tree and house, to wrap and deliver presents, and go to carol services.

We had a quiet Christmas Day, and all the family came after Christmas. I had worked all the New Year functions at the Castle, apart from when I was ill, so we decided to go out now I had left. We went to a local inn, so we could walk; it was a bright frosty night, and we had had a little snow over Christmas so it was lovely to walk down the lane to the green and see my old school. It is now a library, but it brought back memories of my school days when the teacher would warm up our little bottles of milk on the stove in the middle of the classroom. We had a nice evening after dinner, and we had toasted the New Year in, so when the music became loud we decided we would be old bores and go home. We went back out in to the frosty night, and we looked forward to another New Year.

36

FORWARD TO THE FUTURE

This was to be a good year, but also sad. We have been married forty-three years, and I can remember the very first day when I saw Roger. I was thirteen and he was fourteen. A week later, he asked me to meet him and we went for a walk along the river, and from that day we have been together. We have been through so much, and I still look forward to him coming home each night, and get that extra beat of the heart when I see him. We both think that when we made that promise in church, 'to love, honour, and obey until death do us part,' we should try very hard to stand by it.

On February the ninth, it was announced from Buckingham Palace that Princess Margaret had died; she had been ill for some while, and a few weeks later, it was the Queen Mother's funeral - a grand affair with beautiful music.

March, and Roger had an appointment at the hospital as he has a lot of trouble with his sinusitis. Sometimes his face is so swollen and painful; he is to have an operation.

I am so enjoying my retirement, and can plan so many things. I took Lucia and Alex to Maidstone Museum for a Greek day; they were taken to the Greek room to get designs to paint plates and a mask, and had a great time. We had lunch, and then wanted to go back in the museum. Alex wanted to take Lucia and me on a tour. Lucia was most impressed as he had only been once before, but had remembered so much. I drove them down to Julie for tea, and we arrived with them both asleep in the car with their masks on. After tea, I took a very tired girl home.

Another nice afternoon when Ann picked me up, then Michelle and Val. At the Castle, it was the flower festival, so we had a tour around the rooms. We were impressed with the displays, and then it was on to Eastwell

Manor for tea. The old manor house sits in beautiful countryside; it was April and the surrounding fields had clumps of daffodils, primroses, and the first lambs. We had tea in one of the lounges in front of a wood fire.

It was an exciting day when I had a phone call to say Lucia had won a photography competition to feature her on the cover of *Focus* magazine. Nina and I took her to see David Batten, the photographer, to take the photos. He was very pleased with the results, and used one of the photos to advertise his work. She also appeared in other magazines and newspapers.

The other project I had wanted to do, was to learn to swim. I have always been frightened of water since I was at junior school and the teacher pushed me in, so it took all my courage to sign up for lessons. Hazel, my instructor, was very good and patient, so I went along once a week. I would not say I am very confident in the water, but I am getting there.

I was still attending the water-colour classes, and had a nice afternoon when we went to the bluebell woods on the local heath; it was good to get out to paint rather than stay in the studio.

At the end of last year, René and I had gone to visit Sylvia and Colin as he had become ill, but I was not expecting, at the end of May, to get a call from Sylvia to tell me Colin had died. We had been keeping in touch, and I knew he was having treatment which was making him poorly. I felt so sorry for Sylvia. It was only two years since her young daughter had died; how unfair life is sometimes.

Then I had another upsetting phone call from my friend Diane's sister to say that Diane, who had been in a nursing home, had died. I was very fond of her; a special friend who had started at the castle the same time as me. I would miss her. The same day, our neighbour Doug died; he had not been well for some time.

We had a happy day out after all the sadness. Gail and I went to London to the Victoria and Albert Museum for the tiara exhibition. We had such a good day; we went up by coach so we had plenty of time to chat, and we loved the exhibition.

Roger went into hospital for the day to have his operation; all went well, but he had to wait for the biopsy results.

Julie went to the breast clinic and, because of our family history and the fact that she is now over forty, she can have mammograms, which I am pleased about. Roger had the results of his biopsy, and all was well, thank goodness.

Forward to the Future

Another happy event when Roger and I were invited to the wedding of two of Roger's colleagues, Simon and Charlotte. We drove through the village of Doddington, up on the downs; the village was in the Domesday Survey and has some very pretty cottages. We were driving through orchards to reach Sharsted Court, a lovely old house, but it was the gardens that were magical. Within the gardens are little walled gardens and topiary all around; some parts reminded me of a scene from *Alice in Wonderland*.

In September, I had the chance to meet David Essex, the singer, when he was signing his autobiography. When my turn came, I asked him if he would put, 'to Margaret and her Silver Dream Machine'. All my cars have had names and, a few weeks before, I had a new silver car which I called my Silver Dream Machine after the David Essex song; he probably thought I was mad. He was quite a shy person, but he took time to have a word with everyone having their books signed.

I had the most exciting experiences when I was an extra (non-singing) in the opera, Aida. It has always been one of our favourite operas, so when I had the chance to be an extra I jumped at it. Roger thought I was joking when I told him, as he says I cannot sing at all. I let him think for a while that I would be singing. It was the Chisinau National Opera Company from the capital of Moldova in the Soviet Union. There were two performances at the Marlowe Theatre, Canterbury, and one at the Tunbridge Wells Assembly Hall theatre. I was a bit nervous, when arriving at the Marlowe, but soon felt at ease when I met the other extras. We all assembled on stage for a rehearsal; there were four of us women who were to be slaves, plus the men slaves, and the soldiers, although some members of the cast played these parts as well. We had an interpreter because the rest of the cast spoke very little English, but they were friendly. We were given our costumes, had the most awful brown make-up on any visible part of our body, and I had to wear a long black wig. There were some very young girls from a local stage school who were to perform a dance. We were allowed to stand in the wings of the stage to watch the performance until it was time for our entrance. We had to walk to the middle of the stage, down a staircase, and sit on the bottom of the stairs. We had our hands tied and had to look down, but I did have a peep to look at the audience; it was frightening seeing a sea of faces. When I realised we had to walk down the steep stairs, I was really worried, as without my glasses I cannot see very well. Obviously, I could not wear them as Egyptian slaves certainly did not have glasses, but I did not have to worry because we had to look down, and the lighting was so bright I did not have a problem. When standing in the wings, I was enthralled by the whole production, and the wonderful music composed by Verdi (its first performance was in 1871 at the opera house Cairo). I could not believe I was really there.

The next night, only two of us turned up. We had no problems, but it was a bit different when I went to Tunbridge Wells. Arriving at the theatre, the interpreter said I could watch the rehearsals while we waited for the other extras. I was called on stage to find I was the only one, so it was decided, as I was on my own, to put me in the dressing room with the chorus. Last time, we had our own dressing room with the young dancers. What an experience it was; there were ladies being made-up and having their wigs put on, some were in stages of undress, others were practising their singing, but best of all, some were knitting. They tried to talk to me, but it was very difficult. Russian is not an easy language to understand, although the wardrobe and make-up ladies did speak a little English. I was a bit nervous because Roger was in the audience, so I hoped I would not fall down the stairs when I went on stage. He really enjoyed it and said he was very proud of me.

One of the best days out that month was with Ros and Gail when we visited the house of the Bloomsbury Set Charleston Farmhouse. We drove to Alfriston, in East Sussex; along the High Street are old timbered houses, and behind them, on the edge of a large green, is the 14th century Clergy House. By the 1800s, it was being used as labourers' cottages, now a National Trust property. Nearby is the church named Cathedral of the Downs because of its size; the cruciform church has some of the best flint work in the country. We had lunch in one of the timbered buildings, and in the tiny garden was the original outside toilet. At Charlestone, we toured the house with a guide who was very knowledgeable. In 1916, on Virginia Woolf's recommendation, her sister Vanessa Bell and other artists Duncan Grant and his friend David Garett, and Vanessa's husband Clive Bell and their two sons, moved into Charleston Farmhouse. Vanessa remained friends with Clive Bell but the marriage ceased to exist except in name. The love of her life for over fifty years, despite his homosexuality, was Duncan Grant by whom she had a daughter, Angelica. Charleston Farmhouse became known as the country retreat of the Bloomsbury group. After they moved in they transformed the house with their art work, the walls, furniture, ceramics and furnishings. It also had a very pretty garden.

Forward to the Future

I knew Gail and Ros would find the house fascinating. We left the house reluctantly as we all felt we would love to live there. Ros, who was driving, asked if we would like to drive to Eastbourne. We thought it a good idea, but we got a bit lost when trying to leave Eastbourne to go home, and ended back there twice. At last we took the right road to go home; we had had a lovely day.

In October, Richard and Sandy went on holiday to Florida. Luke made us proud by getting an award at school. Lucia won more dance awards. David was planning another trip to Romania. Nina now worked part time at a local school which fits in with the children, plus she really enjoys it. Julie was getting on with her busy life; she has made lots of friends since moving to the new house. Joe is seventeen and still working in antiques, restoring furniture. Alex is now eight and has a great interest in art. Claudia is three; a sweet little girl who loves shoes and handbags.

Breast Cancer Care Awareness Month and Boots stores were having a Marathon Makeover Day with the No 7 make-up ladies doing five-minute makeovers, so Sadie, Flavia, and I went along to support them and offer advice and give out our Breast Awareness leaflets. Over 4,300 makeovers were completed around the UK, raising over £10,000 which was great. The local press supported us, and came to take our photos; it had been a very enjoyable event.

Sadie and I were also models for a mini fashion show, modelling lingerie and swimwear for women who had had surgery for breast cancer, at a large department store. It went really well and we had a great time.

Head Office rang to say a lady had been organising quizzes, and wanted Breast Cancer Care to have the money they had raised. I spoke to Janice, who was the organiser, and she invited me to join them for the last evening of the quizzes. Roger and I went along, and after accepting the cheque for £1055.50, I gave a talk about Breast Cancer Care. It takes time and effort to organise an evening as Janice, Linda, and their helpers had done. It is people like them that make it possible for Breast Cancer Care to offer the services they do.

Becoming a volunteer for Breast Cancer Care, I have met some super people. All the clients are so grateful to have someone to talk to; some have become friends and asked if we could meet, such as Valerie, Sheena, and Pearl. It is not always possible to meet, as most of my clients live too far away, but it would be lovely to be able to at sometime.

It is now twenty-seven years since I heard my stomach problems referred to as cancer. I try not to look back, but had I not had the cancer, would I have been the person I am: tolerant, strong, and confident? I am sure I would not have done lots of the things I have. Before, I was so shy I did not even like going out to eat. The first day I went to the Castle I thought, I hope I do not have to make conversation with anyone. Going to work at the Castle was the best thing I ever did, making myself get up and acting normal when some days I felt so ill I do not know how I walked there. But I had committed myself to do the job, and did not want to let them down and, by working, cooking, and cleaning at home, I was proving to Roger and the family that I would overcome these awful gremlins. I had so much support from everyone. On days at work when I would escape to the toilet to be sick, I would come out to find someone washing their hands, and I knew they were really in there watching out for me. Some years later, when I was supervising a wedding or an important function, and speaking to a member of the royal family, I would think: if my Mum could see me now, she would not believe it was me, and how hard it would have been for her to have to cope with my cancer.

Another memorable day was when I visited my old home, Gidds Hill. I had not been there for years. Kathleen and Bev Wingrove live there now; Kathleen is a Holistic Healer, and had given a talk at the support group. When I realised where she lived, and told her it was my old home, she invited me to go back. Going first into the room I had given birth to Richard and Julie, then my Mum and Dad's bedroom which still has the little fireplace and the original doors and door knobs. Kathleen said, 'just think how many times you have turned those knobs!' Suddenly I was a little girl, seeing the big brass bed that used to be in the room. My room is now a bathroom; the walls are white, but Kathleen said my old wallpaper was still there under the paint. When decorating the other rooms, there were as many as eight layers of wallpaper to strip off! I was transported back in time, looking out of the window and seeing the meadow full of daisies and poppies. It was very emotional. I had a lovely morning with Kathleen and Bev; they brought back lots of memories.

How strong Roger had been when he was told I did not have a one in a million chance of surviving, and I would be lucky to live three months; then for two and a half years to see me constantly sick and in the bathroom. I looked so awful, thin with no hair, and being told I still would not survive. All the time, telling me how much he loved and wanted me, and giving me so much encouragement. Then to have all my stomach removed, and the months of trying to eat. Then another operation, a hysterectomy. To become well, and then, fifteen years later, to tell him I had breast cancer and that I had to have another operation, chemo, and radiotherapy, was one of the hardest things I have had to do. His love and devotion made me more determined to survive, and without all my family and friends I would not have been as strong.

And of course, all the medical profession: Dr. Stevens who found the cancer, Professor Ellis for his wonderful surgery and lovely manner, and always making me feel special. Dr Hanhams, Dr Phillips and Mr Jones for their skills. Dr Vaux, without whose kindness, help, patience, and encouragement, I would not have got through it all.

Without all of these people, I would not have seen our three children married, and enjoyed five lovely grandchildren. I still have problems with my eating; it is a constant battle to keep my weight on, but I am fit and well and have a great life. It is now three years since I retired. My life has been very full, especially with finishing this book, and something happened which I was not expecting; I fell in love again when we bought a yellow Labrador puppy, Fleur. She is now one year old, and every day we go off on our walks across the fields and woods which we both enjoy so much.

I have of course had my bad moments in this book, but the happy moments outweigh the bad ones. It is also to show that there are lots of us who survive. Professor Ellis once told me to live each day to the full, and that is what I have done.

This story is about an ordinary woman, but I feel I have travelled an extraordinary journey with wonderful experiences. I was once asked to give a talk about my life. I asked what I should call the talk, and the gentleman who had invited me said, 'My Wonderful Life'. How right he was. I hope this book will be an inspiration to others facing cancer for themselves, their family, or their friends.